MEDIEVAL ENGLISH COMEDY

PROFANE ARTS
OF THE MIDDLE AGES

Series editors:

Elaine C. BLOCK
Frédéric BILLIET
Paul HARDWICK

MEDIEVAL ENGLISH COMEDY

Edited by
Sandra M. Hordis & Paul Hardwick

BREPOLS

D/2007/0095/74

ISBN 2-503-52427-6

Printed in the E.U. on acid-free paper

CONTENTS

Introduction

SANDRA HORDIS and PAUL HARDWICK

'What thing is it, the less it is, the more it is dread?'
'A bridge'
       [ca. 1550]

'A certain jealous husband followed his wife to confession, who when the priest should lead behind the altar to be displied [disciplined by beating], the husband, perceiving it, and doubting the worst, cried unto him, saying, "hear ye, master parson, I pray you let me be displied for her."

'And kneeling down before the priest, "I pray you," quod the wife to the priest, "strike him hard, for I am a great sinner."'
       [ca. 1583][1]

Save for some notable exceptions – namely Chaucer, fabliaux and the Exeter Book riddles – scholars often miss the pervasive presence of comedy in the creative arts of the English Middle Ages. As is the case at all points of human history, humour, jokes, laughter, and comic images appear in many types of medieval English cultural artifacts, even though the concept of humour as an artistic goal is relatively new.[2] We certainly expect to find medieval humour in the jest books, fabliaux, and riddles of Old and Middle English literary history, as is evidenced by

---

[1] Wardroper, John. *Jest Upon Jest: A Selection from the Jestbooks and Collections of Merry Tales published from the Reign of Richard III to George III* (London: Routledge & Kegan Paul, 1970), pp. 69, 98.

[2] See Jan Bremmer and Herman Roodenburg's Introduction in *A Cultural History of Humor* (Malden, MA: Polity P, 1997) for a thorough summary of the history of humour studies.

the examples above, but we are surprised when we come upon comic scenes in the otherwise serious *Morte Darthur*, sermons, and liturgical drama, and yet more surprised at the comic images in intricate manuscript illuminations and sacred stained glass windows. And as humour researchers would suggest, we laugh as a result of our frustrated modern expectations, and are forced to reevaluate what we know about medieval England.

At precisely this point is where this collection of essays developed. What is humour in the English Middle Ages? Does the comic serve any function other than pleasure? How might we reexamine ideas of identity and cultural complexity in terms of humour in medieval England?

As a basis, the contributors to this volume work within a number of assumptions about the humour of the period. Comedy studies from such diverse fields as sociology, psychology, history, philosophy, and literature, while at first appearing to be a mixed bag of conflicting provinces, for the most part can agree on one thing – that humour, in all its forms, is a social act.[3] A performer crafts words and gestures in such a way that a response is solicited from an audience, sometimes abandoned laughter, and sometimes a groan of mild amusement. A good performer will then use the reactions of the audience to elaborate and expand the humour, thus creating a characteristic model of communication. At times, this performer/audience relationship is clear; the teller of the first joke above expects a response of the listener in the middle of the joke which complies to the joke formula, creates a pause for dramatic effect, and calls the audience into the close dialogue of humour.[4] Indeed, simply the act of writing down a funny story or turn of phrase, as in the second example, expects an audience to react, and while not necessarily evoking a verbal response, the writer expects (or at least hopes for) laughter.

But beyond this rather basic model of simple communication lies a complex picture of cultural mores. First, in comedy there is always present a kind of testing, no matter who performs the humour or who responds.[5] On a personal level of communication, tellers test their audience by presenting jokes which explore the parameters of what is acceptable in a particular environment (one wouldn't get a

---

[3] See A. Rapp, *The Origins of Wit and Humour* (NY: E.P. Dutton, 1951), Kenneth White, *Savage Comedy: Structures of Humor* (Amsterdam: Rodopi, 1978), and Michael P. Wolf, 'A Grasshopper Walks into a Bar: The Role of Humor in Normativity', *Journal for the Theory of Social Behaviour* 32:3 (September 2002), 331-44.

[4] See Mikhail Bakhtin, *The Dialogic Imagination*, trans. by Michael Holquist and Vadim Liapunov (Dallas: U of TX P, 1982).

[5] See especially Michael P. Wolf, 'A Grasshopper Walks into a Bar,' where he argues that jokes are evidence of the normalization by testing, and if necessary correcting, the thinking of members of the dominant culture.

positive reception of an ethnic joke at a gathering of the UN, for example), and likewise, what is acceptable to that particular audience (the ethnic joke may be better received in the company of diplomats whose own culture has similar jokes aimed at the target ethnicity). This may be attributed to the simple social desires of the teller: wanting to 'fit in,' to be accepted by peers, and to avoid calling unfavourable attention to one's self.

On a cultural scale, this works in the same way; jokes and humour poke and prod at the parameters of acceptable thought by calling attention to cultural ideas and soliciting a response which either reinforces conservative views, or opens the way for subtle shifts in cultural thinking. For example, the second joke cited above suggests a number of things about the cultural opinions which created it: beatings were an acceptable punishment for sin, relationships between priests and women carry an implied sexuality, women can be clever manipulators, and jealous husbands will be punished for their skewed perceptions. This joke is conservative in that it presents a situation which appears in a number of comic and dramatic texts and therefore reinforces cultural assumptions; but it also suggests a rethinking of the husband's role in disciplining the wife. Here, the husband assumes that the wife is wicked, that the priest is intending to become her next lover, and therefore, the priest will not punish her as much as he himself would. But the husband's desire for appropriate punishment is chastised by his final predicament. Perhaps the subtle cultural lesson here is that husbands should not meddle in their wives' affairs because doing so may not resolve any problems, and may even lead to further marital dysfunction, in this case, the beatings of the husband made parallel to the wife's frustrated desires.

What this creates is what Christine Davies terms the 'Center' and the 'Outside'.[6] Writing about ethnic jokes, she sees humour as a medium which defines and explores a dominant culture's relationship with those on the fringes of or outside conservative social positions, whether the Center is looking at the Outside contained in another economic bracket, religion, or hometown. These groups need not be distant or separated; Davies argues that 'the two groups may be hostile or in a state of conflict, [but] sometimes they may live as amicable neighbors and sometimes they are indifferent to one another'.[7] What jokes and humorous tales do here is to help define 'us' and the Other, but Davies suggests that the self-definition inherent in jokes continually negotiates and redefines the border between Center and Outside.[8] Humour, in effect, becomes a practical medium for the testing and manipula-

---

[6] See Christine Davies' Introduction to *Jokes and Their Relation to Society* (NY: Mouton de Gruyter, 1998), pp. 1-10, for a survey of her theoretical perspective.

[7] Davies, *Jokes*, p. 1.

[8] Davies' entire book explores this relationship and redefinition; see especially Chapters 2 and 5.

tion of cultural thinking and identity, sometimes reinforcing public normativity and sometimes helping to adapt the culture to the changes which occur in culturally interactive times.

And certainly, England between the years AD 900 and AD 1500 saw not merely interactive times, but culturally tumultuous times. Invasions, wars, conflicting political interests, a developing trade economy, the first stirrings of the Protestant Reformation, and countless other events exposed the English people to a variety of new experiences which redefined their position in the world, and as a result, necessitated their redefinition of themselves. We certainly might point to political, economic, and religious reformations which attempted to accommodate each of these sweeping changes in English culture, but humour reveals not only the general reaction to such changes, but the individual, personal reactions of the English people, who in the end are also the determiners of their culture.

The present volume seeks to contextualise humour within these parameters, 'Center' and 'Outside', public and private. Contributors explore these sometimes elusive complexities using a diversity of critical methods and approaches applied to such diverse literary texts as Malory's *Morte Darthur* and liturgical drama, and visual art such as stained glass and manuscript illumination. The individual essays strive to define clearly the functional breadth of humour in medieval England while developing critical perspectives that inform and develop scholarship concerning both well-known and lesser-known cultural artifacts.

Martha Bayless opens the collection by assessing the evidence for entertainment and merriment among the Anglo-Saxons. Although such activities get short shrift in the surviving literature, evidence of Anglo-Saxon laughter does survive in other forms: chronicles, letters, glosses, saints' lives, and archaeology. By examining these records, Bayless sheds light on such phenomena as dwarf jesters, tightrope walkers, gambling, ale-houses, and entertainment in a variety of contexts, from court to monastery.

Addressing the perhaps more problematic issue of the complex dialogue between the serious and the comic, the sacred and the profane, Christopher Crane suggests that – in contrast to earlier thought – far more than subversion and carnivalesque impulses underlie the instances of humour in late medieval religious literature. Crane argues that understanding of the efficacy of laughter to make the heart more receptive to serious exhortation, the need for a contrast between earthly and divine, and the ultimately comic vision (hopefulness) of Christianity all contribute to the rhetorical employment of humour in these genres. Paul Hardwick's study of the early fourteenth-century Pilgrimage Window in York Minster addresses similar questions concerning the earthly and the divine. Using literary sources, drama records and sermon materials, along with comparisons with other decorative media,

Hardwick suggests that the borders of this window – now celebrated for their playfulness – were intended to provide a detailed marginal gloss which places the viewer in relation to the iconography of individual devotion that fills the main lights.

That humour is, indeed, in the eye of the beholder, is explored by Dana Symons who, by focusing upon the varied approaches to humour – sophisticated or spectacular – of popular romances, illuminates differing expectations about what constitutes pleasure amongst audiences of such tales; a divergence that may be linked to the separate venues of private reading and public performance. These readings emphasize that the comic, like all tastes, must be seen as historically, socially, and culturally produced rather than as arising from a set of universally appealing features.

In the context of a growing mercantile economy, Christian Sheridan highlights the congruity between the circulation of meaning within a pun and the circulation of money as exemplified in Chaucer's late fourteenth-century *Shipman's Tale*. The narrative circulation involves the equalization of differences: money allows different commodities to be compared on an equivalent scale, the pun different meanings to be seen in the same word. Thus, concludes Sheridan, we may make a fundamental connection between currency and humour as signifying systems. A rather less glittering example of 'fundamental' signification is addressed by Laurel Broughton as she investigates the perennial conundrum of scatology in the margins of doctrinal manuscripts. Rather than viewing the 'buttfaces and turd bowlers' as evidence of mankind's fallen state, however, Broughton sees the decorations embodying the entire realm or realms of spiritual and human physical existence, signaling a benign unity within God's creation.

Within creation, however, some are more equal than others, and Sandra M. Hordis looks at a surprising element of transgressing social codes; that of cross-dressing in Malory's *Morte Darthur*. Hordis investigates how laughter weaves together both the apparently stable ideal of chivalry and the surprises and shifts within the comic moment, as when Lancelot dresses as a woman or when Alys strikes Alexander successfully with a sword, and concludes that in these comic moments, strict chivalric gender ideals are forgotten and the actions are reinterpreted to reinforce more ecumenical values. The uneasy laughter that this may provoke is further investigated in Miriamne Krummel's analysis of the comedic within The Croxton *Play of the Sacrament*. Reading the Croxton drama through the lens of Hobbesian 'sudden glory', Krummel reveals that the play enables the socially marginalized spectator to obtain the desires for a lost superiority by watching an already oppressed group make fools of themselves, drawing together a thread which binds many of the previous discussions.

The final two essays emphasise the Englishness of medieval English comedy. Focusing upon Chaucer's embellishment of his Middle Dutch sources, Peter Beidler highlights elements of 'realism' which allow for a more empathic engagement with the English text. When we laugh at the antics of Chaucer's characters, Beidler suggests, we are laughing at the actions of believable people, people who are not so far removed from ourselves and the people we know. The comedy, then, is a human comedy. And this human comedy is perhaps nowhere more vivaciously depicted than in the carvings which cavort on the choir stalls of English churches. Elaine C. Block and Frédéric Billiet return us to the performers with which we began, exploring the variety of musical performances – both sacred and profane – represented on misericords. In so doing, they posit a particularly English strain of musical comedy which not only can still be appreciated, but may indeed reveal a continuity in musical theatre.

We are, after all, outsiders to the culture which created the comic moment and, therefore, we must ask ourselves what we might discover of the intentions of comedy in the English Middle Ages. We might turn to Jacques Le Goff for inspiration here: 'As a cultural and social phenomenon, laughter must have a history.'[9] As scholars, we might discover what shifts occurred in ideas of normativity, ultimately leading to a clearer picture of medieval English identity, and as the Other, we are a part of that comic history, laughing today at the comic renegotiations of culture, thereby redefining our perceptions of the English Middle Ages. This collection addresses this agenda, and in so doing we hope that it will stimulate further research into this rich vein of medieval culture.

---

[9] Le Goff in Bremmer and Roodenburg, *Cultural History*, p. 40.

1

Humour and the Comic in Anglo-Saxon England

MARTHA BAYLESS

Those who have gleaned the field of Anglo-Saxon literature for humour have found slim pickings.[1] The only inarguably comic texts are the double-entendre riddles of the Exeter Book. Other surviving genres, ranging from heroic literature to saints' lives, tend to be martial, elegiac, didactic, or some combination of the three. The brief glints of humour identified in them by scholars have been defended only by lengthy arguments buttressed with numerous footnotes, suggesting that whatever humour they may contain is far from self-evident.[2] T. A. Shippey has characterized Anglo-Saxon secular humour as sardonic, a 'tradition of wisdom finding grim amusement in folly'.[3] Nor do Anglo-Saxon narratives themselves feature humour

---

[1] The field has been surveyed by Jonathan Wilcox, 'Anglo-Saxon Literary Humor: Toward a Taxonomy,' *Thalia* 14 (1994), 9-20 and Jean I. Young, '*Glæd Was Ic Gliwum* – Ungloomy Aspects of Anglo-Saxon Poetry,' in *The Early Cultures of North-West Europe*, ed. Cyril Fox and Bruce Dickins (Cambridge: Cambridge University Press, 1950), pp. 257-87.

[2] Studies identifying humour in texts otherwise thought to be without humour include Raymond P. Tripp, Jr., 'Humor, Wordplay, and Semantic Resonance in *Beowulf*,' E. L. Risden, 'Heroic Humor in *Beowulf*,' Shari Horner, '"Why do you speak so much foolishness?": Gender, Humor, and Discourse in Ælfric's *Lives of Saints*,' and Hugh Magennis, 'A Funny Thing Happened on the Way to Heaven: Humorous Incongruity in Old English Saints' Lives,' all in *Humour in Anglo-Saxon Literature*, ed. Jonathan Wilcox (Woodbridge: D. S. Brewer, 2000).

[3] T. A. Shippey, '"Grim Wordplay": Folly and Wisdom in Anglo-Saxon Humor,' in *Humour in Anglo-Saxon Literature*, ed. Wilcox, pp. 33-48 at pp. 39, 46.

as an important thematic element. Scholars have examined laughter in Old English texts and concluded that it represents triumph, detachment, or other qualities more often than sheer merriment or amusement.[4] Hugh Magennis has attempted to tabulate the examples, citing a mere three that qualify as a response to joy – invariably religious joy – and only four examples of 'Laughter as a Symbol of Happiness or Prosperity'.[5] There are no accounts of laughter as, for instance, a response to obscene riddles. If it were not for the chance survival of the Exeter Book and its double entendres – if the likelihood of such a genre had to be predicted from the character of other surviving literature – the existence of bawdy Old English riddles would seem implausible at best.

Was this truly the character of Anglo-Saxon humour – grim, sardonic, and rare – or is this impression of Anglo-Saxon humour an accident of the survival of the texts? Since the overwhelming proportion of surviving texts are sombre, if not positively gloomy, it stands to reason that any humour found in them would be of a similar character. Of course we know that the literature that has come down to us is only a small fraction of what must have circulated in the period. We do have considerable evidence of a great deal of literature that has not survived in complete form, referred to in works such as *Beowulf* and *Deor*, and preserved in summary in chronicles, historical works, and the like.[6] It is striking that although there is clear evidence of dozens of vanished narratives, not one of them is comic. Were purely comic narratives unknown to Anglo-Saxon England? Or was the comic of such low status – perhaps because it was antithetical to the prevailing mode of martial or religious sombreness – that no traces of it have been preserved?

It should be noted that the literature of Anglo-Saxon England includes other exceptions to the prevalence of sombre genres. Chief among these are the early romance texts, *Apollonius of Tyre*, *The Letter of Alexander to Aristotle*, and *The Wonders of the East*. The widespread Eustace romance, moreover, was known in Anglo-Saxon England in both a prose saint's life and a metrical version.[7] These texts of the mar-

---

[4] See Hugh Magennis, 'Images of Laughter in Old English Poetry, with Particular Reference to the 'Hleahtor Wera' of *The Seafarer*,' *English Studies* 73 (1992), 193-204; Shippey, 'Grim Wordplay'; Susie I. Tucker, 'Laughter in Old English Literature,' *Neophilologus* 43 (1959), 222-26; and Laura Ruth McCord, 'A Study of the Meanings of *Hliehhan* and *Hleahtor* in Old English Literature,' unpublished PhD dissertation, University of Missouri, Columbia, 1979.

[5] Magennis, 'Images of Laughter,' pp. 194-95 and 197-98.

[6] The lost literature has been described by C. E. Wright, *The Cultivation of Saga in Anglo-Saxon England* (Edinburgh and London: Oliver and Boyd, 1939) and R. M. Wilson, *The Lost Literature of Medieval England* (London: Methuen, 1952).

[7] Michael Lapidge, 'Æthelwold and the *Vita S. Eustachii*,' *Scire litteras: Forschungen zum mittelalterlichen Geistesleben*, ed. S. Krämer and M. Bernhard, Bayerische Akademie

vellous all relied on imported plots, but their apparently ready adoption by the Anglo-Saxons is worth noting. Other ostensibly religious texts, such as the exuberantly surrealistic *Poetic Solomon and Saturn II* and *Prose Solomon and Saturn II*, evince a liking for the fantastic, even within the confines of religious discourse; and poems such as *Widsith*, with its telescoping of time, place, and legend, straddle the divide between heroic material and the romance. It is also worth noting that even a text as foundational as *Beowulf* has the fantastic – dragons and superhuman monsters who live in pools – at its core. On the side of gloom, it might be said that even monsters and dragons serve to emphasize the danger and transience of the mortal world. On the side of the fantastic, however, it might be argued that even when danger and transience form the basic themes of a work, the Anglo-Saxons like to add a flourish of the fantastic – monsters and dragons. Even the surviving scrap of *Waldere* has two references to the extra-realistic: giants and the quasi-magical smith Weland. The Old English charms suggest a culture abundant with tales about hags, witches, dwarfs, and supernatural assailants. When the same attention to the outlandish is brought to bear on Scripture, it produces Biblical trivia and apocrypha; the *Prose Solomon and Saturn* and *Adrian and Ritheus* discuss such matters as Mercury the giant, the birth of Jesus through Mary's right breast, and who first conversed with a dog. Even the fascination with numbers and firsts, characteristic of such texts, is a further indication of an Anglo-Saxon love of the extravagant at odds with the muted gloom of texts such as *The Seafarer*.[8]

Literary extravagance is one type of play; the Anglo-Saxons demonstrated their love of play in literature of other types as well. The Durham Proverbs are shot through with sardonic playfulness, typified by such examples as 'Wide ne biþ wel cwæþ se þe gehyrde on helle hriman' (Things are bad all over, said he who heard the screaming in hell) and 'Ne swa þeah treowde þeah þu teala eode, cwæþ se þe geseah hægtessan æfter heafde geo[ngan]' (I would not trust you even if you went properly, said he who saw the witch going on her head).[9] The existence of the hundred or so vernacular riddles, both suggestive and straightforward, is evidence of considerable official approval of play, first in the fact that the riddles were copied into the Exeter Book itself, and then in the fact that the manuscript was pre-

---

der Wissenschaften, philosophisch-historische Klasse, Abhandlungen, N. F. 99 (Munich, 1988), pp. 255-65, reprinted in *Anglo-Latin Literature 900-1066* (London and Rio Grande, Ohio: Hambledon Press, 1993), pp. 213-23.

[8] Anglo-Saxon love of the 'enumerative style' is discussed by Charles D. Wright, *The Irish Tradition in Old English Literature* (Cambridge: Cambridge University Press, 1993), pp. 49-105 and 'The Irish "Enumerative Style" in Old English Homiletic Literature, Especially Vercelli Homily IX,' *Cambridge Medieval Celtic Studies* 18 (1989), 27-74.

[9] Olof Arngart, 'The Durham Proverbs,' *Speculum* 56 (1981), 288-300 at p. 292 (no. 11) and 295 (no. 44). They are discussed as examples of humour by T. A. Shippey. 'Grim Wordplay,' p. 35.

sented to Exeter cathedral by bishop Leofric. The fashion for composing riddles, followed by such learned churchmen as Aldhelm and Boniface, became so widespread that riddle-composition became a schoolboy exercise, with products of the classroom incorporated into manuscripts such as Cambridge Gg.5.35 (the Cambridge Songs manuscript).[10] Although many of the clerical riddles are sedately pious, and none is suggestive, the fact that an innately playful genre could be adapted to religious sensibilities illustrates the reach and flexibility of play in Anglo-Saxon England.

One of the Exeter Book riddles even gives us a context for this type of play. The 'cock and hen' riddle places the unveiling of the riddle in its social setting:

> Nu is undyrne
> werum æt wine   hu þa wihte mid us,
> heanmode twa,   hatne sindon.[11]
> (Now it is revealed to men at their wine how the creatures, the two mean-spirited ones, are named among us.)

This suggests that riddles were enjoyed at social gatherings, a scenario consonant with the fact that Anglo-Saxon merriment of the conventional sort – mirthful, festive, non-religious – is mentioned almost exclusively in the context of communal feasting and drinking.[12] It is this kind of reference that assures us that Anglo-Saxon England was not completely devoid of humour. The topos of the hall-joys serves as a shorthand for the pleasures of life in a variety of sources. In fact, one of the strongest pieces of evidence for the importance of merriment in Anglo-Saxon culture is the mournful tone of the poetry of exile: the exile of which the poets speak is invariably exile from the laughter and joys of the hall. The Seafarer, for instance, uses the joys of the hall to characterize the way of life he has lost, emphasizing his exile from fellowship:

---

[10] On Anglo-Saxon riddles see Martha Bayless, 'Alcuin's *Disputatio Pippini* and the Early Medieval Riddle Tradition,' in *Humour, History and Politics in Late Antiquity and the Early Middle Ages*, ed. Guy Halsall (Cambridge: Cambridge University Press, 2001), pp. 157-78 at pp. 157-60. The verse riddles of the Cambridge Songs manuscript are printed by J. A. Giles, *Anecdota Bedae, Lanfranci et Aliorum* (London, 1851, repr. New York, 1967), pp. 50-53.

[11] Bernard J. Muir, *The Exeter Anthology of Old English Poetry*, 2 vols. (Exeter: University of Exeter Press, 1994), I, p. 321, ll. 15-17.

[12] On this see also Hugh Magennis, *Images of Community in Old English Poetry* (Cambridge: Cambridge University Press, 1996).

<pre>
        ...   Hwilum ylfete song
dyde ic me to gomene   ganetes hleoþor
ond huilpan sweg   fore hleahtor wera,
mæw singende   fore medodrince ...[13]
</pre>

(At times I took the song of the swan for my entertainment, the voice of the gannet and the sound of the curlew for the laughter of men, the mew singing for mead-drinking.)

The lament in *The Wanderer* is similar: 'Hwær cwom symbla gesetu? Hwær sindon seledreamas?' (Where did the seats for the feasting vanish? Where are the joys of the hall?) (94) *The Ruin* similarly characterizes loss in terms of the loss of the merriment and fellowship of the hall, lamenting the vanishing of 'meoduheall monig mondreama full,' (many a mead-hall full of the joys of men) (32). In *Beowulf*, centred on Heorot and Grendel's loathing of its revelry, the merriment of the hall comes to stand most fully for the joys of human life. Beowulf reflects on the merriment in the hall when he first set eyes on it:

<pre>
Weorod wæs on wynne;   ne seah ic widan feorh
under heofones hwealf   healsittendra
medudream maran. (2014-2016)
</pre>

(The warband was joyful; never have I seen in my life under heaven's vault greater mead-joy among those who sit in the hall.)

To deprive an enemy of their mead-benches is to take away all that is worth having: their sovereignty, status, and even their lives:

<pre>
Oft Scyld Scefing   sceaþena þreatum,
monegum mægþum   meodosetla ofteah (4-5)
</pre>

(Often Scyld Scefing deprived bands of enemies, many nations, of their mead-benches.)

When a speaker refers to Beowulf's death, he says that he laid aside 'hleahtor ... gamen ond gleodream' (laughter, merriment, and the joys of music) (3020-3021): again the loss of the hall-joys is the loss of life itself. In Vercelli Homily XI, the soul characterizes its role in bodily life in terms reminiscent of those used in *Beowulf*, in which fun represents the soul's joyous engagement with the world. The passage suggests that the soul expresses its animation on earth through mirth and laughter:

---

[13] Muir, *The Exeter Anthology*, I, 232, lines 19-22.

ic wæs þin feðe 7 þin gang 7 þin staðol 7 þin gemynd; 7 ic wæs þin gamen 7 þin
gladung 7 þin hleahtor 7 þin myrhð. Eall þæt ðu wære, ic wæs þis eall on þe.[14]
(I was your movement and your going and your support and your memory; and I
was your fun and your gladness and your laughter and your mirth. All that you were,
I was this all in you.)[15]

Given that the hall was the *locus classicus* of fellowship and merriment, what can
be ascertained about the source of that merriment? Certainly drinking was a sub-
stantial part of the festivities, as witnessed by the most common Anglo-Saxon terms
for communal revelry, *beorscipe* and *gebeorscipe*. Centred on the term *beor*, the
word suggests that drinking was a *sine qua non* of merriment in the hall.[16] In fact,
the communality of revelry is such that, as Hugh Magennis notes, the verb *drincan*,
'to drink,' is attested only in the plural.[17] The Anglo-Saxons drank in company, and
if descriptions of feasts are any evidence, when in company, they drank. The only
exception to the rule of communal drinking is Grendel, the solitary moor-dweller,
who drank blood alone (742), and whose monstrosity is defined by his hatred of
the festivities of the hall.

The term *gebeorscipe* also denoted feasting; Ælfric uses it to describe the heavenly
feast of the afterlife, and so it presumably did not necessarily imply a feast of which
drunkenness was a feature.[18] The feast from which Cædmon withdrew was also a
gebeorscipe in its Old English translation.[19] Thus it may be that the term could be
applied to a dignified ecclesiastical gathering as well as a roisterous secular one;
or, alternatively, there is significant evidence that ecclesiastical gatherings were just
as likely to be roisterous as secular ones. Indeed, due to the biases of the extant
sources, most of the surviving evidence for drunken and merry feasts is ecclesiastical. It is true that the notices of such feasts are invariably condemnatory; but it is

---

[14] Donald Scragg, *The Vercelli Homilies and Related Texts*, Early English Text Society
300 (Oxford, 1992), Homily XI, p. 224, lines 73-77.

[15] The homily also characterizes the sinful life as one of 'unglædlic hleahter,' 'cheerless
laughter,' but this is surely distinct from the laughter to which the soul lays claim.

[16] On the definition of *beor* see Christine Fell, 'Old English *Beor*,' *Leeds Studies in
English* n.s. 8 (1976 for 1975), 76-95.

[17] Hugh Magennis, *Anglo-Saxon Appetites: Food and Drink and Their Consumption in
Old English and Related Literature* (Dublin and Portland, Oregon: Four Courts Press, 1999),
p. 26.

[18] *Ælfric's Catholic Homilies: The Second Series, Text*, ed. Malcolm Godden, EETS s.
s. 5 (London: Oxford University Press, 1979), p. 217.

[19] *The Old English Version of Bede's Ecclesiastical History of the English People*, ed.
Thomas Miller, 4 vols., EETS o.s. 95-96, 110-111 (London, 1890-98, repr. 1959-63), vol.
95-96, cap. 25, p. 342.

also true that the rambunctious feasts being condemned are invariably conducted by other clerics. It seems that Anglo-Saxon clerical merriment was irrepressible.

Admonitions against clerical merrymaking span the Anglo-Saxon period. In 679, a Roman council on English church affairs directed that bishops and other clergy 'armis non utantur, nec citharoedas habeant, vel quaecunque symphoniaca, nec quoscunque jocos vel ludos ante se permittant'[20] ('should not possess arms, nor host cithara players or other musicians, nor permit joking or shows before them'). Originating in Rome, the edict may pertain to Roman habits more than to English ones, but other evidence of English clerical merrymaking followed on its heels. The Penitential of Theodore, a Frankish compilation attributed to Theodore, Archbishop of Canterbury (668-690), issued an admonition about the secular clergy:

> Jocationes, et saltationes, et circum, vel cantica turpia et luxuriosa, vel
> lusa diabolica, nec ad ipsas aecclesias, nec in domibus, nec in plateis, nec
> in ullo loco alio facere praesumant; quia hoc de paganorum consuetudine
> remansit.[21]
>
> (They should not presume to engage in joking and dancing and races, or base and
> lustful songs, or devilish amusements, neither in churches nor in homes nor in the
> streets nor in any other place, since this remains from the practices of the pagans.)

Bede expressed similar concerns in a letter to Ecgberht, bishop of York, in 734:

> de quibusdam episcopis fama uulgatam est, quod ita ipsi Christo serviant, ut nullos
> secum alicuius religionis aut continentiae uiros habeant; sed potius illos, qui risui,
> iocis, fabulis, commessationibus et ebrietatibus, ceterisque uitae remissioris illece-
> bris subiugatur, et qui magis cotidie uentrem dapibus, quam mentem sacrificiis
> caelestibus parent.[22]
>
> (it is said about certain bishops that they serve Christ in such a way that they have
> with them no men of religion or continence, but rather those who are given to laugh-
> ter, jokes, stories, feasting, and drunkenness, and the other attractions of a loose life,
> and who feed the stomach daily with feasts more than the soul with the heavenly
> sacrifice.)

The Council of 'Clofesho,' in 747, enjoined bishops to insure

---

[20] *Councils and Ecclesiastical Documents*, ed. A. W. Haddan and W. Stubbs, 3 vols. (Oxford: Clarendon Press, 1871), III.133.

[21] B. Thorpe, *Ancient Laws and Institutes of Britain*, 2 vols. (London: Eyre & Spottis-woode,1840), II, 46, cap. 38.

[22] *Venerabilis Bedae Opera Historica*, ed. C. Plummer, 2 vols. (Oxford: Clarendon Press, 1896), I.407.

> ut...monasteria...non sint ludicrarum artium receptacula, hoc est, poetarum, citharis-
> tarum, musicorum, scurrorum...[23]
> (that...monasteries...do not become vessels of the frivolous arts, that is, of poets,
> cithara players, musicians, or clowns...)

The admonitions were reiterated later in the document:

> Unde [non] sint sanctimonialium domicilia, turpium confabulationum, commessa-
> tionem, ebrietatem, luxuriantiumque cubilia...[24]
> (Therefore the dwellings of the religious should not be full of shameful chatter,
> feasting, drunkenness, and dens of excess...)

Alcuin's famous letter to bishop 'Speratus,' written in 797, deplored secular entertainment at ecclesiastical feasts, asking, 'What has Ingeld to do with Christ?' Confirming the presence of entertainers at such feasts, he goes on to reprove Speratus:
'It is better that the poor should eat at your table than entertainers and persons of
extravagant behaviour.'[25]

Clerical merriment was still a concern in the tenth century, when Edgar (ruled 957-
75) complained that churchmen

> ...diffluant in comessationibus et ebrietatibus, in cubilibus et impudicitiis; ut jam
> domus clericorum putentur prostibula meretricum, conciliabulum histrionum. Ibi
> aleae, ibi saltus et cantus, ibi usque ad medium noctis spatium protractae in clamore
> et horrore vigiliae...[26]
> (...expend themselves in feasting and drinking sessions, in beds and shameless acts;
> so that now the houses of clerics are considered brothels of prostitutes, gathering-
> places for performers. There gaming takes place, there dancing and singing, there
> people stay awake until the middle of the night with noisiness and uncouth behav-
> iour...)

---

[23] *Councils and Ecclesiastical Documents*, ed. Haddan and Stubbs, III.368.

[24] *Ibid.*, 369.

[25] Translation from Donald A. Bullough, 'What has Ingeld to do with Lindisfarne?',
Anglo-Saxon England 22 (1993), 93-125 at p. 124. The letter is edited in *Epistolae Karolini
Aevi* II, ed. E. Dümmler, MGH, Epist. IV (Berlin, 1895), no. 124, p. 183.

[26] *Cartularium Saxonicum*, ed. Walter de Gray Birch, 3 vols. (London: Whiting and Co.,
1885-1899), III, p. 573.

Around 992, Ælfric added his voice to the condemnation of clerical carousal:

> Nu doþ men swa-þeah dyslice for oft, þæt hi willað wacian and wodlice drincan binnan Godes huse and bysmorlice plegian and mid gegaf-spræcum Godes hus ge-fylan. [27]
>
> (Now men neverthless behave foolishly too often, so that they stay up and drink madly in the house of God, and make merry disgracefully and fill God's house with foolish speech.)

The Council of Clofesho's 'poets, cithara players, musicians, [and] clowns,' and Bede's enumeration of 'laughter, jokes, stories, feasting, and drunkenness' go some way to explain what exactly might happen at such a gathering. Alcuin's account of clerical games, dancing, singing, boisterousness, and staying up late rounds out the picture. The conundrum comes in the fact that the surviving literature seems much too sombre for boisterous hall-gatherings. Clearly jocularity, high spirits, and laughter were staples of the hall. The clowns mentioned at the Council of Clofesho and in other sources suggest performances by comic entertainers rather than just ad hoc tomfoolery. But do these admonitions indicate the existence of actual comic narrative? And if so, was it composed or performed by specialised entertainers such as *scops*, or was it a more demotic genre, practiced by anyone who remembered a funny story? Last – and related to these other issues – if comic narratives did exist, were they told in verse?

Although much remains mysterious about entertainment in Anglo-Saxon England, there is indisputable evidence of comic performers. How they amused their audiences exactly is less clear. Evidence for anything like secular theatre is extremely tenuous.[28] The most suggestive piece of evidence comes from King Edgar's complaint about the depravity of the clergy, which is so egregious, he reports, that 'Haec milites clamant, plebs submurmurat, mimi cantant et saltant' (The soldiers shout these things, the people mutter them, the performers sing and dance about them).[29] If we understand *mimi* as actors, the passage suggests satirical plays or skits, but if *mimi* here denotes performers in general, as often seems to be the case in Anglo-Saxon England, then the passage could just as well be describing performances of satirical songs or poems accompanied by miming or capering. These performances

---

[27] *Die Hirtenbriefe Ælfrics in altenglischer und lateinischer Fassung*, ed. B. Fehr (Hamburg, 1914, repr. Darmstadt: Wissenschaftliche Buchgesellschaft, 1966), Brief I, no. 107; p. 24.

[28] On this question see Jocelyn Price, 'Theatrical Vocabulary in Old English: A Preliminary Survey (1),' *Medieval English Theatre* 5 (1983), 58-71 and 'Theatrical Vocabulary in Old English (2),' *Medieval English Theatre* 6 (1984), 101-25.

[29] *Cartularium Saxonicum*, ed. Walter de Gray Birch, 3 vols. (London: Whiting and Co., 1885-1899), III.573.

might be enacted by a single performer, and the plural of the statement may refer to multiple performers rather than multiple players in the same performance. However these *mimi* performed, this is a very rare witness to satirical performance in Anglo-Saxon England.

The terminology of entertainers offers further evidence about the kinds of performance in Anglo-Saxon England, but the evidence is often challenging to interpret. Old English terms for performers include *scop, leasere, tumbere, fædel, scericge*, and possibly *þyle, woðbora* and *leoðwyrhta*; the varieties that seem to offer the most evidence of encompassing the comic are *spillere* and *truð*, and in some contexts *gleoman* and *gliwere*.[30] Latin terms in use include *poeta, mimus, histrio,* and *parasitus*, with the terms most certainly related to comedy being *comicus, scurra, ioculator,* and *iocista*. Difficulty stems from the fact that Latin terms could be mapped onto the Anglo-Saxon cultural practices only imperfectly. In addition, Anglo-Saxon authors and translators, unfamiliar with Roman performance traditions, may not have fully understood the conventional uses of the Latin terms. The difficulty of applying Roman terms to Anglo-Saxon practices is demonstrated by one glossator's struggles to explain the term *comicus*:

> Comicus scilicet est qui comedia scribit cantator uel artifex conticorum seculorum idem satyricus .i. scop ioculator poeta[31]
>
> (A *comicus*, that is, is one who writes a comedy; a singer or a creator of secular songs, also a satirist, i.e. a bard, jester, poet.)

It looks as if the glossator understood a *comicus* as, strictly speaking, the author of a *comedia*, also a foreign concept, but then attempted to translate the concept into the world of Anglo-Saxon performance, where the composer of songs or poems might also be a performer. The profusion of ostensible synonyms for the same word make it difficult to identify a precise semantic range for each term, and this complexity afflicts the larger body of Anglo-Saxon glosses. An early eleventh-century manuscript of the *Excerptiones de Prisciano*, for instance, glosses 'tragedus uel

---

[30] The vocabulary of Anglo-Saxons performers and poets has been investigated most thoroughly by Jeff Opland, *Anglo-Saxon Oral Poetry: A Study of the Traditions* (New Haven: Yale University Press, 1980), pp. 230-56. The *þyle* is discussed by Norman E. Eliason, 'The Þyle and Scop in Beowulf,' *Speculum* 38 (1963), 267-84. The *woðbora* is discussed by Ida M. Hollowell, '*Scop* and *Woðbora* in Old English Poetry, ' *Journal of English and Germanic Philology* 77 (1978), 317-329. The identity and vocabulary of medieval performers is also discussed by J. D. A. Ogilvy, 'Mimi, Scurrae, Histriones: Entertainers of the Early Middle Ages,' *Speculum* 38 (1963), 603-619.

[31] From the tenth- and eleventh-century glosses in British Library Harley 3376, ed. Robert T. Oliphant, *The Harley Latin-Old English Glossary*, Janua Linguarum, Series Practica 20 (The Hague and Paris: Mouton & Co., 1966), C1206, p. 84. The edition expands the abbreviation *.s.* to the less likely 'siue'; I have substituted the more likely 'scilicet.'

tragicus uel comicus uel comedus' as 'unwurð scop' (lowly *scop*).[32] Does this mean that a *scop* performed both serious and comic material, and so both tragedians and comedians could be conflated under the same term? Or does it mean that Old English had no term for a performer or composer whose work encompassed both the serious and the comic, and thus *scop* had to be pressed into service to cover an alien concept?

Similar problems are present for most of the glossary evidence, but one term, *truð*, is supplied with intriguing external evidence. The *truð* was a performer or entertainer associated with a trumpet, and the word translates *liticen* (trumpeter) in glossaries.[33] The *truð* was so closely associated with trumpets that the Old English term for trumpet is *truðhorn*.[34] Yet the *truð* seems to have been more than a musician. One piece of evidence is the circularity of the word *truðhorn*; if *truð* were merely a trumpeter, then to call the instrument a *truðhorn*, a 'trumpeter's trumpet,' seems impossibly redundant. It seems more plausible that the *truð* had an identity beyond his instrument, and thus that the word *truð* preceded the naming of the horn. Potential confirmation of this comes from a glossary that identifies *truð* as *histriones*, performers.[35] Of course even trumpeters are performers, but the more general term may imply a larger scope for the performance of the *truð*. A story told by Ælfric may also give witness that there was felt to be something frivolous or profane about the *truð*, which may imply buffoonery more than musicianship. In the story, a sacreligious and gluttonous *truð* disregards Lent and suffers divine punishment:

> On þære ylcan wucan com sum truð to þæs bisceopes hirede, se ne gymde nanes lenctenes fæstenes, ac eode him to kicenan, þa hwile ðe se bisceop mæssode, and began to etenne. He feoll þa æt ðære forman snæde under-becc geswogen ...[36]
> (In that same week a *truð* came into the bishop's household, a man who paid no heed to the Lenten fast, and betook himself to the kitchen, while the bishop celebrated mass, and began to eat. He fell down backwards then, lifeless, at the first morsel ...)

The role of sinner in such stories is often assigned to professions with ungodly reputations. We may compare later medieval illustrations in which unbelievers were

---

[32] L. Kindschi, 'The Latin-Old English Glossaries in Plantin-Moretus MS. 32 and British Museum MS. Additional 32246' (unpublished Stanford PhD dissertation, 1955).

[33] J. Zupitza, *Ælfrics Grammatik und Glossar*, Sammlung englischer Denkmäler 1 (Berlin: Weidmann, 1880); repr. with intro. by H. Gneuss (Hildesheim, Weidmann, 2003).

[34] Ælfric's *Glossary*, ed. Zupitza, *Ælfrics Grammatik*, s.v. *lituus*.

[35] Kindschi, 'The Latin-Old English Glossaries.'

[36] *Aelfric's Lives of Saints*, ed. W. W. Skeat EETS, o.s. 76, 82, 94 (London: N. Trübner and Co., 1881), p. 264 (no. 12, Ash Wednesday).

represented by the fool of the Psalms, dressed as a court fool.[37] In a similar way, Ælfric may have 'cast' a variety of professional fool as the sinner in this tale, and so this may suggest that the *truð* was a kind of comic performer. If so, it is tempting to wonder if the *truðhorn* was like the horns blasted for comic effect by modern clowns.

Other evidence for buffoons or jesters in courts or elsewhere is complicated. *Gliwere* is equated to *scurra* (buffoon) in one set of glosses.[38] *Scurra* is equated with *mimus* and *iocista* in one glossary, and defined as *gligmon*[39] and *sceawere* elsewhere.[40] Although the precise semantic range of these terms is unclear, the Anglo-Saxons do seem to have understood *scurra* as a clown or buffoon rather than a performer in general, as the word appears in texts that may suggest clownish performance. Aldhelm says 'jocistae scurraeque ritu'[41] (in a joking or clownish manner), and the Northumbrian Priests' Law dictates: 'Si presbyter ebrietati deditus sit, vel scurrilis aut cerevisiarius fuerit, hoc compenset'[42] (If a priest is given to drunkenness, or is fool-like or a *cerevisiarius*, he should atone for it.)

A distant but intriguing suggestion of the existence of court fools or jesters comes from Geffrei Gaimar, the Anglo-Norman chronicler who composed his verse chronicle, *L'estoire des Engleis*, for a Lincolnshire patroness around 1140. Geffrai describes an altercation between King Edward the Martyr and a dwarf jester, an altercation which led to the king's death in 978. Gaimar takes some time to elaborate on the skills of the jester, although these more likely reflect jesters in his own day than any knowledge of tenth-century practices:

> Il ert un jur joius e lied,
> En Wiltesire aveit mangied.
> Wlstanet un naim aveit
> Ki baler e trescher saveit,
> Si saveit saillir e tumber

---

[37] On this see, for instance, V. A. Kolve, 'God-denying Fools and the Medieval "Religion of Love",' *Studies in the Age of Chaucer* 19 (1997), 3-59.

[38] H. D. Meritt, *The Old English Prudentius Glosses at Boulogne-sur-Mer*, Stanford Studies in Language and Literature 16 (Stanford, 1959, repr. New York 1967), 1-115, no. 620.

[39] L. Kindschi, 'The Latin-Old English Glossaries.'

[40] J. J. Quinn, 'The Minor Latin-Old English Glossaries in MS. Cotton Cleopatra A.III' (unpublished Stanford dissertation, 1956).

[41] *MGH, Auctores Antiquissimi* XV, no. 5, p. 493.

[42] J. Mansi, *Sacrorum Conciliorum Nova et Amplissima Collectio*, 52 vols. (Graz: Akademische Drunk- und Verlagsanstalt, 1960-62), vol.19, p. 69.

E autres gius plusur jüer.

Li reis le vit, si l'apelat

E a jüer lui comandat.

Lu naim lui dist que nun fereit,

Pur sun cumant ne jüereit.

Cum li reis plus bel l'en preiat,

E il encuntre le ramponad,

Forment s'en est li reis marid.

Wlstanet dunc s'en issit...[43]

(One day he [Edward] was joyous and happy.

He had dined in Wiltshire.

He had a dwarf, Wlstanet,

Who knew how to dance and caper,

And he knew how to leap and tumble

And how to perform many other amusements.

The king saw him, and called him

And commanded him to perform.

The dwarf told him he would not do it,

That he would not perform on command.

As the king asked him more nicely,

And [the dwarf] just insulted him [in return],

The king became very angry because of it.

Wlstanet then went out ...)

The dwarf goes to the house of Ælfthryth, the mother of Edward's half-brother and the instigator of his murder in other legends. Edward follows and is murdered by an unnamed co-conspirator as he speaks with Ælfthryth outside her house. Stories of Edward's murder were embellished as the centuries passed, but this is the only one to mention or implicate a jester.[44] The story of the dwarf jester bears the stamp of legend, but that legend may go back some centuries. The name of the jester, Wlstanet, appears to be the common Anglo-Saxon name Wulfstan (spelled 'Wlf-stan' in late Anglo-Saxon documents)[45] provided with a Norman suffix. The presence of such an archaic name in the text suggests that the legend circulated in the Anglo-Saxon period, when the name Wulfstan or Wlfstan was common. This does

---

[43] Geffrei Gaimar, *L'Estoire des Engleis*, ed. Alexander Bell (Oxford: Blackwell, 1960), p. 127, lines 3983-3996.

[44] On the various Anglo-Saxon versions of Edward's death, see Susan J. Ridyard, *The Royal Saints of Anglo-Saxon England* (Cambridge: Cambridge University Press, 1988), pp. 44-50.

[45] See, for example, *The Vita Wulfstani of William of Malmesbury*, ed. Reginald R. Dar-lington (London: Offices of the Royal Historical Society, 1928), *passim*.

not mean that the legend was true, but, more important for our purposes, that popular legend of the late Anglo-Saxon period found it plausible that a dwarf filled the role of jester, and plausible that a jester was a denizen of the royal household. Thus even if we cannot pinpoint a specific jester in a specific Anglo-Saxon reign, we can come closer to verifying the existence of jesters by noting their appearance in popular legend.

The Old English term for 'jester' was most likely *spillere*, from *spilian*, 'to play,' although other, perhaps broader, terms seem to have been used as well. Glosses suggest more about the status of the *spillere*, giving, for example, *parasitorum: gliwra spilra spillendra*.[46] The *parasitus* was an attendant, and so the *gliwere* or *spillere* must have had an official position. Elsewhere various forms of *parasitus* translated as *þena* (thegns or retainers), *cnihta* (attendants), *incniht* (household retainers), *stiward* (attendant) and *gligman*.[47] In turn, glossaries on Aldhelm define *per gymnisophistas* as *þurh plegemen uel gligmen uel gleawe*.[48] The *plegeman*, *gligman*, and *gleaw* may have been athletes first and foremost, as the term *gymnisophistas* suggests, but it is more likely that they were jesters of the order of Wlstanet, who tumbled and capered as part of their buffoonery. Other appearances of the term *gligman* or its variant *gleoman* in glosses show that the *gligman* was an entertainer. *Gleo* or *glig* denoted play or mirth, and this was closely allied with music; a *gleobeam* was a musical instrument, *tympanistia* is transated *gliwmæden*, and a cymbal-player is a *cimbalgliwere*.[49] The term *gleo* itself does not seem to indicate music per se, however, but something like 'playing'. (We might note that in modern English musicians still 'play' music, although of course the term is not etymologically related to *gleo*.) *Facitiae*, for instance, is glossed *wynsum gleo*, and *luserit* as *gliwode*.[50] In a gloss on Gregory's *Dialogues*, *gligcræft* is defined as *ars musica, histrionia, mimica, gesticulatio*, suggesting that its practitioners were

---

[46] Louis Goossens, *The Old English Glosses of MS. Brussels, Royal Library, 1650* (Brussels: Paleis der Academiën, 1974).

[47] Goossens, *Old English Glosses*, N. R. Ker, *Catalogue of Manuscripts Containing Anglo-Saxon* (Oxford: Clarendon Press, 1957), p. 470.

[48] Goossens, *Old English Glosses*.

[49] Fritz Roeder, *Der altenglische Regius-Psalter*, Studien zur englischen Philologie 18 (Halle: M. Niemeyer, 1904), Ps. 67:26 and C. Sisam and K. Sisam, *The Salisbury Psalter*, EETS 242 (London: Oxford University Press, 1959), and related glossaries; Hans Hecht, *Bischof Waerferths von Worcester Übersetzung der Dialoge Gregors des Grossen* (Leipzig and Hamburg, 1901-07, repr. Darmstadt: Wissenschaftliche Buchgesellschaft, 1965), pp. 10, 61.

[50] For *facetiae*, see J. D. Pheifer, *Old English Glosses in the Epinal-Erfurt Glossary* (Oxford: Clarendon Press, 1974). For *luserit*, see H. D. Meritt, *The Old English Prudentius Glosses*.

multi-talented, even theatrical performers.[51] Jeff Opland attempts to make a case that the *gleoman* was a more lowly performer than the *scop*, writing, 'The gleoman has no connection in the glosses with poetry or indeed with composition; he is a wandering entertainer of dubious repute,' and '*scop* and *gleoman* are kept quite distinct in the glosses'.[52] This may be true of the glosses, but the role of the *gleoman* does overlap with that of the *scop* in other sources, and so the range of the *gleoman* may well have included serious poetry. In *The Order of the World*, the world is interpreted by a man who knows 'gliwes cræft, mid gieddingum' ('the practice of *gliw*, through poems/songs' (11-12)). *Beowulf* has 'Leoð wæs asungen, gleomannes gyd' (the song was sung, the lay of the *gleoman*) (1159-1160), and *Widsith* sums up the role of bards who carry the tales described in the poem: 'Swa scriþende gesceapum hweorfað gleomen gumena geond grunda fela,' (So the people's *gleomen*, travelling according to their destinies, go through many lands) (135-36). It seems likely, then, that *gleoman* was a wider term than *scop* or *scurra*, meaning something like 'entertainer,' and encompassing a variety of performers, from the serious *scop* to the clownish *spillere*. If this is the case, however, why would the 'tragedus uel tragicus uel comicus uel comedus' be glossed as *unwurð scop* rather than the potentially more versatile *gleoman*? It is possible that the *scop*, like the *comicus* and *tragicus*, could compose his own material, where the *gleoman* was a perfomer of stock material. Or it is possible that the glossator considered a *gleoman* and an *unwurð scop* one and the same.

Whatever their names, many of the jests and tricks performed by the more frivolous entertainers are lost, but a few can be discerned from illustrations. In the eleventh-century British Library Cotton Tiberius C.VI, a psalter produced ca. 1060 in Winchester, King David is surrounded by three musicians and a juggler juggling three balls and three knives.[53] The juggler is labelled 'Ethan'; the Ethan in 1 Chronicles 15-16, however, is a cymbal player, which means that the juggling is a purely Anglo-Saxon addition, and undoubtedly reflects actual practice.[54] A second juggler appears in Trinity College Cambridge B.5.26 (olim 172, produced in Canterbury 1070 x 1100), juggling three knives.[55]

---

[51] F. M. Padelford, *Old English Musical Terms*, Bonner Beiträge zur Anglistik 4 (Bonn: Hanstein, 1899), p. 77.

[52] Opland, *Anglo-Saxon Oral Poetry*, p. 244.

[53] fol. 30v; reproduced in Alan J. Fletcher, 'Jugglers Celtic and Anglo-Saxon,' *Theatre Notebook* 44 (1990), 2-10 at p. 5.

[54] Fletcher, 'Jugglers,' p. 4.

[55] Reproduced in C. M. Kaufman, *Romanesque Manuscripts 1066-1190* (London: H. Miller, 1975), ill. 11, and in C. Reginald Dodwell, *The Canterbury School of Illumination 1066-1200* (Cambridge: Cambridge University Press, 1954), p. 106.

Thus although the evidence is complex and fragmentary, comic performers, jesters, and buffoons did ply their trade in Anglo-Saxon England. This leaves the question of whether such entertainers might have retailed comic narrative as part of their performances. Edgar's statement about the *mimi* who 'sing and dance' about the crimes of the clergy gives one small indication that narrative might have been involved; the definition of *gligcræft* as *histrionia, mimica, gesticulatio* may also suggest something acted out, though not necessarily narrated. This is not a great deal to go on. Opland has assembled the vocabulary of various kinds of poem or song (*leoð*), which provides further evidence:

> What of the compounds? There are many: *æfenleoð* (an evening leoð), *bismerleoð* (an insulting leoð), *dryhtleoð* (a lord's leoð), *fusleoð* (a departure leoð), *fyrdleoð* (an army leoð), *galdorleoð* (a charm leoð), *giftleoð* , *gryreleoð* (a terrible leoð), *guðleoð* (a battle leoð), *hearmleoð* (a harmful leoð), *hildeleoð* (a battle leoð), *licleoð* (a leoð for a corpse), *sæleoð* (a sea leoð), *scopleoð*, *sealmleoð* [a psalm-leoð], *sigeleoð* (a victory leoð), *sorhleoð* (a sorrow leoð), *wigleoð* (a battle leoð), and *wopleoð* (a weeping leoð).[56]

Of the nineteen terms, only two are even potentially humorous, the *bismerleoð* and the *hearmleoð*. Both might be satirical, and it is just possible that the *bismerleoð* could be a type of flyting. But it is striking that there are no purely comic genres in this list. It may well have been that humorous narratives were too frivolous to warrant the time of a scribe or the cost of velum, but it is harder to imagine that any mention of such narratives should be excluded from everyday vocabulary. If comic narrative is missing from the list, it may have been missing from the poetic repertoire altogether. There is always the chance, of course, that terms for comic poetry do not appear because the surviving references are found exclusively in serious texts. Although the stock of Anglo-Saxon literary narrative preserved is slim, the number preserved in summary form is quite large.[57] The literary seems to encompass a limited number of themes, the vast majority historical or pseudo-historical: violence, treachery, conflict, and evil women. Wonders, such as the magical cow and the child who changes into a bird (both found in the story of Kenelm), make their appearance in saints' lives, where they can be given a gloss of piety.[58] But although the demands of genre made room for the marvellous, history and comedy are antithetical genres, and none of these forms or interests allows for the comic. Thus it should not be surprising that there was little room for the comic in the of-

---

[56] Opland, *Anglo-Saxon Oral Poetry*, p. 247.

[57] Surveyed by Wright, *Cultivation of Saga* and Wilson, *Lost Literature*.

[58] On the popular motifs found in the life of Kenelm and other Anglo-Saxon narratives, see Catherine Cubitt, 'Sites and Sanctity: Revisiting the Cult of Murdered and Martyred Anglo-Saxon Royal Saints,' *Early Medieval Europe* 9 (2000), 53-83.

ficial political and ecclesiastical landscape. If comic narrative existed, then, it must have done so on a more informal level, perhaps solely in prose. Jokes were no doubt told between friends; entertainers hammed it up when people gathered for *gebeor-scipe*s; kings employed performers who no doubt told comic stories as well as tumbling, capering, and juggling. Entertainers, perhaps *gleomen*, proffered riddles, including joking and bawdy ones, at hall-gatherings. But formal comic verse narrative, such as any form of vernacular fabliau, leaves no trace in the historical or literary record. Analogous cultures with strong traditions of heroic verse, such as some cultures of modern Papua New Guinea, similarly have no comic poetic genres; and thus it is a reasonable conclusion that formal comic narrative simply did not exist in Anglo-Saxon England.

This is not to say that comic narrative per se was unknown in Anglo-Saxon England. As might be predicted from the irrepressibility of the clergy, sophisticated bawdy narrative was introduced by the Church. The indisputable evidence of this is the Cambridge Songs, a compilation of Latin lyrics copied at St. Augustine's, Canterbury, in the mid-eleventh century, from an exemplar most likely of German origin.[59] A number of the songs have musical notation and four include the name of the tune to which they should be sung, although whether these tunes were known in England is unanswerable. It is clear, however, that these were not conceived of nor copied as poems for private reading, but as songs intended for oral, public performance. Though none of the lyrics is Anglo-Saxon in origin, the very fact that they were copied in Anglo-Saxon England provides important testimony to an enjoyment of secular music and narrative. Many of the songs are serious, and include hymns, political songs, and settings of the metres of Boethius; but the collection also contains love-songs, religious humour, and seven comic narratives which can lay claim to being the earliest fabliaux in Europe.[60] They are thus a landmark in sophisticated humour.

As we have seen, there are centuries of testimony to the fact that monastic culture often – perhaps customarily – was open to the same kinds of entertainment that circulated in the secular world. Although post-Conquest culture is never a reliable guide to pre-Conquest practices, it should be noted that, contrary to modern expectations of monastic seriousness, later English monasteries formed one of the three or four most important sources of employment for entertainers in later medieval

---

[59] Jan Ziolkowski, *The Cambridge Songs (Carmina Cantabrigiensia)* (New York and Tempe, Arizona: Garland, 1994).

[60] Peter Dronke, 'The Rise of the Medieval Fabliau: Latin and Vernacular Evidence,' in *Romanische Forschungen* 85 (1973) 275-97.

England.[61] Performers appeared at the monastery of St. Benet of Hulme fifteen times in 1372-73, sixteen times at Selby Abbey in 1397-98, and fifteen times at Battle Abbey in 1478-79.[62] It should be clear from the witness of early medieval writers that monastic entertainment was not a phenomenon imported with the Normans, but had a venerable tradition in Anglo-Saxon England, however much it might have been deplored by the more austere elements in the Church. The Cambridge Songs may comprise the most important piece of evidence for the content of high-status monastic entertainment: it may well comprise a script, or perhaps more accurately a libretto, of one monastery's evening entertainment.

If the comic was for many centuries a low-status, informal genre in Anglo-Saxon England, it is a pleasant irony that the Church that fought against clerical merriment so persistently should be the institution that educated the Anglo-Saxons sufficiently to gain access to the bawdy humour of other nations, and to serve as a vehicle for the *imprimatur* and poetic status the comic had been lacking. Thus, far from being too gloomy to appreciate comic tales, the Anglo-Saxons were among the earliest in medieval Europe to import them, to copy them, and to enjoy them.

---

[61] Sheila Lindenbaum, 'Entertainment in English Monasteries,' *Le Théatre et la cité dans l'Europe médiévale*, ed. Jean-Claude Aubailly, Stuttgarter Arbeiten zur Germanistik 213 (Stuttgart: Hans-Dieter Heinz, 1988) (*Fifteenth Century Studies* 13 (1988)), pp. 411-34 at p. 411.

[62] Lindenbaum, 'Entertainment,' p. 411.

2

Superior Incongruity: Derisive and Sympathetic Comedy in Middle English Drama and Homiletic Exempla

CHRISTOPHER E. CRANE

In the fifteenth-century morality play *Mankind,* which illustrates mankind's need for Mercy in order to obey God's will, the title character defends himself with a spade against three baudy, wicked, and outrageously funny devils who are tempting him, sent by their superior, Myscheff; Mankind wounds them in head, arm, and private parts, and they wail in pain to their leader:

> Neu Gyse: Alasse, master, alasse, my privyte!
> Myscheff: A wher? alake! fayer babe, ba me! [Kiss me!]
>   Abyde! to son I xall it se.
> [...]
> Nought: 3e pley in nomine patris, choppe!
> Neu Gyse: 3e xall not choppe my jewellys, and I may.[1]

This moment and many others like it in the play invite laughter at the expense of the villains. However, other comic moments in the play invite us to laugh at the protagonist, Mankynde, or to partake in the transgressive laughter of these same villains. What exactly is the intended role of such comedy?

---

[1] *Mankind,* ed. by Mark Eccles, *The Macro Plays: The Castle of Perseverance, Wisdom, Mankind,* EETS 262 (Oxford and London: Oxford UP, 1969), ll. 429-40.

In order to illustrate and warn against the sin of sacrilege, Robert Mannyng's four-teenth-century Middle English penitential manual *Handlyng Synne* tells of a hus-band and wife who dare to make love near the church. For their sacrilege God curses them so that 'þey myghte no more be broght asondre / þan dog & bych þat men on wondre'. In order to get unstuck, the husband calls for monks and asks them to pray 'þat þey myght be undoun', a word which also signifies God's forgiveness of their sins a few lines later. Mannyng presents the story as a warning against sacrilege and says specifically that it should make us forever fear 'to do þat dede' in a holy place.[2] This story may appear mortifying, vivid, and potentially quite persuasive, especially for a medieval reader taking it as authoritative and true. However, it is also comic in its depiction of the couple's punishment.

As these examples show, medieval English drama and homiletic exempla provided audiences with vivid, comic illustration of Christian truth in action. The presence of humour in these two genres with the common aim of providing religious instruc-tion and exhortation reveals some patterns in the medieval attitude toward and understanding of the relationship between laughter and persuasion. Bakhtin's pop-ular theory of Carnival misrule to explain medieval comedy, while offering valu-able insights into the culture, does not account for some of the orthodox rhetorical aims of the humour. A comparison of some comic exempla in late medieval English drama and religious instruction literature points to a theory of comedy in which learning and laughing occur interdependently and in which laughing both at oneself and at God's enemies represent effective avenues to spiritual instruction and edifi-cation. Such comedy both arises from and reinforces the essential medieval tension between spirit and flesh, between the heavenly and the earthly, and ultimately, between God and man in order to foster in the audience a better understanding of their human frailty and sinfulness as well as their need for grace and victory over evil through their Christian faith.

Drama and Homiletic Narratives

Though at first glance a simple didactic device, the homiletic exemplum is not easy to define, in part owing to confusion in the Middle Ages themselves.[3] Using stories to teach predates Christianity, though the Middle Ages of course needed no greater precedent for doing so than Jesus Christ, who used stories, parables, to explain the

---

[2] Robert Mannyng, *Handlyng Synne*, ed. by Idelle Sullens (Binghamton, NY: Medieval and Renaissance Texts and Studies, 1983), ll. 8932-9014.

[3] Frederic C. Tubach, 'Exempla in the Decline', *Traditio* 18 (1962), 406-17 (p. 408 n.6).

mysteries of God's kingdom while at the same time himself *being* the quintessential exemplum, the model human life, the story of what God would do, and did do, as a man. Scripture's use of narrative to teach gave authority to the method.[4] The influence of Pope Gregory's *Dialogues*, however, most firmly established the exemplum as a formal element of Christian preaching.[5] Medieval writers also appropriated classical stories by giving them allegorical Christian interpretations, plundering the Egyptians (itself an historical exemplum legitimizing the appropriation of pagan aesthetic and rhetorical forms for carrying the Christian message) as Augustine recommends in *De doctrina Christiana*.[6] Modern scholars do not entirely agree about the definition of the exemplum. In his early descriptive study of exempla in medieval England, J. A. Mosher identifies the essential elements of the exemplum as 'a short narrative used to illustrate or confirm a general statement', going on to identify narrative and human characters as the essential elements.[7] Two decades later, Owst allows inclusion of 'any kind of homiletic simile or illustration' in the term and then identifies 'Narration' as stories about humans, 'Fable' for beast tales, and 'Figure' for lessons drawn from the natural world.[8] More recently, Larry Scanlon has attempted to 'redefine' the term as 'a narrative enactment of cultural authority', recognizing a closer relationship between the narrative, its message, and its cultural context than the earlier definitions do.[9]

A medieval preacher and his audience understood life and history as allegorical, as very exempla of spiritual truth. These homiletic illustrations, in content more like the morality plays than the biblical cycle plays, present readers and listeners with practical portrayals of the good work urged or the evil deeds warned against in the sermon. An exemplum, whether read in a book, heard in a sermon, or watched in performance, shows the audience what the Christian's life should (or should not) look like. Medieval Christianity was not ultimately about educating the mind but about living righteously; an exemplum shows the audience how they can and should do good or avoid evil. The exempla says with Christ (after the parable of the Good

---

[4] G. R. Owst, *Preaching in Medieval England* (London: Cambridge UP, 1926), p. 152.

[5] Tubach, 'Exempla in the Decline', p. 409.

[6] Augustine, *De doctrina Christiana* 2.40.

[7] Joseph Albert Mosher, *The Exemplum in the Early Religious and Didactic Literature of England* (New York: The Columbia UP, 1911), pp. 1, 6.

[8] Owst, *Preaching in Medieval England*, p. 152.

[9] Larry Scanlon, *Narrative, Authority, and Power: The Medieval Exemplum and the Chaucerian Tradition* (Cambridge: Cambridge UP, 1994), p. 34.

Samaritan), 'You go and do likewise'.[10] Paul urged the Philippians to follow his own example.[11] The accounts of God's faithfulness to Israel in the Old Testament were to be passed down not simply as a set of ancient stories to learn but as demonstrations of God's past grace to inspire hope in his grace to come – his help, his involvement in the future – both for the next day and for eternity on which to ground further actions of faith and obedience[12]. These examples along with events recorded in the New Testament, miracles of saints, and classical folk tales in the early centuries of the church were appropriated by the Middle Ages for the same purpose.

The dramatized Bible stories and morality plays function in essentially the same way as does a sermon or homiletic exemplum. The medieval plays enact (or reenact, in the case of biblical drama) scriptural narrative or other orthodox teaching. Certainly some plays teach or edify the audience in different ways than do their more overtly homiletic counterparts; but the application of humour – either to make model characters more imitable or to condemn evil by inviting the audience to laugh at it – is one approach they share. Both genres employ story-telling which, among other things, encourages audience members to practise their faith by showing them what doing so ought to look like.[13] In the Middle Ages, biblical history offered the master story for all of life, that their God had sacrificed himself to defeat the Devil and free all his captives, and that a glorious deliverance awaited the faithful. The cycle plays and morality plays all act, in effect, as exempla of some facet of this very story. They begin with the start of evil (first in heaven, then in Eden); they climax with the near- or seeming-defeat of the King, his glorious resurrection, and his setting free of the captives; they end by showing the eternal destiny of the King's subjects and his enemies. Each pageant within a cycle tells a small piece of that story. The morality plays, while not retelling biblical events, exemplify through allegorical or typological representation the invisible elements in the struggle to live the Christian life: resisting temptation and persevering in God's ways in order to be found faithful at the Judgment.

---

[10] Luke 10. 37, *English Standard Version* (Wheaton, IL: Good News Publishers, 2001). The Vulgate reads, 'vade et tu fac similiter'. *Biblia Sacra Iuxta Vulgatam Versionem* (Stuttgart, 1994).

[11] 'Quae et didicitis et accepistis et audistis et vidistis in me haec agite et Deus pacis erit vobiscum', Phil 4. 9, Vulgate.

[12] John Piper, *The Purifying Power of Living by Faith in Future Grace* (Portland, OR: Multnomah 1995). Though Piper writes about contemporary Christianity, I am indebted to his work for this description of the application of Old Testament narratives.

[13] 'Other things' includes objectives related but not identical to moving the audience's will to practise their faith, such as teaching doctrine, building community, asserting status in the community (especially among competing guilds), or making political comment (in sermons or drama).

When a medieval preacher or writer of a religious manual provides a short narrative to illustrate an abstract spiritual truth, he is giving the audience a concrete picture of the truth acted out. Sometimes the desired emotional response is *Schadenfreude*, the laughter of 'triumphal derision'[14] invited by identifying the sin with a clearly evil character who is opposed to God. In another comic pattern, the message is reinforced through the audience's sympathetic laughter as they recognize the sin in an exemplary character, one much like themselves.

Comic Theory

There is no evidence of a developed medieval theory of comedy, let alone one of rhetorical comedy. Aristotle, Cicero, and Quintilian all treat humour in their rhetorics; however, until almost the end of the fifteenth century, the volumes with the most to say on the subject had little influence on medieval rhetorical theory.[15] Only Cicero's and pseudo-Cicero's brief comments on the use of humour in *De inventione* and *Rhetorica ad Herennium*, respectively, suggest their influence on the medieval employment of it in the genres under consideration here. Both advocate the use of humour to keep the audience listening:

> For, just as a loathing and distaste for food is relieved by some morsel with a bit of a tang, or appeased by a sweet, so a mind wearied by listening is strengthened by astonishment or refreshed by laughter.[16]

Ad Herrenium lists eighteen humorous devices the orator might employ for listeners who have been wearied by hearing (*defessi erunt audiendo*).[17]

---

[14] Hans-Jürgen Diller, 'Laughter in Medieval English Drama: A Critique of Modernizing and Historical Analyses', *Comparative Drama* 36.1 (2002), 1-19 (p. 2).

[15] Aristotle's *Rhetoric*, though translated into Latin and copied, became associated with his other works on ethics and philosophy and was apparently not treated as a text on discourse. In England the earliest indication of its use at Oxford or Cambridge is 1431. James Murphy, 'Artistotle's *Rhetoric* in the Middle Ages', *Quarterly Journal of Speech* 52 (1966), 109-15 (pp. 109-15). Cicero's *De oratore* and Quintilian's *Institutio oratoria* deal most heavily with the use of humour, but they were almost completely inaccessible by all records until the fifteenth century. James Murphy, 'Cicero's Rhetoric in the Middle Ages', *Quarterly Journal of Speech* 53 (1967), 334-41 (pp. 334-41).

[16] Nam, ut cibi satietas et fastidium aut subamara aliqua re relevatur aut dulci mitigatur, sic animus defessus audiendo aut admiratione integratur aut risu novatur. Cicero, *De inventione,* trans. by H. M. Hubell (Cambridge: Harvard UP, 1949), 1.17.25.

[17] *Rhetorica ad Herennium,* trans. by Harry Caplan (Cambridge: Harvard UP, 1954) 1.6.10.

Consistent with these works, the view in medieval preaching manuals and modern scholarship about the purpose of humour in homiletic exempla is that it serves to keep the listeners' attention so they will better attend to the spiritual point that follows. In his fourteenth-century *De forma praedicandi*, Robert of Basevorn cites Cicero in advocating well-placed humour in a story in order to bring the listeners pleasure if they are bored and especially if they are sleepy. Basevorn qualifies this advice with the provision that the stories not be inappropriate.[18]

Although medieval homilists and dramatists certainly employed humour to keep the audience's attention, a more complex relationship between the comedy and the message often underlies the structure of the humour itself. Most of these stories are more than sugar coating on the medicine of dry spiritual truth, and while they indeed keep one's attention better than they would without the use of humour, many of the homiletic exempla also possess a more direct relationship between the humour and the message, a relationship that is fundamentally linked to the core of medieval spirituality and world view. Much of the homiletic literature, both humorous and serious, centres on the contrast and tension between opposites: flesh and spirit, sin and righteousness, devils and saints – some facet of the ultimate opposition between, and incongruous union of, man and God.

Modern comic theory includes a broad range of cultural phenomena, many of which are beyond the scope of literary analysis. No single theory about exactly what makes people laugh and what our capacity to laugh signifies has been settled on, though not for lack of effort on the part of many philosophers, theologians, literary critics, sociologists, and psychologists from Plato to the present. The most common points of agreement are that humour involves elements of surprise and perceived incongruity. Robin Andrew Haig categorizes the historical theories about the nature of humour into five major types, each emphasizing different critical ingredients or sources of the risible: incongruity, superiority, 'changes in affect or tension,[...]social communication,[...]and psychoanalytic approaches'.[19] Haig's study is a psychological one aimed at understanding therapeutic uses of humour, and even his five categories reflect this emphasis; others group his last three into one category – 'relief theories' – alongside incongruity and superiority.[20]

---

[18] Robert of Basevorn, *De forma praedicandi,* trans. by Leopold Krul, *Three Medieval Rhetorical Arts* ed. by James Murphy (Berkeley and Los Angeles: University of California Press, Ltd., 1971), p. 212.

[19] Robin Andrew Haig, *The Anatomy of Humor: Biopsychosocial and Therapeutic Perspectives* (Springfield, IL: Charles C. Thomas, 1988), p. 9.

[20] D. H. Monro identifies Superiority, Incongruity, and Release from Restraint as the three major theories. *Argument of Laughter* (Notre Dame: University of Notre Dame Press,

The oldest statements of comic theory fall primarily under the latter of these, 'superiority theory'. Superiority theorists argue that people laugh in response to some form of perceived inferiority in others or superiority in themselves. Plato's, Aristotle's, and to some extent Cicero's views of comedy fall into this category, but Thomas Hobbes is usually credited with the earliest and best known superiority theory identified as such. He considers laughter the outward expression of 'a passion that hath *no name*', and a kind of joy, which he calls 'sudden glory'. Hobbes' term includes two components of that which produces laughter: surprise or unexpectedness and a sense of relative greatness, of superiority. These produce the 'passion' which arises

> from some sudden *conception* of some *eminency* in ourselves, by *comparison* with the *infirmity* of others, or with our own formerly; for men laugh at the follies of themselves past, when they come suddenly to remembrance, except they bring with them any present dishonour.[21]

He makes similar comments in *Leviathan* when he lists 'sudden glory' among the passions of mankind; it produces laughter in people 'either by some sudden act of their own, that pleaseth them; or by the apprehension of some deformed thing in another, by comparison whereof they suddenly applaud themselves'.[22] Nearly all humour theorists recognize this Hobbesian sense of superiority as one type of humour (e.g. ethnic jokes and other aggressive humour), but many accuse it of failing to account for much other humour containing no apparent criticism or producing no conscious feelings of superiority in the speaker or the audience.

Hobbes' view dominated humour theory until incongruity and relief theories appeared in following centuries. Incongruity theories argue that humour consists of a perceived or felt gap – an incongruity – between expectation and actuality. Laughter, Francis Hutcheson first argued in 1750, is the response to that perception.[23] Kant is most famous, however, for furthering the theory by adding to it the idea that laughter arises from perception of '[s]omething absurd (something in which, there-

---

1951), p. 210. John Morreall identifies these same three as the primary comic theories in *Taking Laughter Seriously* (Albany: State U of New York Press, 1983); Simon Critchley uses Moreall's categories as a starting point for discussing comic theory in *On Humour* (New York: Routledge, 2002), pp. 2-3.

[21] Thomas Hobbes, *On Human Nature* IX, *Restoration and Eighteenth-Century Comedy*, ed. by Scott McMillin (New York: W. W. Norton and Co., 1973), p. 343-44. Italics are the editor's.

[22] Hobbes, *Leviathan* I.6, ed. by Richard Tuck (Cambridge UP, 1991), p. 43.

[23] Peter Berger, *Redeeming Laughter* (Berlin: Walter de Gruyter, 1997), p. 22; Critchley, *On Humour*, p. 3.

fore, the understanding can of itself find no delight)' which produces 'a strained expectation being suddenly reduced to nothing'.[24] For Kant, the tension between expectation and reality is resolved as one realizes there is nothing to fear, that the incongruity is harmless.[25] With regard to Hobbes' superiority theory, Kant's view retains the sense of suddenness but not the required perception of 'glory' as essential to humour.

Henri Bergson produced one of the best known and admired works on the nature of comedy; Peter Berger calls his 1900 essay *Laughter* (*Le rire*) 'the most important philosophical work on the comic in the twentieth century'.[26] The essay is identified by many as incongruity theory, though Bergson himself does not specifically do so.[27] Bergson argues in his famous definition that the essence of comedy is 'something mechanical encrusted on the living'.[28] He states, 'the living body ought to be the perfection of suppleness, the ever-alert activity of a principle always at work'.[29] Bergson sees in all comedy some way in which the mechanical, non-living world is supplanting, imitating, or being imitated by the living. A man slipping on a banana peel is comic because in doing so he acts like a non-living object at the mercy of the laws of physics rather than like a conscious, careful human. Social customs and ceremonies have inherent comic potential for this reason, containing 'rigidity [...]clashing with the inner suppleness of life[...]which is only waiting to burst into full view'.[30] Bergson expands his basic notion of tension between the living and the mechanical to include the relationship between the soul and the body of a person, identifying as comic any incident that 'calls our attention to the physical in a person, when it is the moral side that is concerned'.[31] This element of the comic proves useful in understanding some of the comedy of the Middle Ages.

Both superiority and incongruity theories offer valuable insight for understanding why people laugh and how medieval texts employed humour. Laura Kendrick applies the assumptions of incongruity theory in her essay on Chaucer's comedy,

---

[24] Immanuel Kant, *The Critique of Judgement*, trans. by James Creed Meredith (Oxford: Clarendon Press, 1952), II.332, p. 199.

[25] Haig, *The Anatomy of Humor*, p. 16.

[26] Berger, *Redeeming Laughter*, p. 28

[27] Ibid., Berger, *Redeeming Laughter*; Haig, *The Anatomy of Humor*, p. 17; Critchley, *On Humour*, p. 4.

[28] Henri Bergson, *Laughter: An Essay on the Meaning of the Comic,* trans. and ed. by Wylie Sypher. In *Comedy* (New York: Doubleday Anchor Books, 1956), p. 84.

[29] Bergson, *Laughter*, p. 92.

[30] Ibid., Bergson, *Laughter*, p. 89.

[31] Ibid., Bergson, *Laughter*, p. 93.

noting that 'For their comic effect, goliardic texts praising and reveling in various types of sinful behaviour relied heavily on incongruity and on the audience's capacity to detect irony'.[32] Derek Brewer, too, employs incongruity theory in his discussion of medieval comic tales.[33] Proponents of superiority theory criticize incongruity theory as too broad because not all juxtapositions of incongruous elements and the resulting tension between expectation and reality produce laughter.[34]

Contemporary humour theorist Charles Gruner maintains that superiority theory *best* explains *all* instances of humour and that Hobbes' 'sudden glory' identifies the two components essential 'for any evoking of laughter'. Gruner argues that a sense of superiority is always present even if the audience is not conscious of it, and 'even the most 'whimsical' and 'harmless' joke' contains aggression.[35] F. H. Buckley argues the same; humour may arise from an incongruity, but it is an incongruity in which the two elements are unequal, and one of them always receives ridicule or derision. Buckley addresses objections to the superiority theory that argue for 'innocent laughter' based on the socially uniting, sympathetic component of laughter by pointing out that such humour may indeed unite the jester and the audience, but it is at the expense of the butt, over which both feel superior.[36]

This integration of incongruity and superiority theory provides the approach I use for identifying and understanding the humour in the Middle English texts in this study. Though he labels incongruity as the *sine qua non* for comedy, Brewer sees superiority laughter as a major element in much medieval humour. Medieval comedy that laughs *at* a butt Brewer identifies as 'derision', which is 'a general attitude of humorous, superior contempt, very characteristic of medieval humour [...]. A sense of superiority has rightly been felt to be an important component of a sense of humour, even if not the only component'.[37] Both superiority and incongruity theory are essential to the comedy of a poetics seeking to teach and delight while

---

[32] Laura Kendrick, 'Comedy', in *Companion to Chaucer*, ed. by Peter Brown (Blackwell, 2000), 90-113 (p. 95). Her readings of the Envoy to the Clerk's Tale and the Miller's Tale find the comedy arising from incongruity (pp. 108, 110).

[33] Brewer, Introduction, *Medieval Comic Tales*, 2nd ed. by Derek Brewer (Cambridge: D. S. Brewer, 1996), p. xv.

[34] Charles Gruner, *Understanding Laughter: The Workings of Wit and Humor* (Chicago: Nelson-Hall, 1978), p. 7; Gruner, *The Game of Humor: A Comprehensive Theory of Why We Laugh* (New Brunswick, NJ: Transaction Publishers, 1997), p. 24; F. H. Buckley, *The Morality of Laughter* (Ann Arbor: U of Michigan Press, 2003), p. 29.

[35] Gruner, *Understanding Laughter*, pp. 30, 36.

[36] Ibid., p. 39.

[37] Brewer, Introduction, p. xix.

remaining ever conscious of the fundamental tension between God and man. The juxtaposition of the mechanical with the living, body with soul, letter with spirit, provide the foundation of medieval religious comedy.

Triumphant Laughter

The simplest structural pattern in the comedy of both drama and exempla is one in which evil characters appear ridiculous and invite the audience's laughter at their expense. This humour is generated by the contrast and tension between good and evil, and the rhetorical aim of this humour is to deride evil and exalt good, thereby encouraging in the audience a love for goodness and good behaviour. In a critique of some recent discussions that emphasize Bakhtinian Carnival interpretations of medieval comic drama, Hans-Jürgen Diller argues that, 'The religious literature of the Middle Ages especially is full of the terrible fate that awaits the damned but which apparently is not meant to call forth sympathy; on the contrary, *Schaden-freude,* even triumphant derision, seems to be the intended reaction'.[38] He notes that this is the same laughter ascribed to God himself in Psalms 2:24 and 59:9. Of this type of humour in the biblical cycle plays, V. A. Kolve observes that for the medieval audience, 'severance from God is chiefly a result of man's stupidity, of his failure to be intelligent', and the appropriate response to such stupidity is laughter. This laughter should be and is 'unrestrained and unsympathetic', and it places man in his proper role of concurring with God about the wicked.[39] John Cox's examination of devils in the cycle dramas concurs with Diller's position; he argues that, far from subverting authority, 'the social function of the Devil in the mystery plays is to be the Enemy'.[40] Both homiletic exempla and the drama use comic depictions of evil to evoke *Schadenfreude* in order to reinforce the orthodox submission to and love for God.

Ciceronian rhetoric provided medieval writers with sufficient precedent to justify this strategy (if such justification was even needed). The author of *Rhetorica ad Herennium* lists attacking one's opponent as a rhetorical strategy for securing the hearers' good will.[41] The clear moral division in the Middle Ages between good and evil underlay the use of such black-and-white comedy.

---

[38] Diller, 'Laughter in Medieval English Drama', p. 2.

[39] V. A. Kolve, *The Play Called Corpus Christi* (Stanford: Stanford UP, 1966), pp. 140-41.

[40] John Cox, 'The Devil and Society in the English Mystery Plays', *Comparative Drama* 28.4 (1994-95), 407-38 (p. 434).

[41] *Rhetorica ad Herennium,* 1.4.6.

Some exempla and plays depict devils or bad men as ridiculous or comical; others mock the losers or unfortunate ones in the action of the story. A knight in the Middle English *Gesta Romanorum* is returning from war to claim his betrothed, the daughter of his emperor; along the way he meets the King of Hungary, who is also travelling to the emperor to marry the same woman.[42] They travel together and a rain comes, soaking the king through his clothes. The knight cryptically tells him he is foolish for not having brought his house with him. At a river the king nearly drowns as he rides his horse through; the knight tells him he is foolish for not bringing a bridge. Finally, as they eat together, the knight tells the king he should have brought his father and his mother to dinner. To each of the knight's statements the king incredulously replies by asking how he could possibly have done the impossible. After these events they reach the palace, and the knight manages to beat his rival to the princess and marry her before the king realizes his competition. Her father, the emperor, on hearing the king's story of the knight's statements, interprets them for him: the house he should have brought was an outer garment to protect from the rain, the bridge he should have had was someone else to test the depth of the river, and his father and mother equate to bread and wine with dinner.

The allegorical interpretation provided at the end of the story is that the emperor represents Christ and the knight represents 'every good Cristen man' who is seeking eternal life, represented by the emperor's daughter. The king represents men of authority in the world who go through life without clothing themselves in virtue, who put their trust in the world rather than in God (i.e. the bridge), and who seek eternal life in vain because they lack the necessary humility and hope (i.e. father and mother). The didactic purpose of the exemplum is to build the allegory of the knight as a wise Christian and of the three elements the Christian needs in life.

This exemplum develops part of its humour from the allegory within the story – the enigmatic statements by the knight interpreted later by the emperor. The king's confusion, however, could be removed from the story – either by eliminating the knight's remarks altogether or by having him give the explanation immediately – without sacrificing the plot or the elements needed for the moral at the end. For example, when told (after being soaked through by the rain, a comic image in itself) that he should have brought his house, the king replies, 'Myne hous is large, and maade of lyme and stone; and how shold I haue y-brouȝt myn hous with me? Þou spekiste lewidly'.[43] The king's confusion and the incongruity between what he is

---

[42] *The Early English Versions of the* Gesta Romanorum, ed. by Sidney J. H. Herrtage, EETS e.s. 33 (London, 1879), pp. 37-42. At the beginning of the tale she pledges to wait seven years for her knight, after which she is free to marry another; the seven years are nearly over, so she has agreed to her father's desire that she marry the King of Hungary.

[43] Ibid., p. 38.

thinking and what the knight is thinking (which the audience learns shortly or already knows from very likely having heard the story before) creates humour; the
king is actually the one speaking 'lewidly', so he further makes a fool out of himself. In addition, he first has his clothing soaked because he does not have a coat,
and he then comically rides too deep into the river. This irony is entertaining, but
it does more than simply keep the audience awake for the moral at the end. The
audience is first of all laughing at an authority figure who is humbled; the story
would be less humorous if, for example, the king were replaced by a servant or
even another knight. However, the comedy is not carnivalesque or subversive because the king is the opponent of the hero, the good knight who represents the
Christian. The story (including the humour) ultimately supports the authority of
God, the church, and the preacher who may use this story to extol Christian virtue
and instil it in the listeners. When the text identifies the king with other authority
figures who spurn virtues and faith in God, it is in effect telling the audience, 'even
though some men have power and authority in the world, they do not have what
you have: virtue and faith'. The low comedy of the king's dousing by rain and river
combined with both his inability to understand the knight's statements and the fact
that what appears foolish to the king is really great wisdom create a comic effect
that ridicules the folly he represents and exalts Christian wisdom. The audience's
laughter at the king reinforces the serious condemnation of what he represents and
lifts up the model of virtue, faith, and wisdom exemplified in the knight.

The massive preacher's resource, *An Alphabet of Tales,* a fifteenth-century translation of *Alphabetum Narrationum*, contains over eight hundred exempla arranged
alphabetically by subject.[44] Three out of four exempla on the subject of bailiffs
similarly employ comedy rooted in medieval morality, inviting *Schadenfreude* at
the expense of an immoral character, reflecting the apparently timeless enjoyment
of laughing at corrupt officials. In the most developed of the three, the stated lesson
(offered before the tale begins) is that bailiffs frequently take bribes but do not do
what they promised in return (Tale 99).[45] In this story a bailiff is bribed with a cow
by one man to speak in his favour in court. Meanwhile, the man's opponent gives
the bailiff's wife an ox to secure her husband's favour on his side. The wife agrees
to the request, but she then also takes the cow from her husband, showing her support for the first man. In court the bailiff says nothing on behalf of either man, and
as the case progresses against the man who has given the ox, he says to the bailiff,
'Sur, whi spekis nott þe ox?' The bailiff replies that the cow is so good and fair that
she will not allow the ox to speak, meaning that his wife's preference for the cow

[44] *An Alphabet of Tales: An English 15th Century Translation of the* Alphabetum Narrationum *of Etienne de Besançon,* ed. by Mary Macleod Banks, EETS o.s. 126 and 127
(London: Kegan Paul, Trench, Trübner, and Co., 1904, 1905).

[45] 'Ballivi frequenter munera recipiunt sed non faciunt quod promittunt'.

has outweighed his own voice in the matter. Following the tale is an additional moral in Latin that further illuminates the moral at the beginning: 'This fable is useful to any judges, showing both that bribes pervert justice and that women often take more bribes than men do'.[46]

The humour of this tale actually lies neither in the bailiff's dishonesty, which is treated as a given, nor in the ox-giver's frustration; the audience is meant to laugh at the bailiff's reply, which is humorous both in its witty return of the ox-giver's metonymy (the ox's or cow's 'speaking' stands for the bailiff's speaking for the party who has bribed him with the ox and cow) and even more so in his extension of the figure by having the cow represent his wife's influence on him. In addition, the statement (made clear by the Latin) that the bailiff's wife is more crooked than the bailiff is humorous both in its unexpectedness and in the inversion whereby the woman triumphs over the man. The bailiff, in addition to being typically dishonest, is depicted as a hen-pecked husband – a common humorous motif in medieval literature – who does not even get to keep the bribes for himself or speak the way he wants in response to them. The exemplum therefore satirizes the bailiff by first confirming the reputed dishonesty of the profession and then making him subject to his wife. The other two bailiff tales, though completely different in subject matter, both invite laughter at the expense of these officials for the sole purpose of criticizing them.[47] Although the moral aim of these bailiff tales is less overtly religious than others, their humour clearly arises from and perpetuates a moral standard, inviting derisive laughter in order to reinforce the lesson.

The cycle plays and moralities abound with comic evil characters whose very wickedness invites *Schadenfreude*. Many of these characters assert their own greatness before the audience in an extended speech; the humour comes from the incongruity of their smallness compared to God's and the dramatic irony arising from tension between the audience's complete awareness of and their foolish ignorance of that smallness. Perhaps the most vivid and famous example is Herod, present as a comic boaster in all four cycle plays. In the York Masons play, Herod opens with a highly alliterative, somewhat aureate speech asserting his dominion over the earth and heavens:

> The clowdes clapped in clerenes þat þer clematis inclosis –
> Jubiter and Jouis, Martis and Mercurij emyde –
> Raykand ouere my rialte on rawe me reioyses,
> Blonderande þer blastis to blaw when I bidde.[48]

---

[46] 'Hec fabula valet ad quoscumque iudices, et quod munera peruertunt iudicium, et quod mulieres sepius optinent magis quam viri'.

[47] *An Alphabet of Tales* #s 97 and 98.

[48] 'Herod', *The York Plays,* ed. by Richard Beadle (London: Edward Arnold, 1982), ll. 1-4

His speech continues for eighteen more lines in which he asserts how greatly he is honoured by earthly lords, how physically impressive he is, and that he is 'worthy, witty, and wyse'. Herod's baseless boasting is a sharp contrast to the humbleness of the magi in the preceding play, depicted as sincere worshippers who praise the one who is truly worthy of the kind of praise Herod honours himself with. The extreme claims he makes and the formal excesses in his diction associate him with the formalities of earthly rulers contemporary with the audience and make him laughable to the audience. He is not threatening whatsoever, and in fact his very claims are what most directly underscore his ridiculousness and prove him powerless to the audience. Tricomi asserts that in the N-Town play 'Herod's pride, boastfulness and rant are exaggerated to the point where the king becomes a cartoon tyrant, a thing, one who [...] is *not* like ourselves. The necessary consequence of such invention is to deprive Herod and his henchmen both of their fearsome reality and their humanity'.[49] This irony adds to the humour and reinforces through the contrast the greatness of the true king of the world. In his discussion of laughter in the plays, Diller points out that in the Towneley *Magnus Herodes* play, Herod himself laughs in triumph at the report of the slaughter of the innocents, increasing further his own folly in the eyes of the audience.[50] Spectators' laughter at Herod's boastfulness depends on dramatic irony, not only in superior knowledge about the plot, but in the their superior awareness of Herod's weakness, in contrast to his arrogance.

The Chester Cappers play provides another vivid example of this rhetorical comedy that mocks evil in order to move the audience toward God. The play is one of the most popular segments in the Chester cycle, according to Tricomi, owing to the comic segment of Balaam and the talking ass, played by a 'full sized dummy, which must have waddled onto the pageant place with two human beings, including the ventriloquist, inside the integument'.[51] Though perhaps the most memorable in performance, this humorous spectacle is not the only kind of comedy at work. The Chester cycle presents King Balaak as a Herod-like comic villain as he calls upon Balaam to curse the Israelites.[52] The prophet of course (after his encounter with the angel who warns him not to do so) delivers a prophetical blessing on Israel instead, just as he does in Numbers 23-24. In response Balaak cries, 'What the dyvell ayles

---

[49] Albert H. Tricomi, 'Reenvisioning England's Medieval Cycle Comedy', *Medieval and Renaissance Drama in England* 5 (1991), 11-26 (p. 21).

[50] Diller, 'Laughter in Medieval English Drama', p. 8.

[51] Tricomi, 'Reenvisioning England's Medieval Cycle Comedy', p. 13.

[52] His opening boast follows Moses' receiving of the Ten Commandments; Balaak expresses frustration and anger over the invincibility of the Israelites and ironically serves as an instrument of testimony to God's greatness as he recounts his reasons for hating and fearing them: their defeat of the Amalekites, their passing through of the Red Sea and the destruction of the Egyptians, and their victory over two nearby kings.

thee, thow populart? Thy speech is not worth a farte!'[53] His frustration at having been foiled by God's purposes makes him even more ridiculous and invites laughter that reinforces for the audience the impotence of an evil ruler's will when God is determined to protect and bless. Balaak entertains the audience, but he also reminds them of this important fact in a way that is at the same time aimed at engaging and aligning their emotions with spiritual truth.

Devils are frequently portrayed as laughable compared to God in this comic pattern, as in the Harrowing of Hell plays. Early in the Towneley version, the devils Rybald and Belzabub become agitated and fearful as they hear a great 'dyn'.[54] As with Herod, dramatic irony makes their words and actions comic. The audience knows whom they are about to face, because of the play's opening and because of the theological tradition upon which the action is based.[55] They futilely determine not to let any souls go, and as Christ calls on the gates to open (quoting the Vulgate from Psalm 24), they assert their power to hold them shut against anyone, recognizing nothing special about Jesus and defying his claim as king. They also call on their leader, Satan, to come and help. Jesus eventually effects their defeat:

Iesus.	Devill, I commaunde the to go downe
	Into thi sete where thou shall syt.
Sathanas.	Alas for doyll and care!
	I synk into hell-pyt.
Rybald.	Sir Sathanas, so saide I are,
	Now shall thou haue a fytt.[56]

These devils, whom the audience may be tempted to fear or blame in every day life as they wrestle with temptation, guilt, and suffering, are depicted as impotent, silly, and utterly defeated by the power of the Lord. Laughing at them strengthens the audience's faith emotionally in the didactic message that Christ is more powerful than the devil and demonstrates that they are on God's side. As Diller observes of

---

[53] 'Balaam', *The Chester Mystery Cycle*, eds. R. M. Lumiansky and David Mills, EETS s.s. 3 (New York: Oxford UP, 1974), pp. 296-97.

[54] 'Harrowing of Hell', *The Towneley Plays*, vol. 1, eds. Martin Stevens and A. C. Cawley, EETS s.s. 13-14. (New York: Oxford UP, 1994).

[55] The most immediate source was the Gospel of Nicodemus, which was translated into Middle English verse. Lumiansky and Mills, *The Chester Mystery Cycle*, vol II, p. 262.

[56] 'Harrowing of Hell', *The Towneley Plays*, ll. 357-62

the effects of this kind of triumphant derision, 'having to laugh at the misfortunes of the devil is a proof of holiness'.[57]

In understanding these plays employing humour with this rhetorical effect as exempla, it is important to note that these evil characters are not the direct counterparts to the 'good guys', such as Joseph, Noah, and the shepherds, discussed below. They do not simply represent people that the audience should not be like. These characters, including the human ones, actually represent evil itself: sin, the world, the flesh, the devil. They represent the things one should avoid. No one would for a moment be consciously wondering whether or not he or she might follow Herod's example, let alone that of a devil. Though they do urge us to avoid evil, they do so by *being* evil; their wickedness, though comic, aligns them with God's enemies; they are not redeemable. The counterparts to these characters are not Joseph and Noah and other exemplars of the human struggle with sin; their counterparts are God, Jesus, Mary, and the angels, who are themselves not humorous in the English cycle or morality plays.

Sympathetic Comedy

L. Carruthers states that, although certainly exempla help to make a sermon more entertaining, they carry the more specific rhetorical objective of appealing to the audience's daily experience.[58] A second and more complex major comic pattern invites laughter at good characters in whom hearers or readers see themselves. Rather than inviting derisive laughter, this comedy invites the audience to laugh at themselves in their own human weakness by seeing those weaknesses in others. It is a laughter of familiarity, of identification, of shared humanity, and it connects the audience to the characters who serve as the example to follow.

The exemplum in *Handlyng Synne* about the husband and wife stuck together when they make love near the church, places the exemplary (or non-exemplary) couple in the ultimate domestic and embarrassing plight. Mark Miller observes that Mannyng's rhetorical strategy in a related exemplum calls 'attention to, and interest[s] us in, the incoherence that attends the apparent naturalness of each of these mo-

---

[57] Diller, 'Laughter in Medieval English Drama', p. 4. Kolve says almost the same thing when discussing this type of humour in the plays, p. 139.

[58] L. Carruthers, "'Know Thyself': Criticism, Reform and the Audience of *Jacob's Well*', *Medieval Sermons and Society: Cloister, City, University*, ed. by Jacqueline Hamesse, Beverly Mayne Kienzle, Debra L. Stoudt, and Anne T. Thayer (Louvain-La-Neuve, 1998), 219-40 (p. 221).

ments'.[59] As we laugh at their situation, we laugh both in sympathetic identification with their embarrassment and with the urges which have led them to their predicament, and we laugh with relief that they are not us. The man and wife are *not* comic because of an evil nature the way devils and other villains are; they are comic precisely because they could be us. The couple serves as an example of what not to do (and also, to a small degree, of good behaviour: Mannyng comments that the sin of the couple was not as bad as it would have been had they been unmarried and committing fornication or adultery) and as a warning against sacrilege; the humour of their plight moves readers emotionally by inviting agreement, not with the mind alone but also with the heart.

Similarly, the late-fourteenth-century alliterative poem *Patience* gently yet effectively incorporates comedy into an exemplum through the contrast of the earthly and heavenly in order to invite readers to identify with and therefore learn from and imitate the model character. By retelling the story of the Hebrew prophet Jonah, the poet seeks to illustrate, he announces, the importance of patience. Though the story does not appear in a religious instruction manual or a sermon collection, it can be and usually is classified as an exemplum or even as a kind of sermon.[60] Lines 1-61 and 525-32 provide the introduction and conclusion while the intervening 464 lines present a retelling of the entire scriptural story of Jonah in order to extol the virtue of patience.

Theologically the story is a retelling of the prophetical book; though not uproariously funny, the poem is entertaining compared to the biblical tale. In fact, most of the elaborations on the biblical account consist of adding realism with the general effect of lightening the story.[61] In particular, the poet introduces significant extra-biblical detail about Jonah's state of mind and the description of the ship and sea

---

[59] Mark Miller, 'Displaced Souls, Idle Talk, Spectacular Scenes: *Handlyng Synne* and the Perspective of Agency', *Speculum* 71 (1996), 606-32 (p. 625).

[60] Charles Moorman, 'The Role of the Narrator in *Patience*', *Modern Philology* 61 (1963), 90-95; Ordelle G. Hill, 'The Audience of *Patience*', *Modern Philology* 66 (1968), 103-09; Paul E. Szarmach, 'Two Notes on *Patience*,' *Notes and Queries* 18 (1971), pp. 125-27. In addition, the poem fulfills the descriptive definitions of both Mosher and Scanlon, cited above. A important counter-argument to seeing *Patience* as an sermon with exemplum is David Williams, 'The Point of *Patience*', *Modern Philology* 68 (1970), pp. 127-36. Though he does not consider the poem an exemplum and sees the humour as derisive, Williams does maintain that Jonah 'functions as a representative man, uncomfortably close to both narrator and audience' (p. 133); the reader is to identify with Jonah as he suffers and experiences God's mercy (p. 135).

[61] Marie Borroff, ed. and trans., *Sir Gawain and the Green Knight; Patience; and Pearl: Verse Translations* (New York: W. W. Norton, 2001), pp. 82, 86.

voyage. Two moments especially enliven the narrative with humour. The first is when Jonah is asleep in the cargo hold and must be woken up during the storm:

> Onhelde by þe hurrok, for þe heuen wrache,
> Slypped vpon a sloumbe, selepe, & sloberande he routes.
> Đe freke hym frunt with his fot and bede hym ferk vp;
> Đer Ragnel in his rakentes hym rere of his dremes. (185-7)[62]

The circumstances in the plot are quite serious for all the characters involved. No one is laughing, least of all Jonah. But the poet treats this moment with a light-heartedness that does not undermine the rhetorical objective of making Jonah an example for readers not to emulate. After Jonah is released from the belly of the fish, the narrator describes his arrival on shore with the comic remark,

> Đenne he swepe to þe sonde in sluchched cloþes,
> Hit may wel be þat mester were his mantyle to wasche. (341-2)[63]

These minor extra-biblical details add humour not just to make the story entertaining but to humanize Jonah, to make him more truly an example with whom the reader can identify. The comedy in the description of Jonah as disheveled and needing a bath after he has been vomited by the whale depends on the incongruity between the earthly and the heavenly: the physical detail of being muddy and needing to wash one's clothes contrasts with his status as a prophet, a representative of the Lord, a person of spiritual authority.

Other moments in the poem similarly use humour to develop in Jonah a comic ethos which draws readers to sympathize with him as one of them. When the whale first swallows Jonah, 'He glydes in by þe giles þurȝ glaymande glette [slippery slime]' and slides down the whale's innards, tumbling head over heels until he 'stod vp in his stomak, þat stank as þe deuel' (269-274). Toward the close of the poem, God's response to Jonah's frustration over his lost 'wod-bynde' (shade plant), though a serious rebuke, depicts his folly as laughable:

---

[62] *Patience*, ed. by Richard Morris, *Early English Alliterative Poems*, EETS o.s. 1, (Oxford: Oxford UP, 1969). Borroff's excellent translation of this passage and the next captures the comedy here almost as well as the original: 'Huddled aft in the hold, hard by the rudder, / And there he snoozes and snores and slobbers unsightly. / The man gives him a good kick to make him get up–/ May Ragnel in shackles shake him out of his dreams!' (p. 95).

[63] Borroff: 'Then he was swept onto the sand in beslobbered clothes–/ It would have been as well to have washed his mantle!' (p. 99). This occurrence is the only one listed for *sluchched,* 'beslobbered' in *MED*.

> ʒet oure lorde to þe lede lansed a speche: [let loose]
> 'Is þis ryʒt-wys, þou renk, alle þy ronk noyse,
> So wroth for a wodbynde to wax so sone,
> Why art þou so waymot wyʒe for so lyttel?' [angry] (489-42)

Jonah is not portrayed as evil here; he is not a devil from whom readers should distance themselves through derisive laughter. Jonah is an exemplar of one who will not endure suffering, and his anger is made small and comic compared to God. By elaborating on the sparse biblical account in these ways, the poet invites a chuckle with several rhetorical effects. First, Jonah becomes more human, more similar to the poem's readers than to the distant, holy Old Testament prophets. Martha Bayless observes the pattern that, 'in primarily humorous religious literature the audience's identification with the protagonists is greater'.[64] Even though *Patience* is not 'primarily humorous', these moments achieve such an effect. From reading or hearing the scriptural account alone, one may not immediately see Jonah as an exemplum of patience, albeit a negative one. But through these details that invite laughter at his human weakness, the poet makes him a more vivid, more identifiable example to follow. As readers see and laugh at him as someone who snores and slobbers in his sleep and who gets filthy and needs a change of clothes at times, they may become more emotionally receptive to the message his story conveys – more ready to persevere through trials, including those brought about like Jonah's, through their own disobedience.

Within the biblical drama of the cycle plays, Joseph, Noah, and the shepherds serve as vivid and genuine models of faith for the audience to learn from. Their comic action enhances their effectiveness as exemplars. In all the four major collections of biblical plays, those involving Joseph prior to the nativity generate sympathetic laughter at a character who struggles just as those in the audience might under similar circumstances. The cycles all present Joseph as an old man who believes he has been cuckolded when he learns his young wife is pregnant. Initially unable to believe in the miracle of her divine conception, he comically wrestles with the news; when he questions Mary, her honest but ambiguous answers only agitate him further. Finally an angel tells Joseph of the child's origin, and he repents of his unbelief. The comedy in the different dramatic presentations of this story arises from several sources. The first and most obvious is Joseph's dilemma simply as an old man, the classical *senex amans* who believes he has been cuckolded. The cycles draw upon the fabliau tradition quite clearly here, and this association draws the audience into the 'fun of the fast-paced, familiar story they witness in the context

---

[64] Martha Bayless, *Parody in the Middle Ages: The Latin Tradition* (Ann Arbor: U of Michigan Press, 1996), p. 210.

of the supreme divine mystery'.[65] A second facet of the comedy is the incongruity of Joseph's misplaced suspicions: he is accusing the most virtuous, pure woman of all time, and his 'rival' is none other than God himself. In the Towneley Annunciation play, Joseph questions Mary, and she gives short, simple answers, to which he responds with longer speeches, more questions, and more confusion:

> Ioseph. [...]Who owe this child thou gose withall?
>
> Maria. Syr, ye, and God of heuen
>
> Ioseph. Myne, Mary? Do way thi dyn!
> That I shuld oght haue parte therin
> Thou nedys it not to neuen.
> Wherto neuyns thou me therto?
> I had neuer with the to do;
> How shuld it then be myne?
> Whos is that chyld, so God the spede?
>
> Maria. Syr, Godys and yowrs, withouten drede.
>
> Ioseph. That word had þou to tyne,
> For it is right full far me fro,
> And I forthynkys thou has done so
> Thise ill dedys bedene;
> And if thou speke thiself to spyll,
> It is full sore agans my wyll,
> If better myght haue bene.
>
> Maria. At Godys wyll, ioseph, must it be,
> For certanly bot God and ye
> I know none othere man;
> For fleshly was I neuer fylyd
>
> Ioseph. How shuld thou thus then be with chyld?
> Excuse the will thou can!
> [...]
>
> Maria. Yee, God he knowys all my doyng.[66]

[65] Virginia Schaefer Carroll, *The 'Noble Gyn' of Comedy in the Middle English Cycle Plays* (New York: Peter Lang Publishing, Inc., 1989), p. 130.

[66] 'Annunciation', *The Towneley Plays,* ll. 186-215.

Joseph's confusion is humorous in itself, but it is doubly so when set opposite Mary's simple replies to his accusations. Instead of appeasing him, her words increase Joseph's suspicions. Both the repetition and the escalation of his temper make the already comical even more so. Eventually he laments having been married in the first place.[67] In the York version, he describes the betrothal process as 'a bad barganne': Joseph recalls standing among other unmarried men each holding a wand, 'And I ne wist what it ment'; Joseph's budded when the others' did not, so he was told to marry this young woman who is now great with a child he knows is not his.[68]

Despite Joseph's folly, this comedy does not invite laughter at him in scorn; spectators laugh at him as they ought to laugh at their own unbelief. The plays do not ridicule him for not believing as they do Herod and other villains, but they do portray Joseph's unbelief and confusion about the virgin birth as laughable. In the York play, when the angel appears to Joseph to validate Mary's story, Joseph is tired and frustrated and wants to sleep. Biblical angelic visits were awesome events, usually met with fear in people; and in an age as enamoured of the miraculous and spectacle as the Middle Ages, one would expect just such a reaction from a righteous biblical character. But when the angel appears, Joseph does not realize who it is, and he just complains about having his sleep disturbed:

Angelus	Waken, Joseph, and take bettir kepe
	To Marie, þat is þi felawe fest.
Joseph	A, I am full werie, lefe, late me slepe,
	Forwandered and walked in þis forest.
Angelus	Rise vppe, and slepe na mare,
	þou makist her herte full sare
	þat loues þe alther best.
Joseph	We, now es þis a farly fare
	For to be cached bathe here and þare,
	And nowhere may haue rest.
	Say, what arte þou? Telle me this thyng.[69]

---

[67] In the Towneley play after the above conversation with Mary, he recounts the story of their betrothal. The York pageant features this comic element even more prominently by opening with Joseph's lamenting to himself over the way he ended up married (betrothed) to Mary in the first place, and N-Town actually dramatizes the betrothal in a separate play. In York Joseph immediately identifies himself as an old man woefully married to a younger woman.

[68] 'Joseph's Trouble about Mary', *The York Plays,* ed. by Beadle, Richard. (London: Edward Arnold Ltd, 1982), pp. 21-30.

[69] 'Joseph's Trouble about Mary', *The York Plays*, pp. 246-56.

What is specifically humorous here is the incongruity between the way Joseph should respond to the angel (and how the audience would expect him to respond) and the way he does respond, treating the angel like another human, someone on his level. This humour is generated by essentially the same dramatic irony mentioned above; however, here it is magnified by his casual, ignorant treatment of the angel rather than by his suspicious, unbelieving words to Mary.

Even though spectators' laughter is sympathetic, it is still laughter of superiority; the audience's delights in knowing the correct response, the superior of the two incongruous elements. The comedy of Joseph's dilemma, like the humour in *Patience* and the *Handlyng Synne* exemplum, invites identification with Joseph's struggle by encouraging laughter not at him but at the struggle itself. Joseph's voicing of doubts and struggles, albeit with comic effect, 'encourages the spectators to examine playfully their own doubts'.[70] As Tricomi observes, Joseph serves here as a 'model for humanity'.[71] The Joseph plays inspire a laughter that gently coaxes the audience to agree. Joseph wins spectators' affections through the earthly confusion, doubt, and unbelief they may find in themselves.

Even better known and more often cited for their comedy are the various Noah plays and the shepherds plays of the nativity sequences, the Towneley *secunda pastorum* being of course the most famous of all. The Noah plays in the York, Towneley, and Chester cycles employ a rhetoric of humour similar to that in the Joseph plays. David Bevington identifies Noah as 'at once comic and virtuous; he is a believably imperfect man with whom the audience can identify, and yet he is also a type of Christ'.[72] The humour in the Noah plays comes from two primary elements: Noah's portrayal as an old man struggling to build the ark, and Noah's domestic strife with his wife, particularly his struggle to get her to board the ark. As with Joseph these two sources of humour in the Noah plays accomplish the following: they help the audience identify with Noah's struggle to do the task God has given him, and they present a domestic struggle the audience can relate to and identify with their own.[73]

---

[70] Carroll, *The 'Noble Gyn' of Comedy*, p. 130.

[71] Tricomi, 'Reenvisioning England's Medieval Cycle Comedy', p. 20.

[72] David Bevington, 'Noah', *Medieval Drama* (Boston: Houghton Mifflin, 1975), p. 290.

[73] The Towneley play, attributed to the Wakefield Master, not surprisingly develops the humour most fully; however, it starts out quite seriously with God and Noah introducing themselves and then conversing about God's command to build the ark. However, in the actual work on the ark, both the York and Towneley versions present Noah comically without ridiculing him. He is a model of diligence in doing God's work for the audience to learn from and follow. In Towneley while he is working on the ark Noah comically complains

With the abundance of critical scholarship on the shepherds plays, especially the Towneley *secunda pastorum,* there is hardly a need to detail specific comic moments in this group. Perhaps most vividly of all the comic scenes in the cycles, the shepherds plays create humour through the incongruity of the intersection of heavenly and earthly. The serious and theologically unexpected visitation of the angels to the shepherds and their being honoured as the first to see the king perhaps best capture the comic (in the Aristotelian sense) vision of the entire cycle drama: God himself entering mankind's world as a man in order to save them. The plays open with the shepherds showing their earthiness in various ways, criticizing one another, delighting in a great feast, wrestling each other, and singing – including parodying the angels' song after their visitation and announcement. In the Chester and Towneley cycles, they are transformed into devoted spreaders of the gospel after seeing the Christ child.[74] Though the details vary among the versions, in none of the plays are the shepherds portrayed as evil or ridiculous, despite their need for Christ and grace. Even the scoundrel Mak of the Towneley *secunda pastorum* is a redeemable scoundrel, not a villain like Cain or Herod. The shepherds' earthiness, their humanity, and their responses to the heavenly visitation invite laughter of identification that will encourage the audience to seek the Christ child and his mother for the same transforming grace.[75]

---

about his back hurting and calls himself 'an old dote'. ('Noah', *The Towneley Plays,* pp. 365ff). The York Noah himself is not quite as comic in building the ark, but the pageant portrays him with a similar element of down-to-earthness in his work; both versions do so in stark and humorous contrast to God's role at the beginning of the play. The York, Towneley, and Chester cycles all present Noah's wife as resistant to boarding the ark. The Towneley Noah anticipates strife with her before she even enters the scene; immediately after God leaves the opening scene, Noah says he is afraid of an argument with his wife – because she is so easily angered over small matters – about these instructions (182-88). As soon as his wife enters, they start to bicker. The sharp contrast of this earthly struggle with Noah's heavenly conversation with God and his holy mission to build the ark adds to the humour. In addition, his wife's resistance to boarding the ark is the height of folly, a comic effect dependent more on the dramatic irony of the audience's knowledge of the magnitude of the impending disaster than on the situational irony arising from the warnings and pleading of the other characters. However, once she is on the ark, her relations with Noah become supportive and mutually respectful: the drama uses the same contrast as earlier in the play but now in reverse, placing emphasis on the 'serious' message of the play.

[74] The Towneley First Shepherds Play, that is. In the better-known Second Shepherds Play, they worship the child with sincere praises, but they do not mention going to spread the good news specifically.

[75] Lynn Forest-Hill explains that the shepherds use of crude language, as in the Chester play when the junior shepherd Trowle wrestles with one of the older ones and warns his opponent, 'Keepe well thy score for feare of a fart' (ll. 278-79), entertains the audience with the 'inversion of hierarchy [which] serves the didactic purpose of the play, which is to illustrate the shepherds' transition from disunity, depicted by the flyting and wrestling, to

The pattern of sympathetic comedy applies to characters who themselves are the exempla, the models for the audience to imitate. Their dilemmas, often presented comically, inspire laughter at the familiarity of the dilemma, at the audience members' own weakness, reinforcing their need for the message and making them more ready to appropriate it.

Mankind

The riotous morality play *Mankind*, perhaps more than any other Middle English play, threatens the notion that these comic dramas support the orthodox teaching of the Church and Scripture. Most of the humour in this play is generated by the worldly personifications Neu Gyse, Nowadays, Nought, their leader Myscheff, and the devil served by all four, the formidable Titivillus. Sometimes the play invites the audience to laugh with derision at them as at Herod or at the dishonest bailiff. Sometimes, however, the audience laughs *with* the villains, in spite of and even because of their naughtiness. In addition to the scatological and often blasphemous humour of the villains, one scene in *Mankind* makes the title character himself sympathetically comic much as do Joseph, Noah, and the shepherds. *Mankind* illustrates the effective juxtaposition of both *Schadenfreude* and sympathetic laughter to create a temporary carnivalesque effect in order to move the audience toward greater devotion to God.

The complex comedy of *Mankind* includes a significant use of transgressive language and behavior which evokes both *Schadenfreude* and carnivalesque laughter for this same ultimate purpose.[76] The dialogue between Neu Gyse and Mischyff about Neu Gyse's pained 'pryvetee' invites laughter at the expense of their foolishness and wickedness.[77] However, much of the comedy is more problematic. In the process of harassing and tempting Mankynde, the evil tricksters frequently induce the audience to laugh *with* them, drawing them to participate, by association, in the downfall of Mankynde. In the play's opening scene, the wicked trio and their leader Myscheff mock the holy character Mercy boisterously and crudely: they trip him, creating physical, slapstick comedy (113); they also make fun of his words and language (45-65, 124-34). Mercy reprimands them for their foolish words, and they leave cursing him. Despite the obvious wickedness of treating Mercy – a personification of Divine Mercy – this way, these jokes are surely meant to entertain the audience. Throughout the play, these villains, a kind of medieval Three Stooges,

---

Christian fellowship after the angel's appearance'. *Transgressive Language in Medieval Drama: Signs of Challenge and Change* (Burlington, VT: Ashgate, 2000), p. 64.

[76] Ibid., p. 106.

[77] See the opening excerpt of this essay.

joke among themselves with outrageously transgressive language. They use Latin, mock-Latin, and religious diction to throw crude insults at one another such as 'Go and do þat longyth to þin[e] offyce: osculare fundamentum*!* ['Kiss my ass!'] (141-42) and other crude mis-translations and parodies of Scripture or the Mass. The comedy arises from the incongruity between the formal language, usually associated with the spiritual or holy, and the scatological content, clearly belonging to the fleshly and unholy world of sin and temptation which they personify.

Is there any strategy in such joking to actually deepen the religious edification of the play? Had the dramatist wanted simply to convey that the characters are wicked and should be avoided, he could have given them more ominous and didactic dialogue similar to the speeches by the Seven Deadly Sins in the first half of *The Castle of Perseverance*.[78] Or even keeping the action comic, he could have portrayed them as simply ridiculous, objects of derision like Herod.

However, the play's strategy operates less directly in many cases, actually involving the audience in the action of the play, in true carnivalesque fashion, breaking through the division between the world of the play and the world of the audience.

After further efforts to turn Mankynde away from his faith have failed and Mankynde has defeated the villains with his spade as described above, they decide to summon the devil Titivillus to help them successfully tempt Mankynde. The voice of the devil is heard from off stage, and the tricksters tell the audience members that in order to see this devil, they must put money in a collection plate that is passed around. The contribution is, of course, to pay the actors for their entertainment.[79] However, in the world of the play of which they have become a part, the audience is financing the effort to ruin Mankynde's soul. Rosemary Chaplan explains that involving the audience this way makes them simultaneously 'insiders' and 'outsiders' of the play's action and gives them a 'double perspective, and a choice', in which they must decide whether to side with Mercy and obey God or with the comic tempters and enjoy seeing Mankynde fall.[80] The audience becomes complicit in the moral fall of the hero, who so clearly represents themselves.

Sympathetic comedy occurs midway through the play when, in an effort to disrupt Mankynde's faith and righteousness, Titivillus sneaks a wooden board into the soil

---

[78] *The Castle of Perseverance, The Macro Plays,* ed. by Mark Eccles, EETS 262 (London: Oxford UP, 1969), pp. 1-111; in particular, see ll. 482-1235.

[79] As noted above, Bevington cites this play as the 'first recorded instance in England of openly commercial acting'. 'Mankind', *Medieval Drama,* p. 901.

[80] Rosemary E. Chaplan, "Farewell, Jentyll Jaffrey': Speech-Act Theory and *Mankind*', in *Medieval Englishe Theatre* 11 (1989), 140-9 (p. 146).

where Mankynde is about to till. The devil tells the audience that he himself remains invisible and that he will hold his 'nett' of invisibility before Mankynde's eyes '[t]o blench hys syght'. He seeks to make the hero angry, that he might 'lose hys pacyens, payn of schame' and to 'wene grace were wane' [believe grace is insufficient] (531-40). While Mankynde, completely unaware of the trick, is struggling with the soil, the devil steals his sack of grain from behind his back. At first his attitude is a model of Christian piety. He announces his dependence on God's mercy for success in his labour, and he states that he begins his work in the name of the Father, Son, and Holy Spirit (541-5). Mankynde's frustration at the lost corn and difficult digging quickly distract him, however:

> Alasse, my corn ys lost! Here ys a foull werke!
> I se well by tyllynge lytyll xall I wyn.
> Here I gyff wppe my spade for now and for euer. (547-49)

Mankynde quickly returns to piety by kneeling to pray, but as he does Titivillus whispers that he can shorten his prayers and distracts him with the urge to relieve himself. Mankynde excuses himself, heeding at the most base level his earthly nature instead of his spiritual; when he returns to the stage a few moments later, he announces he prefers eating and sleeping to work and prayer (550-88).

Mankynde's frustration at these hindrances is humorous for the audience, who can easily identify with such difficulties. Like Joseph's struggle with confusion and unbelief, Mankynde's predicament invites laughter at the shared humanity represented by the struggle to do one's work as he ploughs as though there were indeed a board in the earth. In fact, the joke may also have encouraged spectators to persevere more joyfully amid trials, remembering that a devil may be simply playing tricks. How does this comedy persuade the audience of the play's message, of their need to repent of sin and cry to God for mercy and pursue good works? The answer with respect to this play is slightly more complex. Mankynde finally gives in to his tempters after Titivillus's manipulations, meeting the three villains in the ale-house, begging their mercy for his earlier violence against them, and swearing obedience to their orders to go forth and sin. In these comic moments of weakness, Mankynde becomes an even more vivid exemplar, making his later non-comic repentance and restoration by Mercy a more persuasive model for the spectators. As in the other plays using humour in this way, the audience is to identify with Mankynde and then learn from his example in the same situation. Their sympathetic laughter at his difficulties farming the land invites spectators to see themselves in Mankynde's role as he falls into sin and later repents. Without the humour, they may distance themselves from the character as he begins to stray.

However, the play does not end with Mankynde's downfall. Including the audience in the action of the play and inducing their laughter *with* the joking of the villains ultimately serves the stated orthodox Christian aims of the play. While Mankynde is in his pious state, the audience is drawn through the carnivalesque humour of the villains to support, albeit inadvertently, the temptation. Once Mankynde begins to struggle, the rhetoric shifts to sympathetic comedy until Mankynde has exhausted the pleasures of the world and, despairing of his own life, desires death (800-810). At this point, the comedy invites *Schadenfreude*: Mercy appears, and the three villains and Mischeff comically flee much like the devils Jesus defeats in the Harrowing of Hell plays. Just as they are about to hang Mankynde by a rope, they see Mercy enter with a scourge. New Gyse becomes entangled by the rope: 'Qweke, qweke, qweke! Alass, my thrott I beschrew yow, mary!' (808). Unlike the earlier humour, these final comic moments do not invite audience members to laugh sympathetically in collusion with the villains; spectators are simply to laugh derisively at the wicked tempters' misfortune. The goal of the play is no longer to draw the audience into the evil. The rhetorical objective has shifted to that of moving the audience to identify with Mankynde's repentance and restoration.[81]

Mankind is rich with numerous examples of comedy, not all of which serve the same function.[82] The above observations do not imply that performances did not include true carnivalesque, subversive comedy. Readings of the text which focus on Bakhtinian misrule err not in observing such effects but in assuming that such comedy persisted at the expense of any orthodox rhetoric achieved by the comedy. Modern expectations about the intersection of devout religious faith and the comic do not easily make sense out of the kind of juxtaposition we find in fourteenth and fifteenth century drama and homiletic exempla. The confident belief in the existence of the spiritual and of its continuous tension with the fleshly, earthly world of physical temptation, foolish wives (and husbands), and farts made possible a religious rhetoric employing a humour generated from the incongruities inherent in this very opposition.

---

[81] Chaplan observes this effect as well: 'When Mercy's final admonition to Mankynde is turned on the audience, the abrupt return to the 'real' world shows, better than any dispassionate description, how easily one can become involved in sin' (pp. 146-47).

[82] A few examples illustrate *Mankind*'s comedic richness. Linguistic play: Myscheffe parodies Mercy's formal, religious diction by rhyming which his words (ll. 45-6); Myscheff invents phony Latin words in mock proverbs of little value which he then translates: '*Corn servit bredibus, chaffe horsibus, straw firybusque*', meaning, he says, 'the corn shall serve to brede at the nexte bakinge' (ll. 57-59). Slapstick: the three villains' physical defeat by Mankynde when he beats them with a spade (ll. 376-400); their moaning and bickering as Myscheff plays doctor and nearly 'cures' their wounds by chopping off genitals and head (ll. 432-50).

Conclusion: Medieval English Comic Theory

Horace's call for poetry to delight as well as teach was another reason so much religious literature could include humour; in an age which understood dedication to God as the goal of life, these justifications for enjoyment even in the midst of seriousness were important. All poetry should have a moral aim, and it should please. The comedy in these texts confirms for later Middle English what Curtius observes about earlier continental literature: the mixture of jest and earnest was among the stylistic norms which were known and practised by the medieval poet, even if he perhaps nowhere found them expressly formulated.[83] That the Middle Ages was as much a time of laughter as it was of faith is clear. As Beatrice White points out, 'the greatest medieval poet placed the sullen in Hell's lower circle because they had been sad in God's sweet air, and[...]the greatest medieval saint called himself Joculator Dei'.[84]

During the Middle Ages, laughing and learning – indeed, flatulence and faith – were not necessarily opposed. Curtius observes that 'The sacred and the profane[...] is the fundamental division in the medieval intellectual world'.[85] Medieval humour lends itself particularly well to analysis using superiority theory, largely because of the inherently moral world-view of the period. However, this humour (like all humour) also depends on perceived incongruity. The reason both theories are necessary for understanding medieval comedy is that the incongruities of the Middle Ages are not morally equal or neutral. Peter Berger sees comedy in general pointing to two fundamental incongruitites: 1) people's incongruence within themselves and 2) people's incongruence with the universe, humanity's smallness.[86] Scholars of medieval comedy consistently recognize its inseparability from the moral polarity of the period. Robert Miller sees in the *Wife of Bath's Tale* an 'ambiguity which results from the opposition of a fleshly vision and a spiritual vision [and which] provides the pattern for many exempla'.[87] Derek Brewer observes the same tension in his discussion of the structure of medieval comic tales. In all of Chaucer's fabliaux, he asserts, 'The fundamental joke is that man's spiritual nature is in con-

---

[83] E. R. Curtius, *European Literature and the Latin Middle Ages,* trans. by Willard R. Trask (New York: Pantheon, 1963), p. 424.

[84] Beatrice White, 'Medieval Mirth', *Anglia* 78 (1960), 284-301 (p. 301).

[85] Curtius, *European Literature*, p. 430.

[86] Berger, *Redeeming Laughter*, pp. 209, 214.

[87] Robert Miller, '*The Wife of Bath's Tale* and Mediaeval Exempla', *ELH* 32.4 (1965), 442-56 (p. 446). JSTOR. <www.jstor.com>.

flict with his physical nature'.[88] In discussing the liminality of medieval humour, James Andreas observes in it 'a dialectical tension between sacred and obscene, male and female, young and old, and high and low'.[89] He describes the work of Dante, Chaucer, and the *Gawain* poet as turning the paradoxes and inversions of Christian theology (citing the beatitudes as an example) 'into comic structural conventions'.

I submit the following three observations toward a theory of medieval English comedy: first, it is best described (in modern parlance) as superiority-incongruity comedy, for medieval English comedy necessarily depends on and arises from the fundamental incongruity understood in the Middle Ages between God and man. This incongruity appears in various comic texts and other art forms through juxtaposition of spirit and flesh, heaven and earth, or soul and body. Audience members' laughter arises as they identify themselves with the clearly superior of the two incongruous elements. Second, medieval English comedy reinforces that very incongruity, the distinction between the spiritual and fleshly, emphasizing the contrast between the two, often through this very juxtaposition in the text or performance. Finally, medieval English comedy celebrates the superiority of God over man and the Christian hope for man's ultimate reunion with God.

How do these types of laughter qualify as examples of perceived superiority, of Hobbes' 'sudden glory'? This question represents the greatest objection proponents of other humour theories make to superiority theory: in many situations one does not feel superior when laughing, and certainly an infant feels no superiority over anyone in such games. The sense of superiority in such laughter is rooted in the ultimate superiority of God over all enemies and the fact that the faithful Christian is promised a place on God's victorious side of that great incongruity. Berger sees the 'so-called Easter laughter of the medieval church [as] a powerful liturgical expression' of the view that the comic is proleptic, looking ahead to what is to come just as faith does.[90] The texts I consider above all reveal an interdependence among faith, humour, and rhetoric. The comedy arises from the religious tension of moral incongruity and from the audience's joyful identification with the superior side of that incongruity.

---

[88] Derek Brewer, 'Structures and Character-Types of Chaucer's Popular Comic Tales', *Estudios Sobre los Géneros Literarios*. University of Salamanca. *Filosofía y Letras* 89 (1975), 107-18 (pp. 111-12).

[89] James R. Andreas, 'Festive Liminality in Chaucerian Comedy', *The Chaucer Newsletter* 1 (1979), 3-6 (p. 4).

[90] Berger, *Redeeming Laughter*, p. 215.

The deeply rooted faith of the Middle Ages provided individuals with just such a paradigm of the relationship between sorrow and joy, evil and good; the triumph of God's goodness was assured, and with it, the joy of the Christian. The security of this faith not only created a vision of life that made laughter possible, it recognized that laughter as a means of moving a person's tripartite self – mind, emotions, and soul – nearer to the very joy that was its source.

3
Making Light of Devotion:
The Pilgrimage Window in York Minster

PAUL HARDWICK

O f the numerous apocryphal additions and continuations to Chaucer's *Canterbury Tales*, perhaps the most engaging is the anonymous fifteenth-century *Canterbury Interlude*. This lively fabliau of sexual misconduct and mischance in the tavern is punctuated by a scene in which the company reaches its goal, Canterbury Cathedral. As we may expect, whilst the Knight, the Parson, and the Ploughman – exemplary figures all – approach the shrine with due reverence, other pilgrims of more questionable morality provide the opportunity for comedy:

> The Pardoner and the Miller and other lewde sotes
> Sought hemselff in the chirch, right as lewd gotes,
> Pyrid fast and poured highe oppon the glase,
> Counterfeting gentilmen, the armes for to blase,
> Diskyveryng fast the peyntour, and for the story mourned
> And ared also – right as rammes horned!
>> 'He bereth a balstaff,' quod the toon, 'and els a rakes ende.'
>> 'Thow faillest,' quod the Miller, 'thowe hast nat wel thy mynde.
> It is a spere, yf thowe canst se, with a prik tofore
> To bussh adown his enmy and thurh the sholder bore.'[1]

---

[1] *The Canterbury Interlude*, in *The Canterbury Tales: Fifteenth-Century Continuations and Additions*, ed. by John M. Bowers (Kalamazoo: Medieval Institute Publications, 1992), pp. 60-79, ll. 147-56.

The humour here works on the understanding that the reader is not only fluent in the language of Christian iconography, but also assumes that this understanding is common to all. The crooked interpretations of these would-be gentlemen as they attempt to read the narratives depicted in the glass, then, is a clear mark of their 'lewedness' compared with the average churchgoer.

However, whilst in the later Middle Ages images in glass and elsewhere may have been seen as books of the unlearned which all could read,[2] we may wonder whether the viewer would have been expected to interpret every element of the picture surface. For although the main pictorial space of a window or other devotional image may clearly be intended to lead the devout to 'be remembrid on the passioun of Seint Petir or of Seint Poul or of the holi lijf of Seint Nicholas',[3] it is difficult to attribute the same to the '"drolleries", "babewyns" or "grotesques"' which begin to invade glass from the thirteenth century.[4] The present essay will address the so-called Pilgrimage window (nXXV) in York Minster, and will argue that even the 'lively and amusing' scenes which appear as mere comic decoration to the modern viewer may be read as meaningful elements of the overall devotional message.[5]

The Pilgrimage Window

The nave of York Minster retains the most extensive corpus of glass surviving from the early fourteenth century.[6] Particularly striking is the north nave aisle, which exemplifies the prevalent aesthetic of the period, the banded window. The alternating bands of rich historiated panels and delicately foliated grisaille, first recorded in England in the York Minster chapter house at the close of the thirteenth century, create a very light interior, at the same time conveying an impression of artistic coherence

---

[2] This notion may be found as early as c.600, in Gregory the Great's letter to Bishop Serenus of Marseilles. In the later Middle Ages, it is still invoked, particularly by defenders of images against Lollard attacks. See, for example, Reginald Pecock, *The Repressor of Over Much Blaming of the Clergy*, ed. by Churchill Babington (London: Longman, Green, Longman and Roberts, 1860), I, 208-16.

[3] Pecock, *Repressor*, I, 212.

[4] Sarah Crewe, *Stained Glass in England c.1180-c.1540* (London: Her Majesty's Stationery Office, 1987), p. 5.

[5] David E. O'Connor and Jeremy Haselock, 'The Stained and Painted Glass', in *A History of York Minster*, ed. by G. E. Aylmer and Reginald Cant (Oxford: Clarendon Press, 1977), p. 357.

[6] O'Connor and Haselock,, 'The Stained and Painted Glass', pp. 341-64; Thomas French and David O'Connor, *York Minster: A Catalogue of Medieval Stained Glass I: The West Windows of the Nave* (Oxford: Oxford University Press, 1987).

throughout.[7] This impression, however, is true only of the larger scheme, for upon closer investigation of the individual windows it is clear that there is not only a lack of iconographic unity, but also a lack of stylistic unity. This indicates that, within certain formal constraints, individual donors – and the workshops that they commissioned – were allowed considerable freedom.[8] Nowhere does this freedom appear to have been exploited more fully than in the Pilgrimage window (3.01).

As David O'Connor and Jeremy Haselock note, one of the most intriguing aspects of the Pilgrimage window is that

> it so clearly demonstrates the close inter-action between different art forms in the Middle Ages, especially the influence which manuscript painting had upon the more monumental art of glass-painting. In some respects the window is very nearly the page of a manuscript transferred into glass. The border running across the base of the window is clearly derived from the *bas-de-page* scenes which are such a prominent feature of contemporary manuscripts.[9]

This comparison may not only be made in terms of the visual impression made by the window but also, I would suggest, in the way in which the window should be 'read'.

We have seen above that images were deemed to fulfil the same function as books, so we may think of the large pictorial panels as constituting the main 'text' of the window. Reading, as is most commonly the case with stained glass of the period, from the bottom to the top,[10] the window may be read as a text exhorting lay piety.[11]

---

[7] On the evolution of the banded window, see Meredith Parsons Lillich, 'The Band Window: A Theory of Origin and Development', *Gesta* 9.i (1970), 26-33. On its introduction into England, see Richard Marks, *Stained Glass in England During the Middle Ages* (London: Routledge, 1993), pp. 148-50.

[8] O'Connor and Haselock, 'The Stained and Painted Glass', pp. 350-4, discern a similarity between the Bellfounder's window (nXXIV) and the Penancer's window (nXXVII), suggesting that they may be from the same workshop, of which they also see evidence in the west window of the north aisle in Patrick Brompton Church, North Yorkshire.

[9] O'Connor and Haselock, 'The Stained and Painted Glass', pp. 354-7. Marks, *Stained Glass in England*, pp. 56-8, whilst noting that, from the late thirteenth century, glazing became more strongly influenced by painting and architecture, makes the important point that this influence was reciprocal.

[10] Whilst this is generally the arrangement of stained glass windows, this is not always the case; the most notable exception in York Minster being the Great East Window (I), which is to be read from top to bottom.

[11] A full description of the window may be found in John Toy, *A Guide and Index to the Windows of York Minster* (York: The Dean and Chapter of York, 1985), p. 17.

3.01: York Minster Pilgrimage Window (nXXV). Reproduced by kind permission of the Dean and Chapter of York.

The bottom row shows St Peter (3.02), identifiable not only by his customary attribute of the key, but also the less common attribute of the church building, particularly apposite in the Minster, which is dedicated to him.[12] To the left is a knight on pilgrimage with horse and banner, to the right a female pilgrim with an attendant. The upper band depicts the Crucifixion, to the left of which stands the Virgin Mary with two companions, to the right St John with Longinus and Stephaton. The surmounting tracery shows Christ flanked by two angels of the passion. Whilst no donor records remain, it has been plausibly suggested that the window may have been commissioned in lieu of a vow of pilgrimage.[13] Certainly, the iconography of pilgrimage displays active devotion to the Minster, in the form of its patron St Peter, within the context of Christ's own commitment to mankind through the Crucifixion. To the reader, this is clearly an exhortation to similar individual piety with, in the apex of the tracery, the promise of eternal life beyond death as the reward.

However, not only is the window to be read like a manuscript; it also shares design features with contemporary manuscripts:

> During the thirteenth century [the] fantastic menagerie escaped from its cage of the foliate initial and entered the borders. This troupe of monsters, animals, birds, humans and fantastic hybrids multiplied in the fourteenth century until in the second half of that century the fashion for this sort of imagery in book illumination waned.[14]

In common with the decorated page of the period, the devotional text of the window is apparently undermined by the exuberant marginalia which crowds the borders and spills into the grisaille panels which punctuate the main text. This marginalia may conveniently be divided into three regions in order to facilitate discussion: the coloured medallions which stud the grisaille areas; the vertical borders which rise through the window; and the lower border which provides the horizontal boundary between the viewer and the main iconography of the window. I shall address these areas in turn before suggesting how they may contribute to a reading – or, indeed, a misreading – of the window as a whole.

---

[12] This combination of attributes occurs several times in the Minster; most prominently in the Great West Window (wI).

[13] O'Connor and Haselock, 'The Stained and Painted Glass', p. 354, n. 179.

[14] Nigel J. Morgan and Lucy Freeman Sandler, 'Manuscript Illumination of the Thirteenth and Fourteenth Centuries', in *Age of Chivalry: Art in Plantagenet England 1200-1400*, ed. by Jonathan Alexander and Paul Binski (London: Royal Academy of Arts, 1987), p. 150.

3.02: York Minster Pilgrimage Window, St Peter in main central light. Reproduced by kind permission of the Dean and Chapter of York.

The Medallions

The medallions represent a diverse range of subjects, from sacred to profane and from domestic to fantastic. Once more reading from lower left to top right, they depict: (lower) two seated figures; two men wrestling; a man leading a horse; (middle) a figure riding a beast; a woman grasping the ear of a kneeling man; a man with a pile of stones; (upper) a mitred head; an archer seated on fabulous beast; a griffin. Such a range of apparently unrelated images may be seen in terms of Lillian Randall's observation that

> the thirteenth century… saw a diffusion on an international scale of a wide variety of anecdotic material, both in the Church and without, through exempla and fabliaux. The early visual manifestations of themes popularised through fabliaux and exempla can most clearly be observed in illuminated manuscripts.[15]

Although 'most clearly… observed in illuminated manuscripts' in its early stages, this phenomenon spread into all media throughout the fourteenth century, and York Minster is richly decorated throughout with lively carvings. Indeed, many of the carvings in the nave show thematic links with the medallions in the Pilgrimage window, covering a range of subjects from realistic human figures to fabulous beasts.[16] Sophie Oosterwijk's observation that

> [t]here does not seem to be a very clear iconographic programme for the sculptures along the aisle wall… The general impression now seems to be one of a mélange of medieval frolics in no particular order,[17]

is equally true of the smaller scale medallions of the Pilgrimage window. However, we must remember that the modern viewer is approaching these subjects from a viewpoint not unlike that of the Pardoner and the Miller with whom we started. As readers we are both, to an extent, 'lewed' in the reading of devotional imagery and, significantly, unsupervised in that reading. Michael Camille, addressing manuscript illustration in the twelfth and thirteenth centuries, has explored the manner in which, in the later Middle Ages, the pictorial was closely associated with the oral performance of texts.[18] This is a useful caveat to bear in mind when considering

---

[15] Lilian M. C. Randall, *Images in the Margins of Gothic Manuscripts* (Berkeley and Los Angeles: University of California Press, 1966), p. 8.

[16] On the nave carvings, see Sophie Oosterwijk, 'Fourteenth Century Sculptures on the Aisle Walls in the Nave of York Minster', *York Historian* 9 (1990), 2-15.

[17] Oosterwijk, 'Fourteenth Century Sculptures', p. 5.

[18] Michael Camille, 'Seeing and Reading: Some Visual Implications of Medieval Literacy and Illiteracy', *Art History* 8 (1985), 26-49.

the decoration of the Pilgrimage window; all these apparently frivolous images are contained within the devotional framework of the Minster. As with ostensibly secular verse or proverbial material within sermon collections, for example, their meaning is entirely dependent upon context, requiring a clerical interpreter to whom we no longer have access to reveal the didactic meaning.[19]

Whilst the mitred head is the only image which on its own refers overtly to a religious setting, others may find analogues in sermon and other devotional material. G. R. Owst, for example, draws attention to the inclusion of wrestling in sermon lists of the pastimes of urban low-life; it is a base activity to be shunned.[20] Other images are more enigmatic. As Richard Barber and Anne Riches have noted, the monstrous frequently has a more serious face than is immediately apparent to the modern viewer.[21] The figure seated upon the fabulous beast, for example, may act as a general symbol of the need to tame the unnatural within. The griffin, on the other hand, is more enigmatic, for whilst there are many explicit iconographic uses, they are far from consistent. It was commonly employed as an emblem of Scientia during the Middle Ages, whilst also being used as a symbol for both Christ and the Devil.[22] Such a rich iconographic tradition emphasises both the import of such images and, at the same time, the importance of the lost cultural context which would clarify the specific meaning of this ambivalent symbol each time it is encountered. The apparently domestic scene of the woman grasping the kneeling man is an example of the scenes of domestic role reversal which are common in ecclesiastical contexts.[23] Indeed, such scenes appear elsewhere in the Minster nave, including striking examples on the west wall.[24] The lively scene, expressing an ostensible air of fun in expressing the topsy-turvy world, has much in common with

---

[19] See, for example, *Fasciculus Morum: A Fourteenth-Century Preacher's Handbook*, ed. and trans. by Siegfried Wenzel (University Park and London: Pennsylvania State University Press, 1989). The importance of the sermon manuscript context for a full understanding of medieval lyric poetry is stressed by Siegfried Wenzel, *Preachers, Poets, and the Early English Lyric* (Princeton NJ: Princeton University Press, 1986), pp. 3-20.

[20] G. R. Owst, *Literature and Pulpit in Medieval England*, 2nd edn (Oxford: Basil Blackwell, 1961), p. 33.

[21] Richard Barber and Anne Riches, *A Dictionary of Fabulous Beasts* (Woodbridge: The Boydell Press, 1996), p. 5.

[22] Beryl Rowland, *Animals with Human Faces: A Guide to Animal Symbolism* (London: George Allen and Unwin Ltd., 1974), p. 87. See also David Williams, *Deformed Discourse: The Function of the Monster in Mediaeval Thought and Literature* (Montreal and Kingston: McGill-Queen's University Press, 1996), pp. 195-7.

[23] See Christa Grössinger, *The World Upside-Down: English Misericords* (London: Harvey Miller, 1997), pp. 87-95.

[24] Oosterwijk, 'Fourteenth Century Sculptures', pp. 6-9.

many widely circulated misogynist texts of the period, which in spite of assumed levity carried the serious intent of articulating – and thereby perpetuating – male authority.[25]

As noted above, the thirteenth century saw the growth of visual representations of themes taken from fabliaux and exempla. In looking at the subjects of the medallions in the Pilgrimage window it becomes apparent just how fine the dividing line between the two could be. Without guidance, they appear to be frivolous – fanciful beasts and mundane domestic scenes. However, given an appropriate interpretative gloss, they become telling exempla from which the sinful viewer may benefit. In their necessity for explanation the medallions act as a pertinent reminder of the need to look at the window as a whole in the serious manner befitting its context in order to read its moral and spiritual significance. This, however, becomes harder for the modern viewer when our attention is turned to the apparently comic images that inhabit the vertical and lower borders.

The Vertical Borders

When looking at the vertical borders of the Pilgrimage window, the viewer is immediately struck by the difference between those of the central light and those of the outer lights, a pattern which is echoed in the Great West Window (wI). French and O'Connor have suggested that the patterned borders of the Great West Window increase in complexity of design, from the simple zig-zag of the outer lights to the heraldic crowns and lions of the inner lights, in order to add increased importance to the central panels.[26] Whilst the same may be seen in the Pilgrimage window, the effect is more pronounced. For whilst the central light, depicting St Peter, the Crucifixion, and the redemptive Christ of the passion, is bordered by an alternating pattern of English lion and French fleur de lys motifs, the borders of the outer lights are a riot of animal imagery, 'where delightful monkey doctors, monkeys with owls on their wrists aping falconers, and squirrels eating nuts can be seen' (3.03).[27] The dignity of the central lights, therefore, appears to the modern viewer to fall away into exuberant playfulness – be it parodic, satirical, or simply comic – in the outer borders. This impression may be modified, however, if we place these animals within the context of their moralisations during the late Middle Ages.

---

[25] This point is made in relation to Richard de Bury's *Philobiblon* in the introduction to Alcuin Blamires (ed.), *Woman Defamed and Woman Defended: An Anthology of Medieval Texts* (Oxford: Clarendon Press, 1992), p. 1.

[26] French and O'Connor, *York Minster: A Catalogue of Medieval Stained Glass*, p. 7.

[27] O'Connor and Haselock, 'The Stained and Painted Glass', p. 357.

3.03: York Minster Pilgrimage Window, pilgrims with ape physician and squirrels in borders. Reproduced by kind permission of the Dean and Chapter of York.

Debra Hassig identifies the squirrel as one of the small furry animals, along with cats and rabbits, used in both literature and the visual arts as emblems of female sexuality.[28] Certainly, if we adopt this reading, an image in the Luttrell Psalter (fol. 181v) depicting ladies travelling with dogs and squirrels suggests the frivolous, misplaced affection for pet dogs coupled with questionable sexual conduct that is elsewhere hinted at in such figures as Chaucer's Prioress. Camille, however, notes that squirrels and dogs, both common pets, were common visual signs of male sexuality, their focus on the lady's lap signalling the physical object of male desire.[29] However gendered, it is clear that the squirrel is intimately related to the desires of the body – the desires which the viewer should leave in this transitional area between the physical world and the devotional space of the main iconography. More closely still associated with the physical instincts of man are the squirrels' companions in the borders, the apes. Apes, like squirrels, have frequently been associated with both male and female sexuality.[30] However, by the later Middle Ages the ape had become seen primarily as the imitator of man.[31] Indeed, the etymological authority, Isidore of Seville, asserted that the word *simius* derived from *similitudo*, noting that 'the monkey wants to mimic everything he sees done'.[32] The apes' mimicry of humans is particularly stressed in the Bestiary tradition, which again cites etymological authority to claim that 'apes are so called because they ape the behaviour of rational human beings'.[33] This simulation or 'aping' of human activities is vigorously expressed in the borders of the Pilgrimage window, as apes bear owls upon their wrists in mockery of noble falconers or inspect uroscopy flasks in apparent parody of physicians.

At first glance the image of the ape holding the owl aloft may be read as broad satire of the aristocratic pastime of hunting, perhaps metonymically suggesting the kind of frivolous pursuits that should be eschewed in favour of the acts of piety pictured in the window's main panels. However, consideration of the iconographic significance of the owl suggests a more complex reading. In her study of owls and

---

[28] Debra Hassig, 'Sex in the Bestiaries', in *The Mark of the Beast*, ed. by Debra Hassig (New York and London: Routledge, 2000), p. 72.

[29] Michael Camille, *The Medieval Art of Love* (London: Calmann and King Ltd., 1998), p. 96. See also pp. 103-4.

[30] For examples, see Rowland, *Animals with Human Faces*, pp. 8-10.

[31] Rowland, *Animals with Human Faces*, p.11. The most extensive discussion of ape symbolism remains H. W. Janson, *Apes and Ape Lore in the Middle Ages and the Renaissance* (London: University of London Press, 1952).

[32] Quoted in Michael Camille, *Image on the Edge: The Margins of Medieval Art* (London: Reaktion Books, 1992), p. 12.

[33] Richard Barber (ed. and trans.), *Bestiary* (Woodbridge: The Boydell Press, 1999), p. 48

apes in Chaucer's *Nun's Priest's Tale*, Beryl Rowland draws attention to the frequency with which the two creatures appear together in medieval art.[34] The owl is most commonly used to represent the Jews, as it 'loves the night':

> It is a bird which flees from light and cannot bear the sight of the sun. This bird signifies the Jews, who, when our Lord came to save them, rejected Him, saying: 'We have no king except Caesar', and preferred the darkness to the light.[35]

Stressing this association with those who reject Christ, Rowland suggests that 'in the company of the ape it appears to represent … the enemy of all true believers' which, perched like a hunting bird on the wrist of the ape, seeks 'to ensnare the soul and separate it from God'.[36] However, as Mariko Miyazaki has pointed out, 'it would be misrepresentative to suggest that every owl necessarily expresses anti-Jewish sentiment'.[37] Drawing on the writings of Hugh of Fouilloy, Miyazaki sees the owl as more generally representative of sinners, but with particular connotations of excessive carnal desire. As with the squirrel, then, we may read the presence of the owl as a comment upon the pleasures of the flesh which have no place in the devotional focus of the window. So, while the ape's imitation of a knight engaged in the noble pursuit of hunting with the inappropriate owl – which is, of course, dim-sighted by day – may at first sight amuse, it undoubtedly contributes to a reading of the whole window that articulates both the folly and, furthermore, the moral danger of focusing solely upon the physical.

Perhaps nothing expresses this concern with the physical, however, quite as vividly as the final recurrent motif in the vertical borders; the ape physician. Physicians are frequently depicted in medieval art as animals; dogs, rabbits or, most commonly, apes.[38] In many cases these images are surely symptomatic, as David A. Sprunger notes, of 'widespread suspicion of the physician-patient relationship' in the late medieval period and beyond.[39] Certainly, contemporary literature abounds with evidence of the distrust with which physicians were viewed, from Chaucer's wry

---

[34] Beryl Rowland, '"Owles and Apes" in Chaucer's *Nun's Priest's Tale*, 3092', *Mediaeval Studies* 27 (1965), 322-5. This article is developed in Beryl Rowland, *Blind Beasts: Chaucer's Animal World* (Kent State University Press, 1971), pp. 36-42.

[35] Barber (ed.), *Bestiary*, pp. 147-8.

[36] Rowland, 'Owles and Apes', p. 324.

[37] Mariko Miyazaki, 'Misericord Owls and Medieval Anti-semitism', in Hassig (ed.), *Mark of the Beast*, p. 34.

[38] See David A. Sprunger, 'Parodic Animal Physicians from the Margins of Medieval Manuscripts', in *Animals in the Middle Ages*, ed. by Nona C. Flores (New York and London: Routledge, 2000), pp. 67-81.

[39] Sprunger, 'Parodic Animal Physicians', p. 79.

portrait of the mercenary 'Doctour of Physik' who 'lovede gold in special' to Langland's bald assertion that '[t]hey do men deye thorugh hir drynkes er destynee it wolde'.[40] However, as I have argued elsewhere, it is a mistake to see all such depictions as humorous or satirical in intent.[41] Satire alone cannot explain the frequency with which animal physicians are depicted within ecclesiastical buildings, whether on misericords, where they abound, or in more prominent locations such as bench ends or, indeed, stained glass. This puzzle only becomes clearer if we turn to a contrasting yet parallel tradition of references to physicians which, rather than satirical, is allegorical.

Whilst, if we are to believe the surviving literature, the physical remedies prescribed by physicians may have been widely doubted, there was one physician whose efficacy was beyond question – Christ. *Fasciculus morum*, a preachers' manual of c.1300 that was widely circulated throughout the fourteenth and fifteenth centuries, provides a particularly fully realised example of this allegory:

> Christ acts like a physician in the following way. A doctor investigates the condition of the sick person and the nature of his sickness by such methods as taking his pulse and inspecting his urine. Thus when Christ visits a sinner, he first enlightens him with his grace to understand himself and his own sin.[42]

Following this initial diagnosis, *Fasciculus morum* goes on to allegorise all aspects of spiritual health as Christ is described as the ideal physician for the ailing soul. These attributes are elsewhere extended to the clergy as they carry out Christ's work in the world. Indeed, this metaphor for the ministry is firmly enshrined in Canon Law from 1215, in which the clergy are referred to as 'doctors of souls'.[43] Given this allegorical tradition within the Church, we may perhaps read the ape physicians

---

[40] Geoffrey Chaucer, *The Canterbury Tales*, in *The Riverside Chaucer*, ed. by Larry D. Benson (Oxford: Oxford University Press, 1988), I 411-44; William Langland, *Piers Plowman: A Complete Edition of the B-Text*, ed. by A. V. C. Schmidt (London: J. M. Dent and Sons, 1995), B VI 274.

[41] Paul Hardwick, 'Through a Glass, Darkly: Interpreting Animal Physicians', *Reinardus* 15 (2002), 63-70.

[42] *Fasciculus Morum: A Fourteenth-Century Preacher's Handbook*, ed. and trans. by Siegfried Wenzel (University Park and London: Pennsylvania State University Press, 1989), p. 255. *Fasciculus morum* was a widely-circulated preacher's handbook, probably of Franciscan authorship, of which twenty eight known copies survive, the latest of which have been dated as being of the late fifteenth century. For manuscript details and textual history, see introduction to Wenzel's edition, pp. 1-23.

[43] Harry Rothwell (ed.), *English Historical Documents: 1189-1327* (London: Eyre and Spottiswoode, 1975), p. 655.

in the Pilgrimage window as representing – like the squirrels and owls and apes – those who merely 'ape' a concern for their spiritual health whilst looking only to the physical. Exactly how we may interpret this menagerie of physical concerns will be addressed after our consideration of the lower border.

The Lower Border

There are two reasons why the marginalia of the lower border attracts more attention than any other in York Minster. First, it is simply closer to eye level than the examples considered above; an obvious yet, I believe, significant point. Secondly, it exuberantly overflows with lively scenes that delight and puzzle in equal measure. Beginning with the left hand corner – the natural starting-place for the eye to travel through the window – the subjects depicted are: (left) a fox reading from a lectern to a cock; a funeral procession made up of apes; ape physicians attending a sick ape (3.04); (centre) an archer with a horse; a fox with a goose pursued by a woman with a distaff; a monkey with an owl (3.05); (right) a stag chasing a hound; and another archer.

The cock and the fox are one of the most common pairings of animals in late medieval decoration. Most famous in English literature through Chaucer's *Nun's Priest's Tale* of later in the fourteenth century, this is but one variant of the oft-told tale of the beguiling of the vain cock and his subsequent escape which may be dated as far back as the 1170s in one of the earliest branches of the *Roman de Renart*.[44] Along with depictions of the fox making off with the cock, another common image is, as in the Pilgrimage window, the fox preacher, which has literary antecedents dating back to the *Ysengrimus* of around 1150.[45] However, as Kenneth Varty has observed,

> in the earliest adventures of Reynard the Fox, there is relatively little satire of priests, monks and pilgrims… With the arrival of friars in the thirteenth century, sharp satire does appear, and friars are often the object of it.[46]

The frequency with which the preaching fox and his unsuspecting congregation of birds appears in church decoration from the fourteenth century is testament to the

---

[44] On the development of the fox and cock story see Kenneth Varty, *Reynard, Renart, Reinaert and Other Foxes in Medieval England: The Iconographic Evidence* (Amsterdam: Amsterdam University Press, 1999), pp. 31-54.

[45] Varty, *Reynard, Renart, Reinaert*, p. 61.

[46] Varty, *Reynard, Renart, Reinaert*, p. 85.

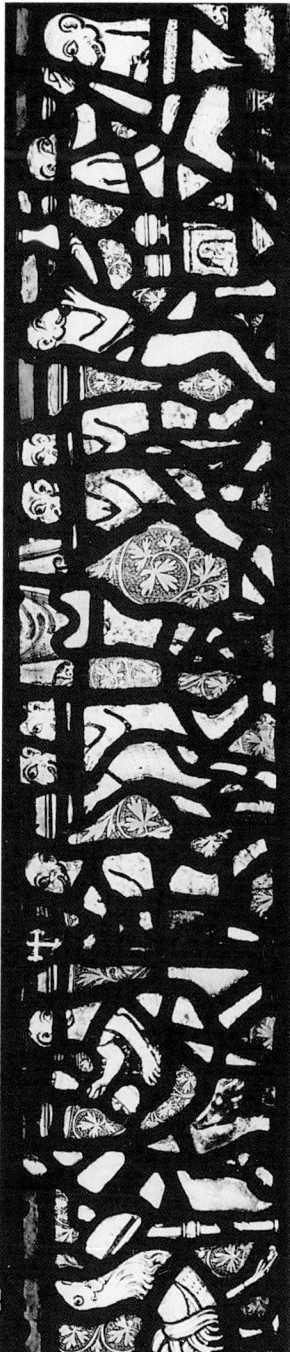

3.04: *York Minster Pilgrimage Window, lower border showing fox preaching to cock, apes' funeral and ape physician. Reproduced by kind permission of the Dean and Chapter of York.*

3.05: *York Minster Pilgrimage Window, lower border showing horse and archer, pursuit of fox and ape with owl. Reproduced by kind permission of the Dean and Chapter of York.*

widespread currency of this tradition.[47] However, we should not let this blind us to another possible reading, in which the emphasis is placed not on the fox, but on the cock. Could this common image, introducing as it does a window referring explicitly to the devotional duty of the individual and implicitly to the choice between the physical and the spiritual, be an exhortation not to be led astray by false interpretation?

Adjacent to this familiar image, the viewer is immediately plunged into less familiar territory with what is undoubtedly the most intriguing scene in the entire window; the 'lively and amusing scene' of the monkeys' funeral.[48] Nowhere does the distance between medieval and modern viewers seem so marked as in this image, for whilst the modern viewer responds with amusement to the apparently parodic antics of the apes, when the iconography is taken into account it is inconceivable that such a response was originally intended. For this is no ordinary funeral; rather, it is the funeral of the Virgin, an apocryphal tale rarely depicted in extant medieval glass. That, of the four surviving examples, three are in the Minster suggests the presence of a fervent local devotion to the Virgin,[49] a suggestion that is further borne out by references to a lost York play of the Assumption, an uncommon episode in English drama.[50] Surely such a public location within the Minster, therefore, would be an extremely unlikely place to find a parody of this episode. However, a clue to a possible alternative reading is provided by examining the role played by St Peter – to whom, we must remember, the Minster is dedicated – within the apocryphal narrative. When St John initially suggests that Peter bear the palm at the head of the funeral procession, he declines, according that honour to John and instead taking his place contentedly as an equal amongst the apostles carrying the bier.[51] Peter,

---

[47] On the depiction of the fox religious in various media, see Varty, *Reynard, Renart, Reinaert*, pp. 55-86; Elaine C. Block and Kenneth Varty, 'Choir-Stall Carvings of Reynard and Other Foxes', in *Reynard the Fox: Social Engagement and Cultural Metamorphoses in the Beast Epic for the Middle Ages to the Present*, ed. by Kenneth Varty (New York and Oxford: Berghahn Books, 2000), pp. 140-8.

[48] O'Connor and Haselock, 'The Stained and Painted Glass', p. 357. This image is discussed in detail in Paul Hardwick, 'The Monkeys' Funeral in the Pilgrimage Window, York Minster', *Art History* 23 (2000), 290-9.

[49] The funeral of the Virgin in C/H nII dates from c.1285; SIV from the middle of fourteenth century. Elsewhere, the scene may be found in an early fourteenth-century window in Stanton St John, Oxfordshire.

[50] See Anna J. Mill, 'The York Plays of the Dying, Assumption, and Coronation of Our Lady', *Publications of the Modern Language Association* 65 (1950), 866-76; Alexandra F. Johnston and Margaret Rogerson (ed.), *Records of Early English Drama: York* (University of Toronto Press, 1979), pp. 23, 47-8, 110, 136 and 143.

[51] M. R. James, *The Apocryphal New Testament* (Oxford: Oxford University Press, 1924), p. 213.

then, is presented as an exemplar of humility. This is expressed further in the narrative's most famous episode, in which a Jew – known uniquely as 'Fergus' in the York drama records – attempts to upturn the bier but instead is struck blind and becomes stuck to the underside of the coffin, the moment represented in the glass:

> And when the apostles lifted the bier, part of him was hanging and part clave to the bier, and he was wrung with extreme torment as the apostles went on and sang.[52]

As the tormented Fergus begs Peter for forgiveness, the apostle replies that only Christ, not himself, may grant this and restore his sight. Peter's role in the ensuing conversion not only reinforces his humility, but also casts him in an intercessionary role, the culmination of which is his commendation of the Virgin's soul to Christ.[53] The figure of humble intercessor is, of course, pertinent to St Peter's place in the main iconography of the window, where he is the focus of the pilgrims, in a direct relationship to the images of Christ above. Yet the monkeys' funeral does not represent St Peter but, rather, a simian imitator. As we have seen above, apes were frequently used to emphasise the physical life of man, and I would suggest that, occupying the marginal area through which the viewer passes between the world and the devotional space of the glass, these figures call for the 'aping' of the holy exemplar above in his humility and charity.

The fox making away with the goose in the central light may suggest a rather less elevated narrative as we turn once more to the world of beast fable. Whilst depictions of the fox carrying off the unwary cock are common in English art of the period, in many instances the cock is replaced by a goose, possibly reflecting a tradition of popular folklore lyrics.[54] That this substitution is made in the Pilgrimage window, with the cock under threat from the preaching fox in the left-hand light becoming a goose in the centre, suggests separate narrative sources and a lack of continuity across the lower border. However, if read at a symbolic level, a conceptual unity becomes apparent. The Bestiary offers a distinction between two types of geese, wild and tame:

> Wild geese fly high and are in strict order, and symbolise those who live remote from earthly rank and follow an ordered life. The tame geese live in villages, and call the

---

[52] James, *The Apocryphal New Testament*, p. 214

[53] James, *The Apocryphal New Testament*, p. 215.

[54] This suggestion is made in Varty, *Reynard, Renart, Reinaert*, pp. 35-8. On the fox's abduction of the cock / goose and the ensuing pursuit, see further, Paul Hardwick, 'Foxing Daun Russell: Moral Lessons of Poultry on Misericords and in Literature' *Reinardus* 17 (2004), 85-94.

> whole time; they often wound each other with their beaks. They symbolise those
> who are happy to lead a communal life, but give themselves up to slanderous talk...
> Divine providence would not have revealed the natural qualities of birds so clearly
> if we had not been required to gain some advantage from it.[55]

Our goose, as we can see from the distaff-wielding pursuer, is clearly of the domestic variety, happy with life but careless and easily led astray. The unwary cock
of the left-hand light, seduced by the false words of the deceiving fox, has become
transformed in the central light into the foolish goose and is seen to suffer the
consequences as he is carried off by his deceiver. The ape physicians and ape and
owl who look on in these scenes provide a reminder, as we have seen above, of the
need to read these exempla correctly and to transcend the concerns of this world.

The right-hand light, showing a classic 'world upside down' motif of the stag pursuing the hound, may perhaps be read as the inversion of the natural order that
results from the lapse into folly described in the previous scenes. The hunter turned
hunted is a common theme on misericords, articulating a fear of instability by
presenting scenes which are 'ridiculous and yet tinged with a sense of apprehension'.[56] In these mixed responses provoked by the images in the Pilgrimage window
may once more be discerned a spiritual dimension. The stag or hart is one of the
most common animal symbols yet, as with the case of the griffin mentioned above,
its meaning is far from fixed. Whilst at times it could symbolise heavenly longing
or even Christ Himself, in the present context it appears more likely that it has the
negative connotations of a general lack of restraint.[57] The dog, however, is less
ambiguous, being traditionally a symbol of virtue and devotion:

> There is no creature cleverer than the dog; they have more understanding than any
> other beast. They also know their name and love their master.[58]

To have this fidelity set to flight by its traditional quarry – lack of restraint – graph-
ically expresses the consequences of a lapse in devotion. All is not lost, however,
for whilst one dog flees, another harries the stag in accordance with the correct
order of things. Rather than presenting a lapsed state, this sequence of images
dramatises a contest, suggesting possible outcomes. The purpose of the apparently

---

[55] Barber (ed.), *Bestiary*, pp. 168-9.

[56] Christa Grössinger, 'Humour and Folly in English Misericords of the First Quarter
of the Sixteenth Century, in *Early Tudor England: Proceedings of the 1987 Harlaxton Sym-
posium*, ed. by Daniel Williams (Woodbridge, The Boydell Press, 1989), p. 75.

[57] On the diverse symbolic uses of the stag, see Rowland, *Animals with Human Faces*,
pp. 94-101.

[58] Barber (ed.), *Bestiary*, p. 72.

unrelated scenes of the lower border is, then, to act as a symbolic narrative of instruction rather than admonition.

Reading the Pilgrimage Window

Elsewhere in the north nave aisle, marginal images explicitly link the patron with his gift. The borders of the Penitentiary window (nXXVII), for example, which in its main lights depicts preaching and administering of penance, shows penitential images mixed with penitentiaries counting coins and craftsmen. The window as a whole is self-referential, recording the money collected by penitentiaries which, in turn, paid for the craftsmen to produce this pictorial exhortation to penance. In a similar way the Bell-Founder's window (nXXIV) depicts in the main lights the casting and tuning of a bell, as well as the donor, the bell-founder Richard Tunnoc, presenting his window to St William of York, whose famed arrival across Ouse Bridge is depicted above. The borders are appropriately filled with bells and apes playing instruments – perhaps acting as a self-referential symbol of humility and aspiration as in the Pilgrimage window. Whilst more enigmatic to the modern viewer, the marginalia of the Pilgrimage window may be read in the same fashion as an integral commentary upon the window as a whole and possibly the status of the donor.

As Naomi Reed Kline has noted, 'most people, whether they could read or not, knew the Bestiary and its Christian symbolism either through sermons or explications of imagery on church surfaces'.[59] The same, unfortunately, cannot be said of the modern viewer, for whom these frequently Bestiary-derived marginal scenes appear as scattered pieces from unmatched jigsaws. However, having explored these scenes and their possible resonance individually, we may now suggest the 'associative connections' through which the contemporary viewer drew them together into a unified picture within the context of the window as a whole.[60] The lower border, just above the viewer's eye level, acts, as we have seen, as an introductory narrative to the complex iconography of the window, exhorting the viewer to a humble 'aping' of the pious acts of the main figural panels, and warning of the consequences of foolish, incorrect interpretation. From this, encircling the main pictorial 'text', is a marginal area, marking the transition between the worldly stone and the illumination of the spiritual. The ambiguously symbolic animals allude to both aspects, drawing the viewer's attention to the physical in order that it may

---

[59] Naomi Reed Kline, *Maps of Medieval Thought: The Hereford Paradigm* (Woodbridge: The Boydell Press, 2001), p. 101.

[60] This follows the model of association suggested in Kline, *Maps of Medieval Thought*, esp. pp. 119-33.

consciously be left behind. Finally, interspersed within the main iconography of
the Pilgrimage window are reminders of preaching exempla, the narratives which
ensure the right interpretations of devotional materials. These apparently diffuse
and flippant images which crowd the borders to a point at which they spill into the
main lights, therefore, cohere to provide a running commentary on the very serious
matter of individual conduct and devotion, all gathered beneath the constant reminder of Christ's passion – the event which gives meaning to the pilgrimage of
Christian life. Such diversity of tone and register within a devotional framework
may be found throughout the art and literature of the later Middle Ages, but nowhere
is it more apparent than in sermon compendia and preaching manuals. Whilst there
is no extant evidence, there is certainly a case to be made for positing a clerical
donor, employing visual representations of preaching exempla in his exhortation
to individual piety.

I have spent much of the present paper so far arguing that the apparently comic
scenes in the borders of the Pilgrimage window serve, when read in context, to
fulfil a serious didactic purpose. Whilst I believe this to be the case, there is, of
course, one important point that cannot be neglected. However serious the message
they convey, the beasts and their antics are undeniably amusing. In this closing
section, I would like to suggest why such a serious subject should be addressed
using humour, before finally addressing the problems raised by this treatment.

It is not only in stained glass that comedy and devotion rub shoulders. The surviving cycles of medieval plays frequently attain dramatic gravitas through the juxtaposition of low humour and spiritual insight. We may observe, for example, the
way in which Noah's wife's comic blustering sharply gives way to the realisation
of the implications of the Flood, or the shock with which we find ourselves in
sympathetic complicity with the bickering soldiers as they stretch Christ on the
cross.[61] Such may be the effect of the marginalia in the Pilgrimage window as the
viewer becomes enthralled by the antics of monkeys, squirrels and foxes, before
realising their didactic import. Yet there is also another way in which laughter is
used for didactic effect in the plays. When Christ is brought before Herod in the
Litsters Play, Herod predicts that they 'shall laugh and have liking'.[62] Christ is
throughout mocked as a fool – not in the sense of the holy innocent defined in St
Paul's letter to the Corinthians,[63] but a sinful fool provided for the court's entertain-

---

[61] Richard Beadle and Pamela King (ed.), *York Mystery Plays: A Selection in Modern
Spelling* (Oxford: Oxford University Press), pp. 23-7; 212-21.

[62] Beadle and King, *York Mystery Plays*, p.182.

[63] 'We are fools for Christ's sake': I Corinthians 4.10. This distinction between the holy
and sinful fool is highlighted by Clifford Davidson in his introduction to *Fools and Folly*,
ed. by Clifford Davidson (Kalamazoo: Medieval Institute Publications, 1996), pp. 1-6.

ment. However, as Christ remains inured to cajolery, Herod himself adopts the role of fool in a futile attempt to elicit a response, thereby dramatising his sin as he reminds the audience of Psalm 52 (AV: 35): 'The fool has said in his heart, There is no God'. In considering this scene, Sandra Billington has noted that

> [had] Christ said a single word, he would have contributed to the Fool-game that he was placed in and so would have betrayed the Christian aspects of the Fool. The audience would have been fully aware of the two sides to the name [of fool] and would have been waiting for any possible slip. One can imagine the humour combined with tension when Herod pulls faces and makes gurgling noises to encourage Christ.[64]

The apparently comic imagery in the Pilgrimage window has this same effect of blending humour with tension. The viewer is at the same time amused by the images and aware of the inappropriateness of laughter within the sacred space. As well as carrying the iconographic significance outlined in this paper, then, it paradoxically uses humour to emphasise dramatically the seriousness of its message.

The resistance of laughter within the sacred space of the Minster is certainly a worthy ideal, and we may see the amusement with which the borders of the Pilgrimage window are viewed today as an indicator of the cultural distance between the present and the later Middle Ages. However, a chance documentary survival from the early fifteenth century suggests that the gulf may not be quite as large as it appears. It has been noted above that one of the scenes from the lower border – the funeral of the Virgin – was the subject of a play in the York cycle. Whilst the text of the play itself does not survive, an entry in the York Memorandum Book for 1431-32 gives us a unique insight into how the play was received by a contemporary audience:

> the Masons of this city have been accustomed to murmur amongst themselves about their pageant in the Corpus Christi Play in which Fergus was beaten because the subject of this pageant is not contained in sacred Scripture and used to produce more noise and laughter than devotion.[65]

The episode itself is considered marginal as it is 'not contained in sacred Scripture'. Furthermore, without supervised interpretation, the sentence is lost. To the observer – and the writer of the Memorandum Book – the Masons are not performing 'the Corpus Christi Play of the Funeral of the Virgin', 'the Corpus Christi Play in which

---

[64] Sandra Billington, *A Social History of the Fool* (Brighton: Harvester Press, 1995), p. 19.

[65] Johnston and Rogerson (ed.), *REED: York*, p. 732.

St Peter intercedes', or even 'the Corpus Christi Play in which Fergus is converted'. Rather, it is 'the Corpus Christi Play in which Fergus was beaten'. Without close supervision, the emphasis of this episode, apparently so significant in terms of local devotion, slips so easily from the spiritual to the slapstick. Rather than achieving the desired end of devotional contemplation, it merely elicits 'noise and laughter'.

So it is with the Pilgrimage window. As we look now at the borders, with our readings 'right as rammes horned', we are like the audience of the fifteenth-century *Masons' Play* as we fail to make the transition from physical to spiritual offered in this marginal area and remain in the world of stone and glass. Like the Pardoner and the Miller with whom we began, we see only the worldly pilgrimage rather than 'thilke parfit glorious pilgrymage / That highte Jerusalem celestial'.[66] In making light of the images we thus resist the light of illumination and, in doing so, the joke is perhaps not on the squirrels, monkeys, apes and owls that crowd the borders, but on the 'lewd gotes' that read them – ourselves.

---

[66] Chaucer, *Canterbury Tales*, X 50-1.

4
Comic Pleasures:
Chaucer and Popular Romance

DANA M. SYMONS

Alan T. Gaylord calls Chaucer's *Tale of Sir Thopas* 'a good bad joke'[1] and concludes, 'No bad poet could achieve this kind of bad poetry'.[2] Chaucer's poem thus escapes the label 'bad' through an understanding of the tale as deliberately bad, a parody of the Middle English metrical romances. In a similar move, Alan Lupack seeks to redeem the popular romance *Sir Tristrem* from critical dismissal by insisting that it 'must be viewed alongside works with similar intent, such as [...] Chaucer's *Tale of Sir Thopas*, rather than as a poor imitation of [Thomas of Britain's] poem'.[3] But, although a poem like *Sir Tristrem* may seem to incorporate elements of parody, when its comic scenes are set next to Chaucer's *Tale of Sir Thopas*, the differences between what the popular romance offers (even if the view of it as parody stands) and Chaucer's highly literary sendup of such tales become clear. The comic possibilities of Chaucer's *Sir Thopas* appear to reside in its evasion of action and in its capacity to create critical distance through its placement in the context of *The Canterbury Tales*. In contrast, the pleasures of a popular tale depend on the enhancement of spectacular features that lend themselves to more immediate enjoyment, as scenes from *Sir Tristrem* illustrate. In one case, Sir Tristrem's

---

[1] Alan T. Gaylord, 'Chaucer's Dainty "Dogerel": The "Elvyssh" Prosody of *Sir Thopas*', *Studies in the Age of Chaucer*, 1 (1979), 83-104 (p. 83).

[2] Gaylord, 'Chaucer's Dainty "Dogerel"', p. 93.

[3] Alan Lupack, '*Sir Tristrem*: Reception and Perception', *Studies in Medievalism* 7 (1995), 49-62 (p. 60).

dog Hodain suddenly materializes just at the moment where he is needed in the plot, appearing in time to drink the dregs of the love potion that Tristrem and Ysonde have just consumed and afterwards apparently joining in when the two lovers 'play' (l. 1690).[4] The comic possibilities of this unusual *ménage à trois* have caused discomfort to a number of critics, all of whom avoid discussing the kind of 'doggie-style' images of love 'play' the scene conjures up. These varied approaches to humour – sophisticated or spectacular – point to differences in audience expectations that may be linked to the separate venues of private reading and public performance. The differences between Chaucer's *Sir Thopas* and the popular romance forms on which his tale relies ultimately emphasize that the comic, like all tastes, must be seen as historically, socially, and culturally produced rather than as arising from a set of universally appealing features.

The disparities between the two tales help explain why *Sir Thopas*, though ostensibly encompassing all the conventions of popular romance, nevertheless fails to charm an audience like Harry Bailly. The Host of *The Canterbury Tales* finds the 'drasty rymyng' (VII. 930) of *Sir Thopas* an unfunny waste of time (it 'despendest tyme' [VII. 931]).[5] Scholars on the other hand usually respond to the tale as witty and clever, understanding the Host's response as a joke on him, with a bit of self-deprecation on Chaucer's part.[6] The discrepancy between Harry Bailly's response and critical reception highlights the fact that *Sir Thopas* is a sophisticatedly 'bad' poem, one that appeals to a highly literate reader. This sophistication points to the way in which Chaucer's tales often deploy strategies that encourage the reader to wonder about meaning, a quality that demands close and careful rereading.

Humour and Taste

Tactics that place heavy demands on readers are evident throughout Chaucer's work, even in tales the Host heartily approves. But the need for diligence on the part of readers has often been naturalized by critics who take Chaucer's rhetorical strategies as evidence of artistic superiority. For example, Richard Daniels points out that the *Miller's Tale* differs from its analogues in its more elaborate plot de-

---

[4] All citations are to the edition of *Sir Tristrem* in Alan Lupack, ed., *Lancelot of the Laik and Sir Tristrem* (Kalamazoo, MI: Medieval Institute Publications, 1992; repr. 1994).

[5] All citations are to Geoffrey Chaucer, *The Riverside Chaucer*, ed. by Larry D. Benson, 3rd edn (Boston: Houghton Mifflin, 1987).

[6] As Gaylord puts it, 'The humour in Chaucer's tale of *Sir Thopas* has always seemed clear enough: when called upon to tell "a tale of myrthe" in his own person, the actual poet gives the fictional poet a good bad joke at the expense of almost everyone, Chaucer included' ('Chaucer's Dainty "Dogerel"', p. 83).

velopment. Daniels shows that Chaucer establishes early on in the narrative the existence of a window of a certain type and height in Alisoun's bedroom, in contrast to the analogues, where the window shows up 'only when needed to advance the plot'.[7] Daniels argues that added details of this type serve to foreshadow later events, add to the realism of the action, and heighten the pleasure for readers: 'our pleasure here stems from the delightful surprise we feel when [a] detail unexpectedly reveals a hidden promise'.[8] But in giving the audience something to anticipate, Chaucer's tale plays to different expectations than those of its analogues, which perhaps rely on the very lack of anticipation for their humorous effects. Such differences show that each version offers its own distinctive appeal.[9] Daniels fails to account for this possibility when he says that 'the *Miller's Tale* pleases all but prudes' and concludes that 'readers across the centuries have been and continue to be moved beyond words – for the greater part they laugh and play – and herein lies the pleasure of Chaucer's text'.[10] These comments suggest that the textual pleasures of the *Miller's Tale* are timeless and offer a kind of inevitably accessible charm, to which all 'good' readers have access, a view belied by the history of the tale's reception.[11]

---

[7] Richard Daniels, 'Textual Pleasure in the *Miller's Tale*', in *The Performance of Middle English Culture: Essays on Chaucer and the Drama in Honor of Martin Stevens*, ed. by James J. Paxson, Lawrence M. Clopper, and Sylvia Tomasch (Cambridge: D. S. Brewer, 1998), pp. 111-24 (p. 122).

[8] Daniels, 'Textual Pleasure', p. 122. The 'hidden promise' of course results from the details of the window anticipating the action in the climactic scene, where first Alison 'at the wyndow out [...] putte hir hole' to be kissed by Absolom (I. 3732), and then Nicholas replays the 'joke', suffering the 'kiss' of Absolom's 'iren hoot', with which 'Nicholas amydde the ers he smoot' (I. 3809-10).

[9] This is not to imply that these audiences are mutually exclusive, but rather to point out that the pleasures of these different tales are distinctive.

[10] Daniels, 'Textual Pleasure', pp. 122-23.

[11] For example, the preface to an anonymous 1791 modernization defends the sexual content by arguing that 'we must take the good and the evil together' (Betsy Bowden, *Eighteenth-Century Modernizations from the 'Canterbury Tales'* (Cambridge, Eng.: D. S. Brewer, 1991), p. 170), though the author admits to some revision:

> In the point, on which the Miller turns his Tale, it has been my study to soften the original thought, as far as the story, which absolutely depends on it, would admit; and to cloath it in language, the most delicate I could find, to express an event so indelicately singular: The passage may be called, and is, *topically* gross; and will, on that very account, be more offensive to nice apprehension, than common-place ribaldry about sexual intercourse, where the anatomical means of such intercourse form no part of the text, and are left wholly to the reader's imagination. (Bowden, p. 169; italics in original)

William Lipscomb excluded the tale from his 1795 edition of *The Canterbury Tales* because of its 'indelicate' subject matter (Bowden, p. 177). Similarly, John Matthews Manly considered the tale 'not fit to be read in a mixed company' and included only the descriptions of Nicholas, Alisoun, and Absolom in his 1928 college edition (Geoffrey Chaucer, *The Can-*

Daniels's views about what constitutes narrative pleasure elide other possible sources of humour. He argues that 'Chaucer took a contemporary story, rooted in European folklore, which was little more than a bawdy joke and artistically flawed even in its best versions, and gave it the complexity and integrity that mark pleasing narrative art'.[12] His label of 'artistically flawed' and his focus on 'complexity and integrity' as indispensable not only define artistic value absolutely but also outline aesthetic criteria that severely limit the range of responses to the 'bawdy joke'. Such a position discounts the possibility that audiences for whom such texts were produced valued different qualities. More specifically, in privileging Chaucer's version, Daniels refuses the possibility that what enhances the scene in the analogues is precisely the wholly unexpected appearance of both the window and the scene that follows. In some cases humour derives not from foreshadowing followed by 'delightful surprise' but from the more extreme surprise offered by the incongruity of surreal, fantastical, or outright silly events, as a look at *Sir Tristrem* will show. In other words, textual pleasures are not universal or self-evident but require the development of specific expectations. Thus, the Host's rejection of *Sir Thopas* suggests that he has not developed a taste for the parodic humour masked by its 'drasty ryming' (VII. 930), while the analogues to the *Miller's Tale* might appeal to him even more, precisely because of their reliance on spontaneity.[13]

Attempting to recover the original appeal of these works offers an alternative to valuing them according to standards developed above all for the appreciation of literary writing. Pierre Bourdieu's work on the history of taste suggests the possibility that 'popular' texts like the analogues to the *Miller's Tale* or the Middle English romances targeted by Chaucer's *Sir Thopas*, instead of catering to indiscriminate readers with no taste, actually offer a distinctive appeal in their own right.[14] The fact that we do not understand that appeal is all the more reason to reexamine our own aesthetic responses. Hans Robert Jauss makes the case that understanding the

---

terbury Tales, ed. by John Matthews Manly (New York: H. Holt, 1928), p. 559). Feminist readers, as will be discussed later, have criticized the tale for its treatment of women. These have all objected to the tale's sexual content, but for vastly different reasons. By defining such readers as 'prudes', Daniels in turn dismisses their assessments as 'bad' reading, or as evidence of a lack of taste, implying that all 'good' readers define 'the pleasure of Chaucer's text' (p. 111) in the same way.

    [12] Daniels, 'Textual Pleasure', p. 111.

    [13] I do not mean to imply that texts have the capacity to direct or guarantee particular responses from readers or listeners, merely that they encourage some responses over others; surely the *Miller's Tale* could be enjoyed as 'little more than a bawdy joke' in the same spirit as its 'artistically flawed' analogues, according to audience taste. On the other hand, it may not lend itself to such enjoyment as easily.

    [14] Pierre Bourdieu, *Distinction: A Social Critique of the Judgement of Taste*, trans. by Richard Nice (Cambridge: Harvard University Press, 1984).

pleasure of medieval writings for their original audiences 'entails the reconstruction of the horizon of expectation of the addressees for whom the text was originally composed'.[15] This is difficult because 'for the modern reader who is accustomed to admire that something new in a work which makes it stand out against the received tradition, it [...] means a reversal of his aesthetic expectations'.[16] When reading medieval chansons de geste, for example, 'the reader must negate the character of the individual text as a work in order to enjoy the charm of an already ongoing game with known rules and still unknown surprises'.[17] Edmund Reiss similarly points out that 'the romance would seem to build on the expectations derived from the traditions and conventions its audience already was aware of'.[18] These positions insist that preferences are historically and culturally produced rather than 'natural'. In this regard, Bourdieu's explanation of the acquisition of tastes as a process of internalisation, where the learning of cues and the development of specific preferences are largely unintelligible, asks us to consider the possibility that what is identified as 'popular' by the dominant culture is also an acquired taste.[19] We cannot continue to dismiss such works out of hand as 'tasteless' entertainments. Because the valuing of one taste above another is always predicated on the rejection or devaluing of that other, we should be suspicious of assessments like those that brand some vernacular entertainments as 'artistically flawed' or simply 'bad'.

---

[15] Hans Robert Jauss, 'The Alterity and Modernity of Medieval Literature', *New Literary History*, 10 (1979), 181-229 (p. 182).

[16] Jauss, 'Alterity and Modernity', p. 185.

[17] Jauss, 'Alterity and Modernity', p. 189.

[18] Edmund Reiss, 'Romance', in *The Popular Literature of Medieval England*, ed. by Thomas J. Heffernan, Tennessee Studies in Literature 28 (Knoxville: University of Tennessee Press, 1985), pp. 108-30 (p. 111).

[19] Bourdieu argues that the dominant culture denies 'lower, coarse, vulgar, venal, servile – in a word, natural – enjoyment' (p. 7). Although the line seems intended to paraphrase the attitudes of elite audiences, it is unclear whether Bourdieu uses the word 'natural' here as simply a part of this paraphrase, or whether it should be understood as his own characterization of those pleasures as against the more obviously negative terms. Bourdieu does refer to the 'socially conditioned inclinations' of the working class, but he does not suggest whether these 'inclinations' are to be understood as taste of a different sort from that of 'legitimate' culture, or simply as lack of taste (p. 41). His definition of the working class aesthetic as 'a dominated "aesthetic" which is constantly obliged to define itself in terms of the dominant aesthetics' (p. 41) would seem to suggest the latter, as does his comment that 'the refusal of nature, or rather, the refusal to surrender to nature, which is the mark of dominant groups – who start with *self*-control – is the basis of the aesthetic disposition' (p. 40), since this implies that a lack of self-control marks the dominated classes, who presumably 'just act naturally'. Still, he does say that one's taste is the mechanism 'whereby one classifies oneself and is classified by others', and that 'each taste feels itself to be natural [...] which amounts to rejecting others as unnatural and therefore vicious', which seems to imply the acquisition of taste for different groups (p. 56).

Like Bourdieu, Mikhail Bakhtin's history of laughter critiques 'official culture' for its tendency to present its own beliefs as 'eternal truths'.[20] At the same time, Bakhtin sees humour arising out of 'elemental popular laughter' or the 'common people's creative culture of laughter',[21] a place where the body is always present, for 'laughter degrades and materializes' and 'the people's laughter' is thus indelibly 'linked with the bodily lower stratum'.[22] For Bakhtin, this turn to corporeality is what distinguishes parody 'from all the forms of medieval high art and literature'.[23] This explanation suggests that humour stems universally from a grounding in the body and inevitably targets its opposite, operating, in Bakhtin's terms, as a process of bringing the 'high art and literature' down to 'the bodily lower stratum'. Thus, the comic moves only in one direction and serves but one purpose: to act as 'the permanent corrective of laughter, of a critique on the one-sided seriousness of the lofty direct word, the corrective of reality that is always richer, more fundamental and most importantly *too contradictory and heteroglot* to be fit into a high and straightforward genre'.[24]

While some of the implications of Bakhtin's argument remain problematic, what is useful is his identification of humour as a critique or 'corrective' to the 'straightforward' or 'straight'. We need not go the step further and identify an indelible connection between so-called 'high' genres and the 'straight', or naturalize the operation of this 'corrective' so that it has to function unidirectionally. In fact, both Chaucer's humour and that of *Sir Tristrem* arguably find their source in Bakhtin's 'bodily lower stratum', and their differences serve to show that the connection between 'popular laughter' and 'reality' or 'the body' is an artificial one. Rather than residing in a folkloric, popular grounding in the body that is 'natural' and immediately accessible, humour instead represents an acquired taste. Bakhtin's equation of the 'bodily lower stratum' with laughter implies a universalised account that sees laughter as transparent and always operating in the same way, rather than a conceptualised understanding of humour as socially, historically, and culturally embedded, operating differentially for different audiences.

---

[20] Mikhail Bakhtin, *Rabelais and His World*, trans. Hélène Iswolsky (Bloomington: Indiana University Press, 1984), p. 101.

[21] M. M. Bakhtin, 'Epic and Novel', in *The Dialogic Imagination: Four Essays*, ed. by Michael Holquist, trans. by Caryl Emerson and Michael Holquist (Austin: University of Texas Press, 1981), pp. 3-40 (pp. 20, 21).

[22] Bakhtin, *Rabelais*, p. 20.

[23] Bakhtin, *Rabelais*, p. 20.

[24] M. M. Bakhtin, 'From the Prehistory of the Novelistic Discourse', in *The Dialogic Imagination: Four Essays*, pp. 41-83 (p. 55); italics in original.

In contrast to Bakhtin's explanation, recent work on the comic suggests that what we find funny is inevitably imbedded within a matrix of historical, cultural, and personal factors. In a summary of humour research, Paul Lewis explains that amusement arises from an incongruity, which is first perceived and then resolved by the audience in a playful (as opposed to serious) way.[25] The key here is not that the target is necessarily serious but that humour depends on playful engagement with the target. He adds, importantly, that perceiving incongruity 'is subjective' because

> there is no such thing as an objective joke (one that will amuse all of us). Every variable of human consciousness that influences our sense of how the world operates – from cognitive and emotional development, to philosophic and scientific knowledge, to moral and aesthetic norms – must play a role in defining what will strike us as a violation of our sense of reality (that is, as an incongruity).[26]

All the factors that Lewis identifies here as crucial to one's sense of humour participate in the development of what I have been calling 'taste'. That both 'cultural and personal' factors play a part in this development is clear because responses to and identification of humorous elements cannot be entirely idiosyncratic, since 'the extent to which we can share humour is based on a common world view'.[27] In other words, taste must be understood to operate differently between cultures as well as within them, an argument Manfred Pfister also makes:

> What may appear as nature only, as mere nature, pure and simple, and is often given out or celebrated as such, on closer inspection proves to be the product of the cultural processing of nature. If there is, therefore, a 'history of laughter,' it can only be the history of social discourses, representations, performances and practices through which such cultural processing of laughter is effectuated.[28]

Ultimately, humour, like other aspects of taste, is both personally and culturally determined rather than 'natural'. This is particularly clear from some feminist reactions to the *Miller's Tale*, which have found its fabliau premise offensive rather than

---

[25] Paul Lewis, *Comic Effects: Interdisciplinary Approaches to Humour in Literature* (Albany: State University of New York Press, 1989), pp. 9-11.

[26] Lewis, *Comic Effects*, pp. 11-12

[27] Lewis, *Comic Effects*, p. 12

[28] Manfred Pfister, 'Introduction: A History of English Laughter?', in *A History of English Laughter: Laughter from Beowulf to Beckett and Beyond*, ed. by Manfred Pfister (Amsterdam; New York: Rodopi, 2002), pp. v-x (p. v).

funny;[29] such readers would likely reject the humour of both the *Miller's Tale* and its analogues on the same grounds. Karma Lochrie, for example, argues that

> for the purposes of both her sexual and textual exchanges, Alison has been reduced to her 'pryvetee,' and, to borrow the Miller's words, of the remnant we do not need to inquire. The tale's humour depends on this reduction, this conversion of woman to secret thing to prank, and on her disappearance.[30]

Rather than indicating that feminists have no sense of humour (as has sometimes been asserted) what is clear from such modern-day reactions to Chaucer's bawdy tale is that fabliau humour is not 'natural', but represents an acquired taste. Establishing one set of aesthetic preferences as 'natural' over another limits from the outset our understanding of whatever does not fit within the characteristics we have already defined. But as Robert Darnton argues, it is often the most opaque aspects of a culture that provide the best starting point for understanding it. Seeing where we are missing something can signal 'where to grasp a foreign system of meaning in order to unravel it'.[31] Darnton suggests that if we treat the narrative as a 'meaningful fabrication' – one that responds to audience expectations about how to tell a story – we have to assume a 'repertory of associations and responses' from the audience, whether or not we share them.[32] Thus, it is precisely because we have difficulty understanding the preferences of romance audiences in terms of our own aesthetic criteria – criteria primarily established for the interpretation of highly literary writers like Chaucer – that we should be looking to them to help broaden and deepen our understanding of the lives and interests of medieval people.

Sir Thopas and Romance

Traditionally, readings of Chaucer have been based on expectations of literary art that focus on reading for high aesthetic pleasure, and most studies of *Sir Thopas* are arguably coming from the point of view of 'elite models' that see *Thopas* primarily in relation to *Melibee*, Chaucer's self-presentation, his revisions of specific

---

[29] See, for example, Elaine Tuttle Hansen, *Chaucer and the Fictions of Gender* (Berkeley: University of California Press, 1992).

[30] Karma Lochrie, 'Women's "Pryvetees" and Fabliau Politics in the "Miller's Tale"', *Exemplaria* 6 (1994), 287-304 (p. 301).

[31] Robert Darnton, *The Great Cat Massacre and Other Episodes in French Cultural History* (New York: Vintage Books, 1984), p. 78.

[32] Darnton, *Great Cat Massacre*, p. 78.

texts that can be uncovered and examined, or his upending of romance formulas.[33] But inquiring more closely into the formulations of pleasure that underlie the 'rym dogerel' (VII. 925) of *Sir Thopas* may help to explain both the Host's rejection of the tale and the sources of its comedy. Clearly enjoyment of the pilgrim Geffrey's sendup of popular romance depends on familiarity with the conventions of the genre, even while the tale's absurd repetition and undermining of those same romance protocols would seem to discourage unselfconscious enjoyment of them. At the same time, the context of the tale establishes critical distance from the outset, framed as it is within the Host's observations about Geffrey as 'popet' and 'elvyssh' (VII. 701, 703), his demands for 'a tale of myrthe, and that anon' (VII. 706), and, finally, his rejection of the poem as 'drasty rymyng [...] nat worth a toord' (VII. 930). E. S. Kooper calls the Host's remarks 'the unsophisticated and somewhat emotional reaction of this disappointed literary censor',[34] which may be an accurate characterization of his response; nevertheless, Harry Bailly's *function* is far from unsophisticated. Not only does he set the stage for the tale and act out the role of audience through his interruption of and commentary on *Sir Thopas*, but he also directs attention to Chaucer's role as pilgrim in a way that emphasizes the critical distance established by the framing of the tale, a distance that would seem to mark Chaucer's text as unequivocally literary.[35]

The literary qualities of the tale are further emphasized by its pairing in *The Canterbury Tales* with *Melibee*, a fact that makes it tempting to read *Sir Thopas* with and against *Melibee*. The two tales taken together point again to Chaucer's role as

---

[33] Carl Lindahl critiques the 'numerous elite models for the structure of the *Canterbury Tales*' Chaucerians habitually identify, suggesting that in doing so scholars have persistently assumed that borrowings from 'the oral traditions of the lower classes [...] were merely details, and that the governing structures into which artists worked these details were always elite' (see 'The Oral Undertones of Late Medieval Romance', in *Oral Tradition in the Middle Ages*, ed. by W. F. H. Nicolaisen, Medieval & Renaissance Texts & Studies, 112 (Binghamton, NY: Medieval & Renaissance Texts & Studies, 1995), pp. 59-75 (p. 60)).

[34] E. S. Kooper, 'Inverted Images in Chaucer's Tale of Sir Thopas', *Studia Neophilologica*, 56.2 (1984), 147-54 (p. 147).

[35] A number of scholars have discussed the Host's role and function. See, for example, Alan T. Gaylord, '*Sentence* and *Solaas* in Fragment VII of the *Canterbury Tales*: Harry Bailly as Horseback Editor', *PMLA* 82 (1967), 226-35; Cynthia C. Richardson, 'The Function of the Host in the *Canterbury Tales*', *Texas Studies in Literature and Language* 12 (1970), 325-44; Barbara Page, 'Concerning the Host', *Chaucer Review* 4 (1970), 1-13; L. M. Leitch, 'Sentence and Solaas: The Function of the Hosts in the *Canterbury Tales*', *Chaucer Review* 17 (1982), 5-20; S. S. Hussey, 'Chaucer's Host'**,** in *Medieval Studies Presented to George Kane*, ed. by Edward Donald Kennedy, Ronald Waldron, and Joseph S. Wittig (Woodbridge, Suffolk; Wolfeboro, NH: D. S. Brewer, 1988), pp. 153-65; and Leo Carruthers, 'Narrative Voice, Narrative Framework: The Host as 'Author' of the *Canterbury Tales*', in *Drama, Narrative and Poetry in the 'Canterbury Tales'*, ed. and introd. by Wendy Harding (Toulouse, France: Presses universitaires du Mirail; 2003), pp. 51-67.

teller – of these two tales in his pilgrim guise, and of the whole *Canterbury Tales* – a point often picked up on by scholars. Lee Patterson, for example, argues that '*The Tale of Sir Thopas* and *The Tale of Melibee* represent a further attempt on Chaucer's part to define both the kind of writing that constitutes *The Canterbury Tales* and, more tellingly, the kind of person who wrote it'.[36] Seth Lerer makes a similar argument, saying that *Sir Thopas* 'is above all a poem about its teller's presence', a poem whose 'phrases redirect the audience's attention away from Sir Thopas' struggle with giants and towards the narrator's struggle with his own line', and whose stanzas reproduce 'both the amblings of Thopas' horse and the circum-navigations of the story's plot',[37] a point made at more length by Gaylord.[38] These readings of the tale point to *Sir Thopas*'s literary status; it is a tale that begs to be taken seriously. In the end, as E. G. Stanley observes, 'No writer of Middle English stanzaic verse shows such versatile technical mastery as Chaucer does in the Pro-logue and Tale of *Sir Thopas* – to demonstrate his incompetence'.[39]

But a number of scholars, Nancy Mason Bradbury most recently, have pointed to the difficulty in locating exactly what is parodic in *Sir Thopas*.[40] Bradbury argues that we cannot assume that Chaucer and his contemporaries shared the 'aesthetic and social judgments [that] have echoed for decades in critical writings on Chaucer and on the metrical romances'.[41] She goes on to point out that many of the 'devices

---

[36] Lee Patterson, '"What Man Artow?": Authorial Self-Definition in *The Tale of Sir Thopas* and *The Tale of Melibee*', *Studies in the Age of Chaucer* 11 (1989), 117-75 (p. 120).

[37] Seth Lerer, '"Now holde youre mouth": The Romance of Orality in the *Thopas-Me-libee* Section of the *Canterbury Tales*', in *Oral Poetics in Middle English Parody*, ed. by Mark C. Amodio, assisted by Sarah Gray Miller (New York and London: Garland Publishing, 1994), pp. 181-205 (p. 185).

[38] See Gaylord, 'Chaucer's Dainty "Dogerel"'.

[39] E. G. Stanley, 'The Use of Bob-Lines in *Sir Thopas*', *Neuphilologische Mitteilungen* 73 (1972), 417-26 (p. 426).

[40] Walter Scheps observes that 'scholars have generally agreed that Chaucer's *Rime of Sir Thopas* is a parody; they have not concurred, however, on the object of the parody' ('Sir Thopas: The Bourgeois Knight, the Minstrel and the Critics', *Tennessee Studies in Literature*, 11 (1966), 35-43 (p. 35)), listing seven earlier claims for *Sir Thopas's* target. Gaylord sug-gests that assuming that *Sir Thopas* 'parodies Middle English tail-rhyme romances' is a mistake, and that by doing so 'we have missed the joke of jokes, and the last laugh remains to be laughed' (pp. 83-84). Mark DiCicco and J. M. Manly, respectively, argue for the ab-surdity of Thopas's arming, but disagree on what exactly is absurd about it (see Mark DiC-icco's discussion in 'The Arming of Sir Thopas Reconsidered', *Notes and Queries* 46/244.1 (1999), 14-16, for particulars).

[41] Nancy Mason Bradbury, *Writing Aloud: Storytelling in Late Medieval England* (Ur-bana: University of Illinois Press, 1998), p. 176.

of minstrel style' in *Sir Thopas* also occur in Chaucer's poetry in contexts that are not parodic,[42] reasoning that the supposed 'absurd minstrel features' are not easy to delimit in *Sir Thopas* 'because, taken collectively, they represent that aspect of Chaucer's own craft that is most closely associated with memory and oral performance, but is by no means limited to ironic or parodic use'.[43] Seth Lerer goes further to suggest that, while to us *Sir Thopas* 'seems [...] a parody' and *Melibee* a serious literary effort, in fact 'for many readers of the fifteenth and sixteenth centuries, it was the tail-rhyme romance that had compelling appeal'.[44] According to Lerer, 'As an example of the popular *avanture* [*sic*] poetry, the *Thopas* held the imaginations of an audience reared on the adventures of Guy of Warwick, Bevis of Hamptoun, and many other appealing errants'.[45] The picture of *Sir Thopas* delineated by Bradbury and Lerer proposes that at least some audiences contemporary to Chaucer, together with later medieval and early modern audiences, would have been more likely to enjoy the tale's formulaic language and adventurous errancy unselfconsciously than to recognize the poem as a sophisticated literary piece with the built-in ironic distance scholars generally take for granted.[46]

As early as the sixteenth century, *Sir Thopas* was associated by writers and audiences alike with those 'rymes of Robin Hood' eschewed by Langland in his portrait of Sloth.[47] For example, in *Schir Thomas Norny*, written with *Thopas* in mind, William Dunbar explicitly mentions some characters from the Robin Hood ballads,

---

[42] Bradbury, pp. 177-79. Bradbury addresses asseverations (e.g. 'I telle it yow' or 'it is no nay'), 'minstrel-style doublets' (e.g. 'game and glee', 'wele and wo', 'joy and bliss'), and platitudes ('bityde what bityde') (pp. 178-79).

[43] Bradbury, p. 180.

[44] Lerer, 'Romance of Orality', p. 182.

[45] Lerer, 'Romance of Orality', p. 182.

[46] In his chapter, 'The Eighteenth-Century Creation of Chaucerian Burlesque', Joseph A. Dane shows that this 'characterization of the poem as a form of literary criticism' (*Parody: Critical Concepts Versus Literary Practices, Aristophanes to Sterne* (Norman: University of Oklahoma Press, 1988), p. 187) is first found in the work of late eighteenth-century antiquarians, critics, and commentators, such as Thomas Warton, William Warburton, Thomas Percy, Thomas Tyrwhitt, and Richard Hurd (pp. 187, 192, 198), who called the poem 'burlesque' (p. 191). Before this time, *Sir Thopas* was seen as 'silly' but not 'as meta-romance' (pp. 198-99). Dane points out that the word 'parody' was not used to describe *Sir Thopas* until the nineteenth century (p. 192).

[47] See Thomas Hahn's extended discussion of the representation of Sloth in *Piers Plowman* in 'Playing with Transgression: Robin Hood and Popular Culture', in *Robin Hood in Popular Culture: Violence, Transgression, and Justice*, ed. by Thomas Hahn (Cambridge, Eng.: D. S. Brewer, 2000), pp. 1-11.

including Robin himself and Guy of Gisborne.[48] This association 'with the ballad poetry of the greenwood' was retained by later sixteenth-century writers, George Puttenham and Michael Drayton, as well.[49] Even more provocative is the fact that a late fifteenth-century manuscript of *Thopas* replaces 'Beves' with 'Robinhood' (VII. 899) in the catalogue of heroes from 'romances of prys' (VII. 897) that occurs near the end of the tale.[50] Puttenham lumps *Guy of Warwick*, *Bevis of Hampton*, and *Sir Thopas* together (along with *Adam Bell and Clim of the Clough*) as 'stories of old time [...] made purposely for recreation of the common people at Christmasse diners & brideales, and in tauernes & alehouses, and such other places of base resort' in his 1589 *Arte of English Poesie*.[51] Of course, there is no way of knowing whether these performances were anything like the written texts that survive; nevertheless, while we cannot assume that the oral versions of *Sir Thopas* to which Puttenham refers were faithful (or even nearly so) recitations of Chaucer's written text, these connections suggest that at least in its early reception *Sir Thopas* was associated with ballads and romances, confirming its cognitive proximity to oral forms. The poem's early modern reception and the presence of so many conventions of romance in the poem itself would seem to ask us to take seriously the possibility that Chaucer's work, despite its apparent mockery of the genre, could have achieved popular appeal as well. Might the deployment in *Sir Thopas* of some of distinctive features of the Middle English metrical romances have appealed directly to audiences that favoured such tales?

Humour and Romance Conventions

Because the humour of Chaucer's tale arises at least in part from its treatment of the features of romance, these characteristics must be understood in order to identify how Chaucer's tale redirects them to comic effect and to ascertain whether *Sir Thopas* could in fact be taken 'straight' (i.e. as 'just a romance'). In other words, we must attempt to reconstruct, in Jauss's words, 'the horizon of expectation' for

---

[48] J. A. Burrow, 'Sir Thopas in the Sixteenth Century', in *Middle English Studies Presented to Norman Davis in Honour of His Seventieth Birthday*, ed. by Douglas Gray and E. G. Stanley (Oxford: Clarendon Press, 1983), pp. 69-91 (pp. 69-70).

[49] Burrow, 'Sir Thopas', p. 70

[50] Burrow, 'Sir Thopas', p. 70 n. 2. The manuscript is London, Royal College of Physicians, MS 13 (c. 1460-80). For references on this, Burrow points to John M. Manly and Edith Rickert, *The Text of the 'Canterbury Tales'* (Chicago, University of Chicago Press, 1940), VII, p. 197, and Albert B. Friedman, 'Chaucer and Robin Hood', *Notes and Queries* 195 (1950), 210.

[51] *Arte of English Poesie*, quoted in *Elizabethan Critical Essays*, ed. and introd. by G. Gregory Smith, 2 vols (London: Oxford University Press, 1904), II, 87.

audiences of Middle English romance insofar as we can. As we seek to understand this possibility, a comparison of Chaucer's *Sir Thopas* to the early fourteenth-century *Sir Tristrem* will help clarify what appealed to early audiences of the metrical romances.[52] Discounting the linking material, *Sir Thopas* is just 207 lines long, a length that seems perfect for oral performance.[53] But in contrast to *Sir Tristrem*, whose first 207 lines encompass a furious-paced story of war, love, birth, and death,[54] in Chaucer's poem the only action that takes place is Thopas's endless riding, 'lead[ing] neither to ogre nor fair lady, but to exhaustion', until we get the impression that 'he may only have been careening heatedly in circles'.[55] The differences here suggest that the evasion of action is one source of the humour of Chaucer's tale. In the description of Thopas as 'a knyght [that] was fair and gent / In bataille and in tourneyment', for example, the narrator highlights Thopas's knightly prowess, but we never see any battles that support this view. *Sir Thopas* instead offers boasts in place of the expected fight.[56] In Thopas's encounter with the giant Olifaunt, the giant threatens Thopas:

---

[52] *Sir Tristrem* appears in the Auchinleck manuscript (Edinburgh, National Library of Scotland, Advocates' MS 19.2.1), which some argue Chaucer may have seen. See, for example, Laura Hibbard Loomis, 'Chaucer and the Auchinleck MS: "Thopas" and "Guy of Warwick"', *Essays and Studies in Honor of Carleton Brown* (New York: New York University Press, 1940), pp. 111-28; and Derek Pearsall and I. C. Cunningham, introd., *The Auchinleck Manuscript, National Library of Scotland Advocates' MS. 19.2.1.* (London: Scolar Press, 1977), pp. vii-xi. Versions of both *Guy of Warwick* and *Bevis of Hampton* also appear in Auchinleck; while it is worth making comparisons to those poems, focusing on *Sir Tristrem* avoids the traditional source-analogue study that tries to identify the particular romances Chaucer may have modified or targeted.

[53] Andrew Taylor argues that it is likely that performers were in the habit of selecting short episodes from longer narratives for live presentation, explaining that 'it would seem [that] minstrels could not rely on bringing their audience back over several nights to hear a complete series of episodes any more than they could rely on having the audience's undivided attention for several hours' ('Fragmentation, Corruption, and Minstrel Narration: The Question of the Middle English Romances', *Yearbook of English Studies*, 22 (1992), 38-62 (p. 57)). He also cites the opening of Chrétien de Troyes's *Eric et Enide*, where the narrator complains of the entertainer who not only 'corrupts the story, falsifying the true version', but is guilty of 'picking the story apart, breaking it into pieces [*depecier*]' (p. 59).

[54] More specifically, in the first 207 lines of the popular poem, Rouland (Tristrem's father) and Duke Morgan feud with one another, establish a truce, journey to England, and meet with King Mark. In England, they joust in a tournament during which Blancheflour falls in love with Rouland. After the tournament, Blancheflour, hearing Rouland is wounded, swoons; Rouland 'comforts' her and Tristrem is conceived. Meanwhile Morgan breaks the truce, Rouland and Morgan fight, and Rouland is mortally wounded, dying in line 208.

[55] Gaylord, 'Chaucer's Dainty "Dogerel"', p. 89.

[56] See Thomas Hahn and Dana M. Symons, 'Middle English Romance', in *A Companion to Medieval English Literature and Culture, c. 1350- c. 1500*, ed. by Peter Brown (Malden, MA: Blackwell Publishing), pp. 341-57 (p. 350).

>   Child, by Termagaunt!
>   But if thou prike out of myn haunt,
>   Anon I sle thy steede. (VII. 810-12)

This threat is only a limited one, since it is not Sir Thopas himself but merely his
horse the giant targets. Still, Thopas's response is to put off the fight: 'Tomorwe
wol I meete with thee, / Whan I have myn armoure' (VII. 818-19). The humour
stems from both the restricted nature of the threat and 'the knowledge that Thopas's
behaviour stands in stark contrast to that of the heroes of popular romance, who
can certainly boast with the best of them, but whose boasting leads to exciting,
action-packed combat' rather than flight.[57] Tristrem not only routinely exchanges
fighting words with his opponents (three of whom arc giants) but also in each case
escalates the encounters into one-on-one combat.[58]

Unlike the avoidance of action that characterizes *Sir Thopas*, *Sir Tristrem* offers a
number of spectacular battles, all of which emphasize Tristrem's valour. During
Tristrem's blow-by-blow fight with the dragon threatening Dublin, for example,
the narrator focuses on details that exemplify Tristrem's superior bravery. The narrator begins by explaining that the dragon is so fearsome people would rather drown
than stay in Dublin to face it:

>   Out of Develin toun
>   The folk wel fast ran
>   In a water to droun,
>   So ferd were thai than. (ll. 1409-12)

Even Tristrem's valiant knights ('his knightes stithe' (l. 1421)) refuse to intervene;
instead 'Alle thai beden lat be; / Durst non himselven kithe' (ll. 1424-25), leaving
Tristrem to fight alone. Thus, by the time we are told that Tristrem is 'an hardi man'
(l. 1430), the comment has already become redundant, for even the fact that Tristrem is willing to face the dragon at all is evidence of his 'hardiness'. The fight with
the dragon quickly ensues. Even though it seems like 'Helle-fere [...] / Fram that
dragoun fleighe' (ll. 1440-41), in the next line Tristrem begins his assault with a
spear, only to find that 'It no vailed o botoun; / Oway it gan to glide' because the
dragon's skin is 'hard so ani flint' (ll. 1448-49, 1452). The spear then breaks apart
on his second throw, after which the dragon strikes back: 'The stede he gan sle' (l.

---

[57] Hahn and Symons, 'Middle English Romance', p. 350.

[58] See his battles with Morgan and the giants Moraunt, Urgan, and Beliagog. Compare
also, for example, *Bevis of Hampton*, where the emperor of Germany threatens to hang Sir
Guy and cut off his head, with the further promise that he will afterwards destroy Sir Guy's
lineage and insult his honour by killing his son and taking his wife as a lover. Sir Guy responds with boasts to protect his family, after which they begin their exchange of blows.

1458). Here, in contrast to *Sir Thopas*, Tristrem's horse is not merely threatened but killed with the first breath. Tristrem responds by cutting off the dragon's jaw; the beast then breathes fire at him, destroying his armour and shield. Unfazed, 'Tristrem raught his brain / And brak his nek bon' (ll. 1479-80). Here, the action of the poem is quick and fierce, leaving no doubt about Tristrem's bravery or ability as a fighter.[59]

This is not to say that the metrical romances never tell about action rather than showing it, but even the paraphrases often put activity on display in a way that *Sir Thopas* persistently avoids. Like the vague description of Thopas as 'a knyght [that] was fair and gent / In bataille and in tourneyment', the portrait of Thopas's father in the next stanza is quite brief: 'His fader was a man ful free, / And lord he was of that contree' (ll. 721-22). Although we are told here that Thopas's father is noble ('ful free'), no evidence of this is given. The character of Tristrem's father, by contrast, is not simply asserted, but also explained and illustrated. We learn right away that his father Rouland would 'thole no wrong, / Thei Morgan lord wes' (ll. 23-24), and the proof of this is that he wreaks havoc on Duke Morgan's lands:

> He [Rouland] brak his [Morgan's] castels strong,
> His bold borwes he ches,
> His men he slough among
> And reped him mani a res. (ll. 25-28)

Although these lines essentially report the action between Rouland and Morgan instead of illustrating it in detail, in this case the paraphrase contains substantive information (castles are razed, strongholds occupied, men killed, and attacks carried out) and acts as a foretaste of conflict to come. The war between the two lasts so long that Morgan sues for peace, but until that moment the two do not hold back:

> Thai spilden mani a man
> Bituen hemselven to
> In prise. (ll. 40-42)

---

[59] Such scenes are typical of many Middle English romances. For example, in *Bevis of Hampton* the plot focuses on spectacular events such as Bevis's father, Sir Guy fighting with the emperor of Germany and his retinue, Bevis's insults to his mother, his defeat of the man-eating boar, his flight from prison, his battle with the giant Ascopard, his days-long struggle with the dragon, or his fight in the streets of London. That these scenes were a particular draw for audiences is suggested by that fact that, as Pearsall points out, amongst the various texts of *Bevis*, 'the range of textual variation is often greatest in the most exciting scenes' ('Middle English Romance and its Audiences', in *Historical and Editorial Studies in Medieval and Early Modern English for Johan Gerritsen*, ed. by Mary-Jo Arn and Hanneke Wirtjes, with Hans Jansen (Groningen: Wolters-Noordhoff, 1985), pp. 37-47 (p. 42)).

Morgan eventually kills Tristrem's father, for which he is killed by Tristrem, who must then defeat Morgan's three brothers, Moraunt, Urgan, and Beliagog, who challenge him in turn. Thus, at the point where *Sir Thopas* is busy describing Thopas's face as white 'as payndemayn' (VII. 725), *Sir Tristrem* offers its first of many servings of battle.

As with the battles, appreciating the comical in *Sir Tristrem* likewise requires cultivating a taste for spectacular display, and two scenes from the tale illustrate particularly well the type of humour such spectacles offer. For the first, I return to Tristrem's fight with the dragon. After the loss of his horse to the dragon's fiery breath, Tristrem defeats the dragon by cutting off its jaw, piercing its brain, and breaking its neck. It is at the end of the mêlée that a touch of the absurd enters in the moment when Tristrem cuts out the dragon's tongue 'bi the rote' (l. 1485) as a kind of trophy and sticks it down his hose: 'In his hose next the hide / The tong oway he bar' (ll. 1486-87). As a result Tristrem loses his capacity for speech: 'No yede he bot ten stride / His speche les he thar' (ll. 1488-89). The phallic possibilities of the tongue cannot be ignored. Tristrem's double 'phallus' makes him doubly virile, yet strangely impotent: impotent because, on the one hand, having put the tongue down his pants renders Tristrem speechless and at the mercy of the steward's boast that it was *he* (and not Tristrem) who killed the dragon; virile because, on the other hand, it conveniently provides proof that it *was* Tristrem who vanquished the beast, and not the steward who absconded with its head. Upon hearing about the tongue, Ysonde and her mother the queen both 'loke' (presumably down Tristrem's hose), after which 'The Quen [...] / Out of his hose it toke' (ll. 1527-29). Although the scene may seem suggestive to us, it is difficult to know how medieval audiences may have responded to it. Certainly it seems to play deliberately with the convention of the hero cutting off the giant's head as a trophy – proof of his heroic deed. The fact that Tristrem takes the tongue instead seems to have comic resonance, with the possibility for laughter created in the 'doubling' of Tristrem's 'unit'. In favour of the comic reading, it is worth noting that the proof provided by the presence of the dragon's tongue in Tristrem's hose is not really needed, since Ysonde figures out the real hero in a matter of seconds, and the discovery of the tongue merely confirms her reasoning.[60] In any case, whether comic or not, these moments vividly

---

[60] Before even sighting the speechless Tristrem, Ysonde immediately questions the steward's story; afterwards, when she does see Tristrem, she recognizes at once that he is the dragon-killer:

'Dede the steward this dede?'
'Certes', quath Ysonde, 'nay.
This ich brende stede
No aught he never a day,
No this riche wede
Nas never his, sothe to say'.
Forther als thai yede,

convey the sensationalized, action-packed character of the popular Middle English romance narrative.

In place of action, *Sir Thopas* offers a literary performance in its repeated use of the verb *priken*, which, as Katherine Hanley has pointed out, occurs eight times in fairly rapid succession. Hanley notes, 'Eight times in eighty-three lines the word "prick" appears, each time with new shades of meaning and always with comic effect'.[61] When Hanley argues that 'Chaucer achieves both unity and comic variety through one of the most difficult rhetorical devices: the pun',[62] she clearly sees the locus of the humour in the tale as wordplay, with the variety of meanings contained in the verb *priken* generating an elaborate set of jokes.[63] As Gaylord points out, '"pricking" is a perfectly normal verb to ride out from the romances, yet one that obviously tickled Chaucer'.[64] Chaucer's overuse of the word not only entails multiple forms – 'priketh', 'pryked', 'prikynge', and 'prike' – but also gathers extra resonances from its context, as the following two passages illustrate:

> Sire Thopas fil in love-longynge,
> Al whan he herde the thrustel synge,
> And *pryked* as he were wood.
> [...]
> Sire Thopas eek so wery was
> For *prikyng* on the softe gras,
> So fiers was his corage. (VII. 772-74; 778-80; italics added)

A man thai founde whare lay
And drough.
'Certes', than seyd thai,
'This man the dragoun slough'. (ll. 1508-18)

[61] Katherine Hanley, 'Chaucer's Horseman: Word-play in the "Tale of Sir Thopas"', *NEMLA* 2 (1970), 112-14 (p. 112).

[62] Hanley, 'Chaucer's Horseman', p. 112.

[63] This is not to say that this type of wordplay must be necessarily understood as 'elite'; in fact, its status as such is by no means guaranteed, for, as Jonathan Culler points out, puns were regarded by eighteenth-century writers, such as Alexander Pope, Sydney Smith, and Jonathan Swift, 'as the lowest form of wit' ('The Call of the Phoneme: Introduction', in *On Puns: The Foundation of Letters*, ed. by Jonathan Culler (Oxford; New York: Basil Blackwell, 1988), pp. 1-16 (p. 4)); hence the book's stated commitment 'to the view that puns are not a marginal form of wit but an exemplary product of language or mind [...]. The pun is the foundation of letters, in that the exploitation of formal resemblance to establish connections of meaning seems the basic activity of literature' (p. 4). This shows that notions of 'literariness' are culturally produced, and that Hanley's identification of the pun as 'one of the most difficult rhetorical devices' is a view that doubtless helps generate current appreciation for Chaucer's wit, but is not one universally acknowledged.

[64] Gaylord, 'Chaucer's Dainty "Dogerel"', p. 91.

In addition, readers of Chaucer encountering the line 'pryked as he were wood' would recall a similar line from the *Reeve's Tale*, where John the clerk 'priketh harde and depe as he were mad' with the miller's wife (I. 4231). The word 'priken', with its penetrating sexual overtones, repeated in such a way suggests repetition with a difference; that difference is in turn the source of the comedic effect.[65] The resonances here between the two lines heighten that effect by bringing the larger context of *The Canterbury Tales* to mind. Chaucer's punning use of *priken* is in contrast to the verb's (in Bakhtin's terms) 'straight' appearance in popular romances, such as *Guy of Warwick*, *Amis and Amiloun*, and *Bevis of Hampton*, where it refers to riding on horseback or spurring a horse in battle.[66] Thus, in Bakhtin's terms, Chaucer's wordplay is a 'corrective' version of repeating words that targets 'straight' repetition of the type that occurs in the metrical romances.

Rather than thriving on the type of ambiguity the punning on *priken* provides, the popular romance has its own 'spice' of a kind that emphasizes its spectacular features. This brings us to the second comic scene from *Sir Tristrem*, one that illustrates even more clearly the humorous potential of spectacle. Like the window in the analogues to the *Miller's Tale*, Sir Tristrem's dog Hodain suddenly materializes just at the moment where he is needed in the plot. When Tristrem and Ysonde drink the love potion, the dog Hodain slurps up the last few drops:

> An hounde ther was biside
> That was ycleped Hodain;
> The coupe he licked that tide
> Tho doun it sett Bringwain. (ll. 1673-76)

Following this, Tristrem and Ysonde happily 'play miri [...] / In boure night and day' (ll. 1686-88), but instead of being kicked out by the lovers, the dog falls in love and joins in as if it were the most natural thing in the world: 'Thai loved with al her might / And Hodain dede also' (ll. 1693-94). This scene, one of tender af-

---

[65] Hanley's article enumerates the various meanings of the word 'prick', including the sexual, that she argues resonate in *Sir Thopas*.

[66] In her discussion of the sources and analogues of *Sir Thopas*, Loomis covers examples from a number of romances of the treatment of the hero's riding, including the use of *priken* ('Sir Thopas', *Sources and analogues of Chaucer's Canterbury Tales*, ed. by W. F. Bryan and Germaine Dempster (New York: Humanities Press, 1958), pp. 486-559 (pp. 511-13)). As one example, see Bevis's joust against the giant Ascopard (which Loomis does not include) in *Bevis of Hampton* (Ronald B. Herzman, Graham Drake, and Eve Salisbury, eds., *Four Romances of England* (Kalamazoo, MI: Medieval Institute Publications, 1999)):
> Beves prikede Arondel a side,
> Aghen Ascopard he gan ride
> And smot him on the scholder an high,
> That his spere al to-fligh. (ll. 2533-36)

fection (need I say *sans* dog) in many of the Tristan analogues, in some ways resembles the doubling of lovers found in the *Miller's Tale*. But because it raises the prospect that where the dog loves he also 'plays', the comic possibilities of this curious *ménage à trois* call up 'doggie-style' images of love 'play' that rely on different expectations from those Chaucer uses in constructing his plot in the *Miller's Tale*. In the case of *Sir Tristrem*, rather than a series of substitutions or potential substitutions amongst lovers, we have an *additional* lover in the person of the dog. But critics, who insist on reading the scene innocuously and asexually, have consistently avoided the possibilities offered by this scenario. Thus, including the dog in the love scene becomes 'an obvious attempt to give some rational explanation for the unusual faithfulness of Tristrem's dog',[67] or reflective of a 'tendency to portray lovers' commitment coexisting easily with other kinds of devotion',[68] or simply a 'wonderfully comic' parody of courtly love.[69] These readings deflect attention from the kind of preposterous questions the extra in this scene raises, such as, once they are under the influence, how do we tell the difference between Sir Tristrem and his dog, or what did the three of them do when 'Thai loved with al her might'? What makes this episode especially suggestive is the fact that the addition of the dog as a double of Tristrem, unlike the dragon's tongue, has no function in the plot. The 'extra' in the love scene merely serves to open the door to comedic effect, laughter invited by doubling.

As in the analogues to the *Miller's Tale*, the humour here derives in part from the wholly unexpected nature of this display – the dog appears without warning and just as suddenly laps his way to love. Laughter here is only possible, however, against the ground of the normative human couple. In other words, the source of incongruity in this 'menagerie à trois' stems from the expectation of two lovers not three, and the assumption that no animals will enter the picture. When the single position of lover doubles and one of the lovers turns out to be a dog, one could argue that here *Sir Tristrem* acts as a 'corrective' to the 'straight' couple of official culture, where the field is limited to two (human) lovers. By providing an image of 'doggie-style' love, of playful unselfconscious sexuality (what could be more 'natural'?), this 'corrective' in turn suggests that there is nothing inherently 'natu-

---

[67] Thomas C. Rumble, 'The Middle English *Sir Tristrem*: Towards a Reappraisal', *Comparative Literature* 11 (1959), 221-28 (p. 225).

[68] Susan Crane, *Insular Romance: Politics, Faith, and Culture in Anglo-Norman and Middle English Literature* (Berkeley: University of California Press, 1986), p. 194.

[69] Lupack, 'Reception', p. 52. Like Bakhtin, Lupack seems to use parody in a formalist sense, with the notion that something is either 'straightforward' or 'parodic'. His equation of *Sir Tristrem* with *Sir Thopas* when he suggests that the former 'must be viewed alongside works with similar intent, such as [...] Chaucer's Tale of Sir Thopas' ('Reception', p. 60) suggests that he does not see parody as socially embedded or operating differently for different audiences.

ral' about the normative couple. By the same token, because the incongruity of the love scene in *Sir Tristrem* itself plays out against this non-natural backdrop (in other words, exists always in relation to the normative couple), neither can the 'menagerie à trois' be defined as 'natural' in the way that Bakhtin (or possibly Bourdieu) would have it.

This is where the operation of humour as 'corrective' diverges from Bakhtin's definition, which depends in some way on a subversive critique of the 'straightforward' that offers 'a different and contradictory reality',[70] for the love play in *Sir Tristrem* is in direct opposition to Chaucer's treatment of a potential *ménage à trois*, yet they both produce 'correctives'. When we consider the 'obscenity' of the *Miller's Tale*, where the 'double' is momentarily 'tripled' (John, Nicholas, Absolom), next to the playful absurdity of inserting a dog between Tristrem and Ysonde, we can see that Chaucer's wit depends at least in part on refuting the spectacle of a *ménage à trois* in favour of a more traditional male rivalry that has to be resolved, ultimately, by the repudiation of the 'extras'. In this way, Chaucer's humour is at least partially dependent on making the unofficial official, and the scene seems to offer a 'corrective' that 'straightens out' the potential for unconventional love play. Though it brings up the possibility, the *Miller's Tale* finally rejects the *ménage à trois*, which is instead reduced to the 'official' two in a way that re-emphasizes or reconstitutes the normative. Furthermore, in the *Miller's Tale* it is clear that the rivalries that exist between Nicholas and the other two men are not the result of random events, and that the rejection of the 'extras' becomes the source of the joke as well as an exercise in power relations between Nicholas and Absolom or Nicholas and John.

Yet even as it rejects the 'corrective' possibilities of a *ménage à trois* in favour of one *à deux*, Chaucer's tale, in its pairing, however briefly, of Absolom with Nicholas at the window – with the penetration effected there – offers a different 'corrective', in this case to the heteronormative couple represented by Alisoun and John / Nicholas / Absolom. And even as it depends on the possibility for the 'un-straight' pairing of the two men, at the same time the humour of Chaucer's tale is equally contingent both on rejecting that homoerotic possibility and on the image of bacchanal love play that lies behind / beneath Alisoun and her multiple lovers in much the same way that *Sir Thopas* relies on the formulas of popular romance for its humour. Chaucer's *Miller's Tale* in this way offers a multivalent humour that challenges readers to make sense of its variety, just as his puns on *priken* generate ambiguity and multiple readings in *Sir Thopas*. Ultimately, each of the lovers in the *Miller's Tale* ends up 'uncoupled' altogether, suggesting yet another 'corrective' reading: at some level such 'uncoupling' puts all the potential pairings on the same

---

[70] Bakhtin, 'Prehistory', p. 59.

level, suggesting that none of them is 'natural', but that each arises out of cultural structures.

But, however we read the end of the *Miller's Tale*, it is clear that, even in Chaucer's bawdiest moments, spectacle, rather than operating in a purely incidental or episodic fashion – seemingly for the sheer enjoyment of it – must serve a purpose. Despite its fabliau status, this retelling of the familiar love-triangle produces levels of sophistication that require added effort on the part of readers. In fact, the comic possibilities of the *Miller's Tale* in some measure depend on the audience's capacity to pay prolonged attention to the narrative at the same time as they sustain simultaneously a number of possible readings of the tale's climactic scene. In many ways the humour of the *Miller's Tale* and its use and elimination of the extra rival rely on the classic romance plot of adultery (as would any *fabliau*). Chaucer's tale here depends partly on our taking such plots seriously (as in *Troilus and Criseyde*, *The Franklin's Tale*, or even *The Knight's Tale*), whereas *Sir Tristrem* does not. As Derek Pearsall points out, romance and fabliau 'seem to exist in a complementary relationship', where 'romance asserts the possibility that men may behave in a noble and self-transcending manner; fabliau declares the certainty that they will always behave like animals'.[71] *Sir Tristrem* suggests, on the other hand, that men and animals are simply duplicates, interchangeable with and possibly supplementary to one another.

Humour does, then, seem to operate, as Bakhtin says, as a 'corrective', but its object can be multifarious, and the 'corrective' works in an equally multifaceted way (closing down some possibilities even as it opens others up). Chaucer's choice to place the 'obscene' tale in the mouth of the Miller, as opposed to, say, the Knight or the Prioress, signals the conventional nature of what Bakhtin identifies as 'natural' (i.e. the connection between the demotic and the body). In *The Canterbury Tales* Chaucer plays the role of the mediator who claims he will retell the Knight's, Miller's, and Reeve's tales, for example, but is not 'responsible' for them. What seems implicit in Chaucer's presentation is that he recognizes that it is better, because it seems more natural', to tell the bawdy or obscene tale through the drunken churl than the stately knight. By telling his readers in the prologue to the *Miller's Tale* to 'Turne over the leef and chese another tale' (VII. 3177) if they are offended, Chaucer offers the *Miller's Tale* in the guise of a story whose lewdness can be attributed to its 'low' origin in the mouth of the drunken Miller. But we all recognize that this is a guise rather than a natural connection. Seeing these conventions used by Chaucer, in reality the generator of all these tales, shows such representations to be mediated rather than absolute. Chaucer, in some sense, offers a 'corrective'

---

[71] Derek Pearsall, 'Versions of Comedy in Chaucer's *Canterbury Tales*', in *Chaucer's Frame Tales: The Physical and Metaphysical*, ed. by Jeorg O. Fichte (Tübingen: Gunter Narr; Cambridge, Eng.: D. S. Brewer, 1987), pp. 35-49 (p. 49).

to the naturalization of taste and humour. Similarly, the differences between the popular romance and Chaucer's tales point to the limitations entailed by the use of universalizing aesthetic criteria to assess the pleasures of both literary and popular texts. One could argue, finally, that the obscenity of the *Miller's Tale* is no more 'popular' than the skewed chivalry of *Sir Thopas*.

Audiences and Expectations

When *Sir Thopas* takes romance tropes, such as 'love at first sight' or the pre-battle boast, and makes a hash of them, humour arises from the incongruity between what is and what convention leads us to expect: Sir Thopas never sees his lady before he falls in love with her because she exists only in a dream, and his confrontation with a giant becomes an arena for bluster rather than the prelude to a spectacular battle. *Sir Tristrem* turns these same romance tropes into a site of comic effect through the incongruity of the extra: 'love at first sight' introduces a dog-lover into a tender love scene, and fighting a dragon results in the taking of a strange trophy that renders the hero speechless just when he should be celebrating his victory. These different manipulations of generic conventions signal distinct approaches to humour that provide clues about how such tales pleasured their audiences. *Sir Tristrem*'s focus on action and spectacle in place of the intensely psychological drama of Thomas of Britain's highly literary twelfth-century Anglo-Norman version of the tale shows that the tale's emphasis is on qualities that appeal more readily in the context of live performance than in that of silent reading.[72] In contrast, as the emphasis on wordplay and irony illustrates, *Sir Thopas* makes every effort to shut down spectacle, the very quality these ludicrous scenes in *Sir Tristrem* emphasize. This suggests that, despite its connections with oral formulas and the potential appeal the text could have had when read aloud, *Sir Thopas* is a narrative, like *Melibee*, whose ultimate focus is on silent reading and the creation of literary value. Lerer suggests that in the highlighting of its performer *Sir Thopas* represents the oral in Chaucer, while *Melibee* is a 'retreat of the narrator into the absence that controls the written' whose 'overarching fiction is that it in fact is no telling at all, but rather a piece of writing [...] meant not to be heard but read',[73] but the distinction, as Lerer himself points out, would seem to be only a fiction. In every way possible – with its context next to *Melibee*, its teller so pointedly Chaucer himself, its lack of real action, and the subtleties of its wordplay – Chaucer signals against reading the poem as a performative piece. His anxiety on this score perhaps stems

---

[72] For a detailed comparison of these two versions, see Dana M. Symons, 'Does Tristrem Think, or Doesn't He? The Pleasures of the Middle English *Sir Tristrem*', *Arthuriana* 11.4 (2001), 3-22.

[73] Lerer, 'Romance of Orality', pp. 184-85.

from the fact that there is overlap in the audiences of Middle English works, while the potential for mingling of 'high' and 'low' within the works themselves means that that poets like Chaucer must work to establish the distinctiveness – and credibility – of their writings.[74]

Thus, despite his reliance on oral expressions, Chaucer's poem actually works against these to create a virtuoso 'Chaucerian' literary performance. In his note on the formulaic tag 'Listeth, lordes', used at the beginning of *Sir Thopas* (VII. 712), J. A. Burrow observes that the phrase is repeated as 'Yet listeth, lordes' (VII. 833) just over a hundred lines later.[75] According to Burrow, Chaucer is 'imitating, humorously, one of the favourite alliterating collocations in the poetry of his day', and the addition of 'yet' in the second instance 'strikes a fresh note of comic anxiety' by rendering the phrase 'keep on listening'.[76] This appropriation of the oral illustrates Chaucer's dependence on inverting or redeploying popular forms as part of the shaping of his literary art. Bourdieu argues that the dominated always define their taste in relation to that of the dominant,[77] suggesting that 'as much by the absence of luxury goods [...] the working-class life-style is characterized by the presence of numerous cheap substitutes for these rare goods'.[78] This presupposes that popular art, even when a knock-off, creates its meaning through opposition to elite art, rewriting or resisting it, but the converse is equally true, because literary works depend in turn on the existence and repudiation of the popular in order to legitimate themselves. In this way, Chaucer rivals medieval romance by turning its own conventions against itself. But Chaucer is not involved simply in a kind of formal ex-

---

[74] Lerer suggests that Chaucer is concerned with forms of public performance, arguing that 'Chaucer's references, allusions, and citations to the species of late fourteenth-century theater [...] are calibrated not so much towards articulating the theatricality of his own project as they are towards locating that project among competing and potentially disruptive forms of dramatic public expression' (Seth Lerer, 'The Chaucerian Critique of Medieval Theatricality', in *The Performance of Middle English Culture*, ed. by James J. Paxson, Lawrence M. Clopper, and Sylvia Tomasch (Cambridge, Eng.: D. S. Brewer, 1998), pp. 59–60). He goes on to argue that in *The Canterbury Tales* Chaucer deliberately 'silences his Guildsmen not out of neglect but out of purpose, and that by denying them the chance for tale-telling performance, he effectively removes one source of competition for official literature' (p. 60). While cycle plays differ from romances in a number of ways, it seems clear from *The Knight's Tale*, *The Wife of Bath's Tale*, *The Squire's Tale*, *The Franklin's Tale*, *The Tale of Sir Thopas*, and *Troilus and Criseyde* that Chaucer has a vested interest in retelling romance.

[75] J. A. Burrow, '"Listeth, Lordes": "Sir Thopas", 712 and 833', *Notes and Queries* 15 (1968), 326-27 (p. 326).

[76] Burrow, 'Listeth', p. 326.

[77] Bourdieu, *Distinction*, p. 41.

[78] Bourdieu, *Distinction*, p. 386.

periment, nor is he borrowing 'mere details', to modify Carl Lindahl's phrase;[79] *Sir Thopas* depends on the repetitions and formulas that constitute the basis of the pleasure of popular genres, even as it undoes them. Chaucer has stripped these conventions of their purpose and effectiveness as narrative tools, since they no longer move the story along. The fact that his tale offers puns, rhetorical elaboration, and effete language that feminises Thopas in place of spectacle suggests that *Sir Thopas* is calculated to defeat romance audience expectations and undermine the kind of enjoyment that relies on such performative features. Perhaps what makes the Host's 'eres aken' (VII. 922) is the substitution of the very contradictions and tensions that interest a 'literary' reader in place of the anticipated action. What the Host wants is a 'straight' story; what he gets is a 'corrected' version of popular romance.

Although at least some late medieval and early modern audiences may have seen *Sir Thopas* as a 'straight' romance, in connection with other popular ballads and romances, the manuscript evidence suggests that for at least some of Chaucer's early audiences the literary qualities of the tale must have been both evident and of some interest. Judith Tschann explains that the complicated presentation of *Sir Thopas* in some of the *Canterbury Tales* manuscripts 'does more than indicate the verse form; it comments on it'.[80] Tschann suggests that the contrast between the rhyme royal stanzas the Host uses in speaking to the pilgrim Chaucer makes 'Chaucer's doggerel [...] even more glaring and its conspicuous display more incongruous', while the layout's intricacy 'adds to the joke'.[81] Tschann explains that the layout used for *Sir Thopas* is not normally used for tail-rhyme romance[82] and argues that the use of such a design implies that the scribes of these manuscripts deliberately 'called attention to the drastiness of the rhyme through the presentation of the

---

[79] Lindahl, 'Oral Undertones', p. 60 (the original phrase is 'merely details').

[80] Judith Tschann, 'The Layout of *Sir Thopas* in the Ellesmere, Hengwrt, Cambridge Dd.4.24, and Cambridge Gg.4.27 Manuscripts', *Chaucer Review* 20 (1985), 1-13 (p. 7). The manuscripts on which Tschann focuses her discussion are Ellesmere (San Marino, CA, Huntington Library, MS EL 26 C 9), Hengwrt (Aberystwyth, National Library of Wales, MS Peniarth 392D), and Cambridge, University Library, MSS Dd.4.24 and Gg.4.27 because of their 'landmark' status, but she notes that there are fifteen manuscripts with 'a separate column of tail lines' that 'also mark the bobs', eleven of these with consistency (p. 2). In addition, twenty-nine of the fifty-three witnesses 'use brackets to join rhymes', while twenty of these 'write the tail-rhyme lines to the right, making a separate column of tail lines' (p. 2).

[81] Tschann, 'The Layout of *Sir Thopas*', p. 7.

[82] Tschann, 'The Layout of *Sir Thopas*', p. 6.

tale', highlighting 'the skill of the poet who is so good at being so bad'.[83] Tschann in fact argues that

> what [these scribes] thought about the tale is no doubt what we think, that it is a masterful display of incompetence and an excellent joke all around, on Chaucer the pilgrim, on the rest of the pilgrims, on jogtrot tale-rhyme romances, in short that it is drasty rhyme *par excellence*.[84]

The arrangement of tail-lines to the right, with bob-lines marked further to the right makes it seem as if 'the poem is written in double columns, and that one ought to read it column by column', and Tschann points out that this kind of reading 'does not really do [the poem] much injustice',[85] so that such 'horizontal reading has much the same effect finally, with even a little more trouble for readers, who must find their way through an architectural maze, reading across the page as well as down'.[86] Thus, the visual component of the tale emphasizes both its status as an object for reading (rather than for performance) and its difficulty. Tschann suggests that

> a reader encountering the layout and the tale for the first time might even have trouble deciding just where the 'tails' fit into the first column, since they do not actually follow but rather come next to and in between the two preceding lines.[87]

Here, arguably the simplest verse form that occurs in Chaucer's poetry becomes the most difficult to interpret, requiring multiple readings and attention to detail. According to Tschann the layout adds further possibilities 'for reading and interpreting the text', which becomes 'a kind of punctuation poem, one that can be read in different ways depending on how one points it or otherwise indicates the relationship between syntactic units'.[88] In this layout the repetitive, nonsensical qualities of *Sir Thopas* turn out to heighten its ambiguity and multiply potential readings, making this deceptively simple tale, if possible, even more literary.

---

[83] Tschann, 'The Layout of *Sir Thopas*', p. 7.

[84] Tschann, 'The Layout of *Sir Thopas*', p. 7.

[85] Tschann, 'The Layout of *Sir Thopas*', p. 8.

[86] Tschann, 'The Layout of *Sir Thopas*', p. 9.

[87] Tschann, 'The Layout of *Sir Thopas*', p. 9.

[88] Tschann, 'The Layout of *Sir Thopas*', p. 10.

Conclusion

As I mentioned in the beginning of this chapter, in order to redeem *Sir Tristrem* from critical dismissal, Alan Lupack suggests reading it as a parody 'alongside works with similar intent, such as [...] Chaucer's *Tale of Sir Thopas*'.[89] But the differences between the popular romance and Chaucer's tales point to the limitations entailed by the use of the same aesthetic criteria to assess the appeal of both literary and popular texts. Inverting Lupack's paradigm offers the possibility of understanding why *Sir Thopas* might fail as a popular piece and how it achieves its particularly literary brand of humour. In this model, examining Chaucer's poem alongside the metrical romances it is said to mock operates not as a way of uncovering parodic intentions in the popular tales, or of ascertaining the sources of echoes and resonances in Chaucer's poem, but rather as a method of understanding how *Sir Thopas* differs from Middle English romances that favour a performative context over a literate one. In other words, we must discriminate among comic modalities and contexts: humour is not universal. There may have been medieval readers who found delight in *both* the similarities of *Sir Thopas* and *Sir Tristrem, and* in their differences, but my emphasis here falls on the fact that both the 'simple' and 'sophisticated' tastes are acquired.

Sir Thopas reproduces the conventions of popular romance but fails to entertain Harry Bailly. Not being the sort to enjoy exploring the nuances of the word *priken*, the Host considers *Sir Thopas* a waste of time, and its literary pleasures fail to offset the 'drasty ryming' (VII. 930) he finds so offensive. Despite its pitiful attempt at 'horsing around', events in *Sir Thopas* become uneventful because, 'for all Thopas' apparent confrontations with the monstrous, there are hardly any battles here, no clearly definable actions of chivalry'.[90] This lack of action would seem to lead to the inevitable end of the tale's contracting in on itself, as Burrow suggests.[91] Yet, given its dependence on popular romance conventions, the possibility of reading *Thopas* against its own grain, as 'merely' a popular tale, lingers. It is impossible either to confirm or deny conclusively the poem's possibility of being read 'straight', because to do so would entail identifying the answer as textually based, with the poem having a given and invariable 'ontological' meaning. But in fact any meaning – including parody – depends on audiences reacting within interpretive communities; that is, meaning is social and transactional, and can therefore change according to context, venue, and audience. Chaucer seems to have had some anxiety on this score, for, just in case anyone is tempted to enjoy *Sir Thopas* in this way, he

---

[89] Lupack, 'Reception', p. 60.

[90] Lerer, 'Romance of Orality', p. 189.

[91] See J. A. Burrow, '"Sir Thopas": An Agony in Three Fits', *Review of English Studies* 22 (1971), 54-58.

has built-in markers that indicate its elite status, including its proximity to *Melibee* and the Host's reaction. Presumably Harry Bailly, like Sloth, is the kind of audience who prefers hearing the rhymes of popular heroes to reading poems like Chaucer's. As Gaylord writes, 'it will take a closer attention than Harry's to determine if there has been hidden, in plain sight, more than meets the eye.'[92] All this points to *Sir Thopas* as a sophisticatedly 'bad' poem – one that seems designed to appeal above all to a highly literate listener or reader; that Chaucer's pilgrims do not appreciate it points to their preference for something with less *priken* and more 'play'. Yet, seeing *Sir Thopas* as 'sophisticatedly bad' has as its corollary the view of *Sir Tristrem* and other 'low-end' tales or romances as 'simply bad', for what marks Chaucer's poem as one and not the other? The context provides the key. A failure as a romance *Sir Thopas* may or may not be, but as one of *The Canterbury Tales* it is an unqualified success. After all, would even scholars take this poem so seriously if it did not have Chaucer's name on it, or if it were not in a literary context like that of *The Canterbury Tales*? Familiarity with romances is necessary for full enjoyment of this poem, but it is not sufficient. It is its context as a poem by Chaucer and readers' intimate knowledge of his other works that delight a literate audience. The fact that Chaucer has the fictional version of himself tell the tale emphasizes that one must know Chaucer – and have developed a 'taste' for him – in order to relish the joke.

---

[92] Gaylord, 'Chaucer's Dainty "Dogerel"', p. 90.

5
Funny Money:
Puns and Currency in the *Shipman's Tale*

CHRISTIAN SHERIDAN

Critical attitudes towards the *Shipman's Tale* have ranged from the censure suggested by E. Talbot Donaldson, who notes that 'the reduction of all human values to commercial ones is accomplished with almost mathematical precision,' to a more benign view exemplified by Gerhard Joseph.[1] Joseph writes that 'in a tale full of sexual and financial chicanery none of the cheerful amenities of this life are ruffled,' and that reading the tale calls for a 'patient deferral of high sentence.'[2] No matter what their take on the *Tale* might be, critics seem to agree that it portrays a world, as Lee Patterson writes, in which all things and all people can be had for the right price.[3] It is, in short, a tale of commodification. I certainly agree with this assessment, but my argument differs in that I trace this commodification not so much to the debasement of humanist values, as in Donaldson's case, nor in the tale's representation of an undefined bourgeois subjectivity as in Pat-

---

[1] E. T. Donaldson, 'Commentary' in *Chaucer's Poetry: An Anthology for the Modern Reader*, 2e. (New York, 1975), p. 1095.

[2] Gerhard Joseph, 'Chaucer's Coinage: Foreign Exchange and the Puns of the Shipman's Tale,' *Chaucer Review* 17 (1983), pp. 345, 347. For a comprehensive overview of critical discussions of money in the tale, see W.E. Rogers and P. Dower, 'Thinking about Money in Chaucer's Shipman's Tale' in *New Readings of Chaucer's Poetry*, ed. by Robert G. Benson and Susan Ridyard (Cambridge: D.S. Brewer, 2003), pp. 119-38.

[3] Lee Patterson. *Chaucer and the Subject of History* (Madison, WI: University of Wisconsin Press, 1991), p. 351.

terson's argument, as to the way the tale uses language itself, particularly its many puns and double entendres. In this I follow Joseph, Willam Woods and other critics who have focused on the *Tale*'s puns and its language in general. [4] However, in this essay I am less interested in any single pun in the *Shipman's Tale* than I am in theorizing the connection between the comic and the commercial within the *Tale*. Specifically, I argue that the *Tale*'s use of the pun as its signature rhetorical figure and its reliance on the movement of one hundred franks to structure its plot indicate a common logic underpinning the workings of money and humour in this fabliau. Both are linked by the potential threats they pose: the pun that language is ulti-mately meaningless, money that all value is relative. But in both instances that potential threat is contained by context and the faith of the users of language and money. This raising of a threat but never following through on it explains why we both laugh and groan at a good pun and why many scholastic writers praised money while at the same time deploring its potentially divisive social effects. For both the medieval and the modern, puns and money produce pleasure and anxiety simultane-ously.

Many scholars have proposed that we view money and language as equivalent systems of signification. For instance, Jean-Joseph Goux argues that 'the monetary metaphor that haunts discussions [...] of language seems to betray an awareness of the correspondence between the mode of economic exchange and the mode of signifying exchange'.[5] Furthermore, Goux suggests that we view the relationship between money and language not as one of analogy, but as isomorphism.[6] In other words, money and language do not mean the same, but they do create meaning in the same ways. This connection between words and money is nowhere more ap-parent than in the pun, and its ability to highlight this connection explains why it figures so prominently in this most mercantile of Chaucer's works.

As a rhetorical figure, the pun operates by requiring its audience either to recognize two (or more) different meanings in the same word or to recognize a connection

---

[4] William Woods, 'A Professional Thyng: The Wife as Merchant's Apprentice in the Shipman's Tale,' *Chaucer Review*, 24 (1989), pp. 139-149.

[5] Jean-Joseph Goux, *Symbolic Economies after Marx and Freud*, trans. by Jennifer Cur-tiss Gage (Ithaca: Cornell University Press), p. 96. See also Allen Hoey, 'The Name on the Coin: Metaphor, Metonymy and Money,' *Diacritics* 18, no. 2 (Summer 1988), p.28. Marc Shell's *The Economy of Literature* (Baltimore: The Johns Hopkins University Press, 1978) and R. A. Shoaf's *Dante, Chaucer and the Currency of the Word* (Norman, OK: Pilgrim Books, 1983) are two other prime examples that have greatly influenced my thinking.

[6] Goux, *Symbolic Economies*, p. 110.

between two different, but similar words.[7] Within the context of the *Shipman's Tale*, the (potential) pun on cosyn/ cozen (in modern spelling) represents the first type while the play on tally/tail (meaning genitalia) represents the second.[8] But once we have recognized the similarity/ difference the pun embodies, we cannot ignore one meaning in favour of the other. Rather, for the pun to retain its humour we must keep both meanings in mind, moving constantly between them. As Richard Lanham explains, the pun forces its audience to negotiate between two poles of potentially opposed meaning: one pole represents the mundane world of denotation, the other the more fanciful world of connotation which gives the pun its charge.[9] Only by having its audience shuttle between these poles will a pun work. If the audience stops circulating between the connotative and denotative poles of the circuit inscribed by the pun, the figure loses its humorous charge. Here we begin to see the connection between puns and money: both rely on circulation in order to be effective.

In fact, we might say that circulation is constitutive of both the pun and of money. Money, in one of its key social functions, acts as a medium of exchange, as both medieval and modern thinkers have recognized.[10] In a barter economy, each person with something to trade must find someone else who not only wants what the first trader has, but has what that trader wants. Since this perfect correspondence is unlikely to occur except in the smallest societies, the need for a means of comparison arises, and the money form is born.[11] By allowing disparate commodities to be compared, money provides the ground upon which goods can be traded without people's needs and desires for commodities having to coincide directly. Rather, money allows those commodities to circulate until they do find a match. Of course,

---

[7] Jonathan Culler, 'The Call of the Phoneme', in *On Puns: The Foundation of Letters*, ed. by Culler (Oxford: Blackwell, 1988) p. 2; Derek Attridge, 'Unpacking the Portmanteau, or Who's afraid of *Finnegan's Wake*?' in *On Puns*, ed. by Culler, p. 140. See these two essays for further examples of the different categories of puns discussed here.

[8] The existence of both of these puns has been contested by scholars, but as my argument will show, I believe the debate itself is instructive and suggests the power of puns and the ways in which the *Shipman's Tale* draws on that power.

[9] Richard A. Lanham, *A Handlist of Rhetorical Terms*, 2e. (Berkeley: University of California Press, 1991), pp. 126-28.

[10] See for instance Michael J. Haupert, 'Determining Efficient Property Rights Systems for Money,' in *Money: Lure, Love, Literature*, John Louis DiGateani (ed.) (Westport, CT: Greenwood Press, 1994), p. 16.

[11] See Glyn Davies, *A History of Money: From Ancient Times to the Present Day* (Cardiff: University of Wales Press, 1994) and John Chown, *A History of Money from A.D. 800* (London: Routledge, 1994) for historical accounts of the evolution of the money form. My discussion here draws on Marx's description of money in *Capital, Volume 1*, trans. Ben Fowkes (New York: Vintage Books, 1976).

once it has facilitated one exchange, money does not rest; once sellers have received a sum for a commodity, they will use that sum to purchase some other commodity. Money has value only when and where it can be circulated just as the pun creates its value, its humour, only when the audience recognizes the meanings circulating within the punning words.[12] But as we will see below, both types of value, monetary or humorous, can also create some anxiety in those who use money or laugh at puns.

Another connection between puns and money is highlighted by a second type of pun in which the humour depends upon a similar but not identical spelling or, more commonly, an identical pronunciation but different spelling of two or more words (in modern English, know/ no serves as an example). This category of puns forces us to recognize the word not as a whole that smoothly connects to an idea, but as a collection of letters that are arbitrarily yoked to the object or concept they represent.[13] This type of pun separates the Saussurean sign into its constituent parts, the letters themselves – the signifier – and what they represent – the signified – and underscores the dual nature of all words as a collection of sounds or marks on a page in a particular order and as the ideas they represent. Duality also marks money's social function. As we have seen in the previous paragraph, it acts as a medium of exchange, but it also can act (and this was especially clear when currency was made of precious metals) to store value.[14] Like the duality of words, these two functions arise because we are able to distinguish between money as a physical form (its signifier) and its value within a given currency system (its signified). When made of or convertible to a precious metal, money itself stored value, regardless of its ability to circulate. But in order to circulate, money must represent not only the value of its material, but also the reliability of the whole monetary system. That is, to be accepted as money, any form must represent, to use the terms of modern United States currency, 'legal tender' and the guarantees of reliability that phrase implies. Currency ensures that reliability through its inscriptions, in the case of medieval coins, the image of the issuing ruler. Before it has been minted, a coin is like scrambled letters on a page: we may sense an incipient word, but what we confront lacks form and thus is unintelligible. Likewise, the gold or silver that comprised coins would have been valuable in undifferentiated form, but once stamped as a coin, it becomes even more valuable because it is inherently fungible.[15]

---

[12] Joseph makes this precise point about the 100 franks and the puns within the Tale, 'Chaucer's Coinage', p. 350.

[13] Attridge, 'Unpacking the Portmanteau', p. 143

[14] A recognition of (and often confusion over) this dual nature of money exercised medieval thinkers and continues to occupy scholars today. See Rogers and Dower, 'Thinking about Money', for discussion.

[15] Hoey, 'The Name on the Coin', p. 31.

Both coins and words must be parts of a recognized system in order to have their full effect. In this way we see that like the punning word, coins are valuable both for what they are, a commodity, and what they represent, a means of exchange.[16]

However, while money's dual nature as store of value and medium of exchange certainly made it a necessity for social growth, it also generated concern regarding potential social problems. These problems fall into two broad areas for medieval thinkers: dissolution of boundaries and improper reference.[17] Scholastic writers recognized the necessity of money for social interaction. To use an Aristotelian example, often cited by scholastic authors, money allows the farmer to trade with the doctor, although what each has to offer differs so greatly. However, in facilitating this exchange, money makes the farmer and the doctor equal, even if only temporarily. This equality posed a threat as it undermined the hierarchy that ordered medieval society. Such considerations of money's role created an 'awareness of specialization and market dependence [that] brought not the celebration of economic individualism, but an uneasy feeling that private virtue and social order were under threat'.[18] Scholastic thinkers thus held a radically dualistic attitude towards money: celebrating its ability to secure economic order through equal exchanges, but also bemoaning its threat to dissolve social hierarchies.[19]

The second concern raised by money, that of improper reference, arose from the recognition that money was an arbitrary system and as such was open to manipulation. Forgery represented one such manipulation and the sovereign's debasing of the coinage represented another.[20] Both of these abuses posed a danger because they could cause currency to be misvalued or, in keeping with the linguistic connection I have been pursuing, to be misinterpreted. Nicholas Oresme suggests how aware scholastic thinkers were of this issue when he writes that new coins 'should

---

[16] As Marc Shell writes, 'Both coins and letters may be understood as symbols and also as material things: coins, for example, as commodities interpreted apart from any symbolic mediation of economic exchange, and letters as designs without phonetic meaning,' *The Economy of Literature*, p. 74. As should be clear, I wholly agree with this assertion, but stress that this aspect of currency and language is not one we normally consider, unless forced to, as when we are confronted with a pun.

[17] In the discussion that follows, I rely heavily on Joel Kaye's *Economy and Nature in the Fourteenth Century: Money, Market Exchange, and the Emergence of Scientific Thought* (Cambridge: Cambridge University Press, 1998).

[18] R. H. Britnell, *Commercialization of English Society, 1000-1500*, (Cambridge: Cambridge University Press, 1993), p. 172.

[19] Kaye, *Economy and Nature*, p. 18.

[20] Given the *Shipman's Tale*'s French setting, unique among Chaucerian fabliaux, it is interesting to note that debased currency was a rampant problem in 14th Century France, but not as great a problem in England. See Chown, pp. 37-8.

be given a different stamp, so that the common people should be able to know one from the other'.[21] Currency can only perform its salutary function as a medium of exchange if all parties value it equally. If one party misinterprets currency as having more or less value than it should in a given monetary system, money's ability to create an equal exchange is sabotaged. When that happens, money ceases to fulfill its ability to create equality out of the willed inequality of commercial interactions and loses its one redeeming quality in the eyes of medieval thinkers.

Thus it is not surprising that as a topic money often produced an ambivalent response in the scholastic writers who considered it. And it is not coincidental that the *Shipman's Tale*, in which money figures so prominently, has generated so little agreement among critics. As Rogers and Dower write, the *Tale* makes it difficult for us to decide if 'Chaucer [is] praising or blaming money. This is "the thing about" the *Shipman's Tale*, the peculiar feeling that at the end we do not know quite what to make of it'.[22] Rogers and Dower trace that peculiar feeling back to our confused definitions of money, and while I agree that money does create ambivalence here, we must also examine its connection with another frequent cause of discomfort, the pun.

In fact, in the pun we see the two concerns raised by money, that of dissolution of boundaries and of improper reference, being connected. As we have seen, puns function by forging connections, either in meaning or in form, between words that we may not link in everyday discourse. Because it depends upon our recognizing more than one meaning in a word, the pun exposes any illusions we might entertain about the univocality of language as pure fantasy. The pun uncovers a fact that we ignore in our everyday use of language: that signifiers and signifieds are bound together by the most arbitrary of bonds.[23] To put this idea in Chaucerian terms: the word does not have to be 'cosyn to the dede'; rather, the pun suggests that words may be cousin to many deeds. That is, the pun erases the lines that link a signifier to a single signified, dissolving the boundaries that define a word's meaning just as money could dissolve the social boundaries that distinguished one class from another. We can push this connection a bit further when we recall the dual nature of coins, valuable both for what they are and what they represent. That duality allowed currency to be manipulated, thus causing anxiety for medieval thinkers. Puns also reveal a dual nature: puns on similar sounding, but differently spelled words remind us that the material out of which words are formed, letters and sounds, convey

---

[21] '...esset facienda impressio differens, ut uulgus sciret per hoc distinguere inter istam et illam.' *The De Moneta of Nicholas Oresme and English Mint Documents*, ed. and trans. by Charles Johnson (London, 1956), p. 14.

[22] Rogers and Dower, 'Thinking about Money', p. 118.

[23] See the discussions in Culler and Attridge, cited above.

meaning in a way that normally does not draw our attention. When it does, when we 'get' a pun, we see in the figure 'an illustration of the inherent instability of language'.[24]

However, this illustration is itself something of an illusion as the pun does not actually represent language spinning out of control; rather, like all words, the pun has its meaning circumscribed by the context in which it appears.[25] The pleasure of the pun lies in its raising 'the specter of an unruly and ultimately infinite language only [to] […] exorcize it'.[26] The pun may point to multiple meanings for a single word, but not unlimited ones. Likewise, money may suggest that all value is relative, but context – the state of the market or the rate of inflation for instance – limits that relativity. It is this sense of averted danger that connects the use of money and puns in the *Shipman's Tale*.

Many critics have discussed the *Tale's* puns and often cannot agree as what is or is not a pun.[27] The debate whether we should read a pun in 'cosynage' to mean both kinship and deceit stands as an excellent example. Such a pun seems quite likely, given the *Tale's* propensity for them, but linguistic evidence argues against this possibility: the *OED* gives the first recorded usage of 'cozen' to deceive as 1573.[28] I do not propose a resolution to this debate, but merely suggest it tells us something crucial about this *Tale*: it prompts us to go pun hunting. In other words, it suggests that its readers need to pay especially close attention to its diction for fear of missing a joke. In raising the reader's awareness to such a pitch, the *Tale* also has the possibility to make its readers anxious. As David Benson notes, 'by exploiting the treacherous ambiguities of seemingly proper language, the *Shipman's Tale* puts the reader on his guard.'[29] This unease can be traced back to a concern raised by the

---

[24] Culler, 'The Call of the Phoneme', p. 3.

[25] Attridge, 'Unpacking the Portmanteau, pp. 141, 142.

[26] Attridge, 'Unpacking the Portmanteau, p. 148.

[27] Again, see Rogers and Dower, 'Thinking about Money', for a useful overview of the issue.

[28] *OED* online, s.v. 'cozen' <http://dictionary.oed.com>. For a summary of the issue, see Joseph, 'Chaucer's Coinage', pp. 351-2; for a reading of the tale that ties the structure of the tale itself to this pun, see David Abraham, 'Cosyn and Cosynage: Pun and Structure in the Shipman's Tale,' *Chaucer Review* 11 (1977), pp. 319-27.

[29] C. David Benson, *Chaucer's Drama of Style: Poetic Variety and Contrast in the Canterbury Tales* (Chapel Hill: University of North Carolina Press), p. 114. Benson continues to argue that the wariness evoked by the Tale has a pedagogic function, 'train[ing the reader] in intellectual and moral judgment.' Such an argument depends upon having a firm moral

Tale's use of puns and money: that value, whether it is moral, monetary, or humorous, may be a relative quality.

The final couplet of the *Tale* illustrates many of the points raised in the preceding section. The narrator concludes by declaring 'Thus endeth my tale, and God us sende/ Taillynge ynough unto oure lyves ende' (VII. 433-34).[30] Of these lines Joseph writes that in this 'epitomizing and summarizing pun [on the word 'taillynge'] [...] one hears not merely a double but a triple context – God send us not only business and sex enough, but also an abundance of entertaining stories'.[31] Of course, as Joseph rightly points out, this would not have been an aural pun since 'tale,' 'tail,' and 'tally,' the words at the heart of the pun, do not share a common origin or pronunciation in Middle English. But, he continues, it could very well be a visual pun, and as such it can demonstrate the importance of both form and meaning for puns discussed above. An audience listening to the *Tale* would most likely not find a pun in the closing couplet. But someone reading the *Tale* would, based on the orthographic similarity between 'tale' and 'taillynge.' The identification of a visual pun here also recalls the pun's reliance on context. If 'tale' did not appear in the preceding line, there would be no question of a triple play on 'taillynge.' In fact, the original play on tally as a business practice and tail as genitalia here and in the wife's response to her husband that he can 'score [the hundred franks] upon my taille' (VII.416) only exists because it appears at the end of a narrative that has insisted on a connection between sex and commerce. Behind this obvious point lurks the deepest connection between humour and money, one that is specifically enacted in the *Shipman's Tale* – both the joke and the coin depend upon context for their value.

If we think about money's role as a signifying system built on discernible differences between denominations of currency, we can easily grasp this point. The value of a penny only makes sense if we see it in relation to a nickel, dime, quarter, and so on. Outside of its given monetary system, a piece of currency has no value just as outside of its originating context (or, more generally, its original language), a pun loses its humour. Both pun and coin may be translated into a different system, but in either case not without radical changes. But beyond this structural similarity between the workings of money and the pun, there exists a more subjective connection between the two. Not all readers will react in the same way to a pun. For instance, while critics such as Joseph see the puns of the *Shipman's Tale* as being

---

ground on which to stand while rendering judgment; I read the tale as contesting the solidity, or at least the fixity, of that ground.

[30] *The Riverside Chaucer*, 3rd ed., gen. ed. Larry D. Benson (Boston:Houghton Mifflin, 1987). Cited parenthetically throughout the text.

[31] Joseph, 'Chaucer's Coinage', p. 354.

fairly light-hearted, others, such as David Benson, see them as 'doublespeak' covering the 'dishonorable and disgusting'.[32] Neither critic denies the *Tale* is full of puns, but they differ on those figures' effects. Similarly, all participants in a given economic system can agree to the monetary value of a set amount of currency, but for each user that amount may have a different psychological value.[33]

The movement of the hundred franks in the *Tale* provides an example of this principle. As they move from merchant to monk to wife and finally back to the merchant, their meaning for each character shifts subtly. When the merchant initially tenders the loan to the monk, the money represents his good will towards his friend ('My gold is youres, whan that it yow leste'[VII. 284]), but it also represents his good name ('We [merchants] may creaunce whil we have a name, / But goldlees for to be, it is no game'[VII. 289-90]). At this moment, the hundred franks represent literally both his faith in his friend and the faith in him that others must have for his business deals to succeed. For the monk, the money represents, in relatively straightforward fashion, sexual pleasure, as the terse description of the negotiations between him and the wife and the actual sexual encounter itself reveals:

> This faire wyf acorded with daun John
> That for thise hundred frankes he sholde al nyght
> Have hire in his armes bolt upright;
> And this acord was parfourned in dede. (VII. 314-17)

The wife's relationship to the hundred franks is more complicated. She has no problem equating them with the sexual use of her body (one of the prime reasons critics read the *Tale* as rampantly commercial and often disturbing) as she sells sex twice, once to the monk for the hundred franks and then to her husband in place of the franks. But in substituting her body for the money not only has she extricated herself from one predicament, but also has suggested a way out of any future entanglements she may encounter. In other words, as much as we might like to condemn the wife for her betrayal and calculated approach, within the context of the fabliau, she triumphs.

She accomplishes this triumph because of a simple fact; by the time her husband confronts her, the hundred franks have become a fiction within the context that invested them with meaning, the triangle of merchant, monk, wife. Trading amongst themselves, the three characters appear to form their own self-contained market, but the hundred franks have actually fallen out of this circuit when the wife uses

---

[32] Benson, *Chaucer's Drama of Style*, p. 113.

[33] Richard Doty, 'Money: How do I Know It's OK?' in *Money*, ed. by DiGaetani, p. 41.

them to pay her nameless, faceless creditors. In fact, we never actually see the wife spend the hundred franks; once she obtains them from the monk, they appear in the *Tale* only in characters' speeches, specifically the monk to the merchant at line 354 and following and again in the final scene when the merchant reproaches the wife and she responds. Because it is no longer mentioned by the narrator – that is, by a voice beyond the *Tale's* plotline – the money has literally become a figure of speech.[34] The physical hundred franks may have fallen out of the circuit of merchant, monk, wife, but figuratively they continue to circulate indefinitely, both in the wife's promise of sex to her husband and in the monk's hint of blackmail. That is, once the merchant has accepted the monk's half-truth and the wife's bargain, the hundred franks have become a fiction, present within that seemingly closed circuit only as a product of the merchant's imagination. They have become infinitely exchangeable because they exist solely as nominal value.

In this way, the hundred franks have become what the Middle Ages would have known as money of account or, more poetically, ghost money.[35] As opposed to actual coin which, as we have seen, was recognized both as a medium of exchange and as store of wealth, ghost money was solely a measure of value. Ghost money never existed in physical form, but was used to satisfy debts, conduct large transactions, and balance a merchant's books. One suspects modern accountants and Chief Financial Officers would be quite comfortable with the concept of ghost money. However, ghost money does have one large advantage over specie in that it can never be debased. Again, as discussed above, the value of currency in the Middle Ages could be manipulated in any number of ways – forgery of impure imitations, coin clipping, so-called sweating, or, if done by the prince, simply being recalled and recast with a lower percentage of precious metal. Thus a merchant never knew if the frank he accepted as payment one day was worth the same as the frank he accepted a week later because it may have a different metal content, and so coined money became, to use Howard Bloch's phrase, 'a free-floating signifier'.[36]

---

[34] There appears to be an oblique reference to the one hundred franks when the narrator describes the merchant's reasons for visiting the monk: 'Unto daun John he first gooth hym to pleye;/ Nat for to axe or borwe of hym moneye' (337-8). But the lack of a definite article before 'moneye' (he does not ask for the money; compare the monk's 'the same gold ageyn' in 357) and the inclusion of the verb 'borwe' works against this being a clear reference to the loan; how can one borrow money back from the person one loaned it to?

[35] R. Howard Bloch, *Etymologies and Genealogies: A Literary Anthropology of the French Middle Ages* (Chicago: University of Chicago Press, 1983), pp. 168-9; Peter Spufford, *Money and Its Uses in Medieval Europe* (Cambridge: Cambridge University Press, 1988), p. 411.

[36] Bloch, *Etymologies and Genealogies*, pp. 168-9.

Yet for the commercial system to work, merchants must assume that each frank equals every other frank. In general terms, money functions because all users assume that all coins 'are ontologically equal to each other'.[37] The *Tale* plays with this idea in the determiners it attaches to the hundred franks. Before the loan takes place, the money is referred to as '*an* hundred frankes' (VII.181; 201; 271; emphasis added), in other words, a specific sum, but not a specific group of coins comprising that sum. Immediately after the loan, the money is referred to as '*thise* hundred frankes'(VII. 293; 315; emphasis added) in the negotiations between the monk and wife quoted above to ensure that we connect the money the monk borrows with the incipient adultery. And when the monk tells the merchant that he has repaid the money, he says that '...I took unto oure dame,/ Youre wyf, at hom, *the same gold ageyn*' (VII.356-7; emphasis added). The joke here, of course, is on the merchant because he assumes that the monk simply refers to the same amount of gold while we know that John means the exact same coins.

This joke at the merchant's expense might be read as a sign of his gullibility, but I prefer to look at it in light of his earlier speeches about the importance of trust in commercial exchanges. More precisely, he notes that merchants must appear to be trustworthy and successful in order to succeed:

> We [merchants] may wel make chiere and good visage,
> And dryve for the world as it may be,
> And kepen oure estat in pryvetee,
> Til we be deed, or elles that we play
> A pilgrymage, or goon out of the weye.
> And therefore have I greet necessitee
> Upon this queynte world t'avyse me,
> For everemoore we moote stond in drede
> Of hap and fortune in oure chapmanhede. (VII.230-39; see also 287-90)

Given the random dangers that may assail the merchant in his pursuit of profit, his desire to have others view him as successful and trustworthy, as a secure business partner, comes as no surprise. But what is left unstated is that as much as he wants others to believe he is financially stable and safe to do business with, he must believe the same about others. If the parties in a financial transaction do not trust one another, the deal does not get done. All exchanges, whether of love, money, or language, require faith to take place.[38]

---

[37] Shell, *The Economy of Literature*, p. 86.

[38] Shoaf, *Dante, Chaucer and the Currency of the Word*, p. 13.

Sometimes that faith requires that one party take a leap for the exchange to succeed. That is what the merchant appears to do when he accepts the wife's bargain:

> This marchant saugh ther was no remedie,
> And for to chide it nere but folie,
> Sith that the thyng may nat amended be. (VII.428-9)

The merchant here accepts and forgives the wife's liberality with, as he believes, money. But the use of the word 'thyng' complicates this straightforward reading. The word's semantic range (the *MED* lists sixteen possible senses) allows it to refer to a wide variety of objects and phenomena. Within the *Tale* this range includes the gifts Daun John the monk brings for the members of the merchant's household (he gives each one 'som manere honest thyng' [VII.49]); the merchant's accounts (in urging him to quit his counting room, the merchant's wife asks that he leave 'youre sommes, and your bookes, and youre thynges' [VII.217]); and finally, prayer (just before he and the wife reach their agreement concerning the hundred franks, the monk walks in the garden where he 'hath his thynges seyd ful curteisly' [VII.91]).[39] Given its catchall nature, 'thyng' depends even more than most words on context to limit its meaning. But the context here seems designed to promote not clarity, but ambiguity between at least two possible meanings. That is, like a pun, 'thyng' suggests language's inability to assign words a single meaning, but also its ability to keep meaning from multiplying indefinitely.

For the reader, the context ensures that 'thyng' here contains limited meanings – the wife's adultery and deceit and her extravagant spending are the most obvious. But for the merchant, it is his trust that limits meaning, so that when he implores his wife to 'Keep bet thy good' (VII.432) we sense that he intends to refer to money only and not also to her marriage vows in the way readers may interpret his remark. The *Tale's* many puns and near-puns, such as the ambiguity surrounding 'thyng', seem designed to distance the reader from the characters because when we get the pun, we have access to a level of meaning denied to them. This seems especially true of the merchant who is lied to twice, but never questions his wife or friend too deeply. But we ought to realize that the merchant must display this faith in order for the *Tale* to maintain its humour and not descend into the bitterness that characterizes, for example, the *Merchant's Tale*. If the merchant were to examine the path his money took, the delicate equilibrium the wife's lie has established would collapse. Similarly, if a reader analyzes a pun too deeply, the boundaries between the different meanings that have been joined in the punning word would be reinforced and the pun lose its charge. Thus, readers find themselves in much the same position

---

[39] See Woods, 'A Professional Thyng', pp. 141-2 for discussion of the way the use of 'thyng' heightens the sense of commodification that pervades the tale.

as the merchant in the *Shipman's Tale*: caught between two liars, he believes them both simultaneously and is rewarded with sexual pleasure; confronted with potentially contradictory meanings, the audience of a pun must grasp them all in order to be rewarded with the joke.

This need for faith, or more accurately, willingness to overlook certain unpleasant truths, marks the final congruity between the workings of a pun and the role of the hundred franks in the *Shipman's Tale*. In both cases, humour depends upon circulation, but again in both cases, thinking too deeply about either puns or money threatens to stop their circulation and rob them of their effect. Both puns and money can cause anxiety by hinting at some unpleasant truths about the systems they represent, and these worries, even as they remain vague and unspecified, cause us to groan even as we laugh at the *Shipman's Tale*.

6

Joan's Drolleries: Humour in the Margins of Fitzwilliam MS 242

Laurel Broughton

S ometime in the early fourteenth century, an illuminator or group of illuminators produced a book of hours to commemorate the marriage of John de
Pabenham to Joan Clifford.[1] We know very little of Joan Clifford beyond her
name. She became John's second wife in 1314-15, at which time we may conjecture
the book was commissioned. The couple most likely lived in Bedfordshire, in relatively close proximity to East Anglian illuminators' workshops where this book of
hours most likely was produced. Although little written evidence concerning Joan
remains, heraldic evidence in the manuscript's margins suggests her family was
more important than John's.[2] Joan and John appear portrayed throughout the manuscript, Joan more frequently than her spouse.

We might assume both John and Joan were literate, given evidence produced by
M. T. Clanchy from Walter of Bibbesworth's teaching vocabulary:

---

[1] Ownership of this book of hours, Cambridge, Fitzwilliam MS 242, more commonly
known as the Grey-Fitzpayn Hours, has been mistakenly ascribed to Richard de Grey and
thus mistakenly dated to 1308. On the basis of the heraldic elements included in the manuscript, J. A. Goodall, 'Heraldry in the Decoration of English Medieval Manuscripts,' *Anti-
quaries Journal* 77, deduces the manuscript was made to commemorate the marriage of John
de Pabenham to his second wife, Joan Clifford, thus dating the manuscript to 1314-14. The
Fitzwilliam Museum notes this emendation in its online description of the manuscript (http://
www.fitzmuseum.cam.ac.uk, accessed 5/31/04).

[2] Goodall, p. 180-81

> The knowledge of languages which Walter expected upper class Englishmen and
> women of his day to have was: some acquaintance with Latin and the book learning
> of the clergy, a knowledge of colloquial French which required extending and refin-
> ing, and an effortless facility in English because it was the mother tongue. Walter's
> work underlines generalization which characterized English culture in the thirteenth
> century.[3]

Clanchy also suggests a possible practical use for Joan and John's book when he
posits that women in medieval families used books of hours to teach their children
to read.[4]

When Joan opened her book, her eyes would first have rested on a full page illumination of the Annunciation to the left and on the right page, a large capital D
containing the Virgin and Child, surrounded by elaborate marginal decoration. Like
many of its counterparts, this manuscript, now missing some portions, contains not
only full-page devotional images and historiated capitals, but marginalia of a less
elevating nature. Many marginal illustrations depict single animals, grotesques and
hybrids at the bottom of the page, exuberant, suggestive, and serpentine. In addition
to these reptilian drolleries, block line endings contain fish, lizards, and snakes,
both real and wildly imaginative.

Fitzwilliam MS 242 is one of a number of manuscripts associated with the East
Anglian school of illumination.[5] In addition to the stylistic similarities and quality
of the illuminations, these manuscripts share certain social similarities, including

---

[3] Michael Clanchy, *From Memory to Written Record* (Oxford: Blackwell Publishing,
2nd edition, 1993), p. 200.

[4] Clanchy, p. 111-12. He argues that many if not most books of hours were owned by
women and then states, 'Through Books of Hours, ladies introduced their families and
children to prayer—and hence to literacy—in their own homes. This domestication of the
liturgical book was the foundation on which the growing literacy of the later Middle Ages
was built . . .' (p. 112). The idea of the Book of Hours as a teaching tool is underscored by
the popular visual trope of St. Anne teaching the Virgin to read.

[5] Sidney Cockerell, in *The Gorleston Psalter*, (London: Chiswick Press, 1907), p. 2,
includes Fitzwilliam MS 242 in his discussion of manuscripts emanating from the East
Anglian workshops. Related manuscripts include but are not be limited to: the Rutland
Psalter (London, BL Add. MS 62925, 1250-70), the Vaux Psalter (London, Lambeth 233,
ca. 1300), three Peterborough Psalters (ca. 1300 Brussels, Bibliothèque Royale MS 9961-62;
Oxford, Bodleian Library MS Barlow 22; and Cambridge, Corpus Christi College MS 53),
Queen Mary Psalter (London, BL MS Royal 2.B.vii, ca. 1310-1320), Ormesby Psalter (Oxford, Douce MS 366, ca. 1310-1325), Gorleston Psalter (London, BL Add. MS 49622, ca.
1300), Douai Psalter (Douai, Bibliothèque Publique MS 171, 1322-1325) and Luttrell Psalter (London, BL Add. MS 42130, ca. 1340).

the fact that many of them were commissioned for or owned by clerics or women.[6] Given the number of drolleries or marginal grotesques that populate these manuscripts, images that might strike the modern reader as inappropriate if not offensive, we might ask ourselves what their early readers saw cavorting through the margins of their prayer books. Did Joan Clifford smile, chortle, laugh out loud when she reached folio 36r of her prayer book and saw a rabbit with a lion face on its tail end (6.01)? How did she read these images as (we assume) she recited the prayers written on these pages? This chapter will address these questions by investigating the context for marginal images and show that these may not have been as inappropriate for a woman reader as post-Victorian/post Freudian interpretations suggest.

What's funny?

To come to terms with questions regarding Joan Clifford's relationship to her book of hours, we need to understand what she and her contemporaries might have found humorous. Human bodies and bodily functions have long provided the material for humour. In the Middle Ages this humour manifested itself not only in fabliaux, comic plays and other texts, it filled the margins of manuscript pages, where images of lewd or scatological behaviour often accompany sacred texts, which are also illustrated with traditionally religious capitals and miniatures. In manuscripts like the Rutland Psalter, the Ormesby Psalter, the Gorleston Psalter, and their continental counterparts, the reader sees buttfaces mingle with courtly ladies, naked men expose their anal openings, sharp objects penetrate bare rear ends, and excreted faeces cascade down the margins. While the marginal images in Fitzwilliam MS 242 less overtly transgress the boundaries of what we might consider 'good taste' than those in related manuscripts, Joan's drolleries suggest the body. The book presents the tension between the comic use of body and the idea of bodily acts as sinful. Examining the marginalia in Fitzwilliam MS 242 in the context of related manuscripts, their relationship to other objects and texts on the actual page, with other pages of the manuscript and within the larger context of the incarnational aesthetic that pervaded Middle English culture, suggests possible readings of the tension between sacred and profane.

---

[6] More famous examples of Books of Hours associated with women include the Hours of Mary of Burgundy, the Hours of Catherine of Cleves, the Hours of Jeanne d'Evreux. The Vaux Psalter may, like Fitzwilliam 242, commemorate a marriage. See Lucy Freeman Sandler, *Gothic Manuscripts, 1285-1385*, 2 vols. (London: Harvey Miller, 1986), and Cockerell, *The Gorleston Psalter,* for patronage and provenance of specific East Anglian manuscripts.

Attempts to understand the paradoxical juxtaposition of the physical images with their religious contexts have led to a wide range of critical commentary. Art historians from Emil Mâle to Michael Camille have put forth theories about the origin and intention of marginal images. Scholars tend to fall into a number of camps when discussing medieval marginalia. Some, like Mâle, suggest that the artists created them as fanciful decorations.[7] Others see them not as humorous, but as moral satire or signs of the diabolical.[8] Still others, following the theories of Bakhtin, read the grotesques as images of carnival, celebrating physicality, but within a spiritual context.

This physical exuberance had critics in its own time, most notably Bernard of Clairvaux, who, in writing about church decoration, specifically for monasteries, says:

> Ceterum in claustris, coram legentibus fratribus, quid facit illa ridicula monstruosi-
> tas, mira quaedam deformis formositas ac formosa deformitas? Quid ibi immundae
> simiae? Quid feri leones? Quid monstruosi centauri? Quid semihomines? Quid
> maculosae tigrides? Quid milites pugnantes? Quid venatores tubicinantes? Videas
> sub uno capite multa corpora, et rursus in uno corpore capita multa. Cernitur hinc
> in quadrupede cauda serpentis, illinc in pisce caput quadrupedis. Ibi bestia praefert
> equum, capram trahens retro dimidiam; hic canutum animal equum gestat posterius.
> Tam multa denique, tamque mira diversarum formarum apparet ubique varietas, ut
> magis legere libeat in marmoribus. quam in codicibus, totumque diem occupare
> singula ista mirando, quam in lege Dei meditando . Proh Deo! si non pudet inepti-
> arum, cur vel non piget expensarum?
> [But apart from this, in the cloisters, before the eyes of the brothers while they
> read—what is that ridiculous monstrosity doing, an amazing kind of deformed
> beauty and yet a beautiful deformity? What are the filthy apes doing there? The
> fierce lions? The monstrous centaurs? The creatures, part man and part beast? The
> striped tigers? The fighting soldiers? The hunters blowing horns? You may see many
> bodies under one head, and conversely many heads on one body. On one side the tail

---

[7] Mâle, Emile. *The Gothic Image*, trans. Dora Nussey, (New York: Harper and Brothers, 1958). Mâle writes that many imaginary creatures of the thirteenth century 'bear the mark of a gay invention or good-humoured raillery' (p. 59). He goes on to say 'Neither satire nor indecency had any part in the artist's jesting and the hideous obscenities which have been discovered in the cathedrals exist only in the imagination of a few prejudiced archaeologists' (p. 62).

[8] Karl P. Wentersdorf, 'The Significance of "Figurae Scatologicae." in Gothic Manuscripts', *Word, Picture, and Spectacle*, ed. Clifford Davidson (Kalamazoo: Medieval Institute Publications, 1984), pp. 1-19. Wentersdorf says of scatalogocial images: 'It seems likely that they concretize commonplace Christian views about sin and the Devil in a long-standing religious tradition' (p. 5).

of a serpent is seen on a quadruped, on the other side the head of a quadruped is on the body of a fish. Over there an animal has a horse for the front half and a goat for the back; here a creature which is horned in front is equine behind. In short, everywhere so plentiful and astonishing a variety of contradictory forms is seen that one would rather read in the marble than in books, and spend the whole day wondering at every single one of them than in meditating on the law of God. Good God! If one is not ashamed of the absurdity, why is one not at least troubled at the expense?][9]

Other contemporary texts take Bernard's sense of absurdity further to equate laughter with moral deficiency. Moral tales like 'The King who Never Laughed' and the entry on 'Risus' in *An Alphabet of Tales* teach that laughter distracts the mind from salvation.[10] The *Cursor Mundi* reminds us that Christ never laughed.[11]

Although it may have indicated lack of moral fibre, laughter seems to have permeated medieval culture, but there's no clear definition of what medieval audiences might have found funny. Modern definitions abound. E. L. Risden offers a working definition of humour: sudden, pleasing mental catharsis experienced in safety.[12] Raskin posits that humour results from the overlay of two scripts to create ambiguity, which is then resolved in an unexpected way, producing sudden recognition and pleasure.[13] Leacock suggests that humour derives from the perceiver's sense of superiority,[14] and both Booth and Frye emphasize the importance of irony to humour. But do these twentieth- and twenty-first century theories of humour apply to the Middle Ages? Not necessarily. D. W. Robertson, writing of Peter Abelard's 'jocularity' in *History of My Misfortunes*, suggests a discrepancy between modern and medieval understandings of the comic:

> Today many persons think of laughter, the fruit of humour, as a product of release from tension. But this laughter requires a purely emotional kind of humour, not based on the intellectual perception of the ridiculous, but based on feelings. Humour of

---

[9] As quoted by Conrad Rudolph, *The 'Things of Greater Importance'* (Philadelphia: The University of Pennsylvania Press, 1990), pp. 282-83.

[10] 'The King Who Never Laughed,' *Jacob's Well*, ed. Arthur Brandeis, EETS O.S. 115 (London: Kegan Paul, 1900), pp. 220-222. *An Alphabet of Tales*, ed. Mary Macleod Banks, EETS OS 126/127 (London, 1904, 1905, rpt. Kraus, 1987), p. 458.

[11] V. A. Kolve, *The Play Called Corpus Christi* (Stanford: Stanford University Press, 1966), p. 126.

[12] E. L Risden, 'Teaching Anglo-Saxon Humour.' *SMART*, Spring 2002, p. 23.

[13] Victor Raskin, *Semantic Mechanisms of Humour* (Dordrecht, Boston, Lancaster: D. Reidel, 1985), as cited by Risden, p. 23.

[14] Stephen Leacock, *Humour and Humanity: An Introduction to the Study of Humour* (London: Thorton Butterworth, 1937), p. 23.

> this kind is actually rare in medieval literature, and its absence has led to the mistaken impression that medieval people had little sense of humour.[15]

He adds:

> Before the Renaissance the Devil and his cohorts were often comic characters and the vices are often portrayed with comic overtones in medieval art. When medieval people laughed at vice of any kind, they were only sharing the laughter of God, for, as the second Psalm tells us (Douay version), when rebellious worldings seek to break their bonds, 'He that dwelleth in Heaven shall laugh at them.'[16]

Medieval humour then, as Robertson sees it, depends on the gap between what the audience sees portrayed and the religious truth it knows should be, an intellectual rather than an emotional experience.

Robertson is not alone in his reading of medieval humour within a religious context. V. A. Kolve, in *The Play Called Corpus Christi*, notes that medieval writers like Notker Labeo thought that laughter separated man from other animals.[17] He makes a case for linking laughter with medieval concepts of well-being and delineates two responses to the humour in the Corpus Christi cycles: the internal, that which occurs within the plays themselves, and the external, that which occurs within the audience. The two may occasionally coincide, but not always: 'Audience and stage characters may sometimes laugh together, but they need not always do so'.[18] He notes the significance of where the audience places its laughter:

> Here we need only notice that never in these plays is one invited to laugh at God the Father, Christ, or the Virgin. They move in a mimetic world which includes the comic, the violent, the noisy, the grotesque, but though that world acts upon them, it never really touches their characters.[19]

So, while these human and fallible creatures incite the audience to laughter, those functioning on the divine plane do not. They remain above the joking level.

---

[15] D. W. Roberston, *Abelard and Heloise* (New York: Dial Press, 1972), p. 110.

[16] Robertson, p. 111.

[17] Kolve, p. 127. See also Lisa Perfetti, *Women and Laughter in Medieval Comic Literature* (Ann Arbor: University of Michigan Press, 2003), pp. 4-12, for a discussion of the relationship of humour to the body.

[18] Kolve, pp. 137-38.

[19] Kolve. pp. 138-39.

Fitzwilliam MS 242, folio 55v

In Joan's book of hours we find subtle, isolated images of animals and grotesques populating block line endings, bottom margins and the more elaborate decorations of the remaining section pages. The animals are, for the most part, realistic—for example, the puppies on folio 39, or the bear on folio 49. Even the more exotic animals like the giraffe and the elephant bear a reasonable resemblance to their real counterparts. Interspersed with these animals are grotesques, usually hybrids, that mingle some human characteristics with those fantastical.[20] Three hunchbacked, legless heavies roam the early pages of the manuscript (6.02). These give way to hybrids, many of which creatures have hooded heads, attached to lizard- or salamander-like bodies, usually with two legs and a tail. These creatures wear human, cheerful, whimsical faces, resembling hybrids in the Gorleston Psalter.[21] Unlike the grotesques in some manuscripts (the Queen Mary Psalter, for instance), these aren't designed to suggest fright or terror. However, the marriage of the human with the serpentine suggests the ambiguity modern critics identify as a key element of humour, and the discrepancy between what the viewer sees on the page and what she knows actually exists, coupled with the apparent attractiveness of the serpent, allows her to recognize the potential for vice (6.03).

Fitzwilliam MS 242 follows the use of Sarum. Some leaves are missing and some sections are imperfect. The Annunciation on the first page begins the incarnational cycle celebrated throughout the standard form of books of hours.[22] In addition to the grotesques scattered throughout the manuscript, Fitzwilliam 242 may have

---

[20] For a complete description of MS 242, see Francis Wormald and Phyllis M. Giles, *A Descriptive Catalogue of the Additional Illuminated Manuscripts in the Fitzwilliam Museum Acquired between 1895 and 1979* (Cambridge: Cambridge University Press, 1982), Vol. 1, pp. 157-60. With the exception of foliage, the marginal whimsey all but disappears after fol. 54.

[21] See, for example, fol. 128v, as reproduced in Sidney Cockerell, *The Gorleston Psalter.*

[22] Hours of the Virgin are often pictorially associated with significant scenes from Mary's life and the life of Christ from the Annunciation through the Flight into Egypt. Compline is usually associated with the Assumption/Coronation of the Virgin. The Hours of the Cross carry through this cycle, beginning with the betrayal and ending with the deposition. Fitzwilliam MS 242 contains the Hours of the Virgin, Hours of the Trinity, Hours of the Holy Spirit, Seven Penitential Psalms, Litany, Gradual Psalms, Office of the Dead and the Prayer of Bede of the Seven Words (added in the fifteenth century). Most books of hours included a calendar, Gospel lessons, Hours of the Virgin, Hours of the Cross and Hours of the Holy Spirit, the devotional prayers to the Virgin 'Obsecro te' and 'O itemerata,' Penitential Psalms and Litany, Accessory Texts, Suffrages and Office of the Dead. See Roger Wieck, *Painted Prayers* (New York: Braziller, 1997), for detailed discussions.

contained historiated capitals and elaborate marginal decoration for each major
section of the book. Those remaining include:

> Fol. 3, the Hours of the Virgin, historiated D with full border, grotesques, birds, and
> shields.
> Fol. 29, Hours of the Trinity. Large initial D containing Christ in blessing. Scenes
> of hunting decorate the border.
> Fol. 55v. Historiated initial with full border: Crucifixion, cross flanked by Virgin and
> St. John the Evangelist. Shields, animals, and grotesques in border.

These remaining section pages include in addition to grotesques, animals such as
squirrels and rabbits commonly associated with lustful behaviour.

Of these pages, folio 55v, which introduces the Seven Pentitential Psalms,[23] most
commands our attention (6.04). This page presents the Crucifixion, the climax of
the salvation cycle, depicted in the capital that opens the Seven Penitential Psalms.
Around the margins play a tambourine-beating babewin astride a fox, wrestling
beasts, a buttface and veiled lady locked in eye-contact, all interspersed with accurate and detailed realizations of animals including a doe, bear, hedgehog, and
outsized bluejay; heraldric elements and Joan and John themselves, presented in
prayerful attitudes.

Of particular interest is the face-off in the lower right hand corner. Here a hairy
gryllus sends a dirty look to a large, disembodied female head in fantastical, peaked
headdress, veiled from the eyes down. While this may be suggested by the text
above, 'Turbatus est a furore oculus meus (My eye is disturbed in anger)' (Psalm
6:8), there is no clear evidence that the image reflects this verse of Psalm 6. [24]
Whatever the tenor of the exchange, it occurs under the eyes of the dying Christ,
an opposition illustrating the tension involved between the marginal images and
the material they surround.

Although the margins crawl with things of this world, the Crucifixion dominates
the page, a domination that reminds the viewer that all things within and without
the margins are subject to the sacrifice enacted in the initial. The efficacy of the
Crucifixion stems from the incarnation itself, the Word made flesh. Thus the physicality the grotesques celebrate throughout this and similar manuscripts paradoxically becomes the enabling factor of sacrifice and redemption. Salvation history

---

[23] The seven penitential psalms include 6, 31, 37, 50, 101, 129, and 142. For a detailed
discussion, see Wieck, pp. 91ff.

[24] Michael Camille, *Image on the Edge* (London: Reaktion Books, 1992) p. 37, who
notes that the gryllus dates to the classical tradition (p. 37), suggests that this exchange reflects the text immediately above it (Psalm 6:8).

teaches the viewer that these figures retain no power. In fact we see them as cowardly and inept, precisely because we know they are in the end reduced to butts of laughter, like Satan who cracks farts for fear in the N-Town creation play.[25]

Looking at Fitzwilliam MS 242, folio 55v next to the closely-related Vaux Psalter Beatus page (6.05) underscores the incarnational thrust behind the illuminations and may help to put together these seemingly opposing concepts.[26] This page plays with many of the same ideas and includes the same gryllus that faces the veiled lady in the Fitzwillliam hours. Additionally, the shape and ornamentation of the initial suggests a close relationship to Fitzwilliam MS 242. The page presents the beginning of Psalm 1, 'Beatus vir qui non abiit [Blessed is the man who has not walked].' The capital B contains a Tree of Jesse surrounded by tile and foliage. Hybrid beasts play along the top margin, foliage and abstract designs tumble down the right margin. The bottom margin contains from right to left, a naked man crowned and holding a staff, a sleeping lion, and two grylli facing each other.[27] The leftmost matches exactly that found in Fitzwilliam 242, folio 55v, but he directs his gaze not at a lady, but at a fellow gryllus, capped and bearded, with human legs but a beast's tail. The initial B, with its Tree of Jesse, incorporates incarnational imagery that encompasses the cycle of salvation with its inclusion (somewhat unusual for this often-used visual) of a Crucifixion within the Jesse Tree itself.

The relationship of vice to the divine, within the possibility of divine laughter as noted by Roberton, can help us understand that pages where buttfaces cavort under the eyes of the crucified Christ represent unity, not discontinuity. Both pages illustrate incarnational piety which formed the foundation for devotional practices and an aesthetic sense that characterized East Anglian culture in the later Middle Ages. The growth of this aesthetic can be charted through increasingly popular Marian piety to which books of hours and psalters enthusiastically attest.

Incarnational Piety

Although he was clear in his disapprobation of art in religious contexts, Bernard of Clairvaux articulated a devotional practice that influenced much late medieval art.

---

[25] 'For fere of fyre I crake a fart!' Play 1, line 81. *The N-Town Play*, ed. Stephen Spector, EETS S.S. 11 (Oxford: Oxford University Press, 1991). See also Play 2, line 355, 'With a fart my brech I breke!'

[26] London, Lambeth Palace Library MS 233, fol. 15r.

[27] Grylli may be seen as a reference to Satan. David Williams, *Deformed Discourse* (Exeter: Exeter University Press, 1996), pp. 137-38, identifies the human-headed snake that appears in representations of the Fall as a gryllus.

In his sermons on the Annunciation, he urges his audience to become active participants in the incarnational moment. In doing so, he puts himself in the place of both Gabriel and the Virgin as they enact the Annuciation drama.[28]   By the late Middle Ages, this participatory impulse had blossomed into a number of religious practices. This incarnational piety became the hallmark of East Anglian religious experience and gave rise to an aesthetic sensibility well. As Gail Gibson notes,

> In fifteenth-century devotion, in the visual arts, in the religious drama, it is the Incarnate Son rather than the Godhead who is ever fixed before the eyes of the beholder. Instead of God the Pantocrator with his book of mysteries, the relevant central image for the late Middle Ages is a suffering human body racked on a cross; the book has become his body, its secrets red, fresh, and bleeding if still mysterious to minds of man. And it is one characteristic of this fifteenth-century mind that the incarnational focus—the insistence on particular, corporal religious image perceived in the world—is extended as far as, quite literally, the human eye can see. The spiritual object of meditation is held earthbound for as long as human ingenuity (and pious curiosity) will permit.[29]

The manuscripts emanating from East Anglian workshops are imbued with and reciprocally contribute to the aesthetic sensibility Gibson defines. Fascination with the physical body of Christ marks the major pages of Fitzwilliam MS 242. When viewed in the context of the time and place in which they were created, these pages with their seemingly contradictory visual messages, embody the paradox of the body. In order to enact salvation, God becomes man, enfleshed through the body of the Virgin. In order for that body to exist, 'red, flesh and bleeding', it had to be human, and being human, it encompasses the entirety of human experience.

East Anglia also nurtured Julian of Norwich, Margery Kempe and the creators of the N-Town Play, all of whom open windows on possible readings of the Fitzwilliam 242 decorations. Julian of Norwich expresses the understanding that Christ's humanity encompasses Adam's sin. As she tells it, as Adam fell, so Christ falls: Adam and Christ are one in the same and we face the result with holy laughter.[30]

---

[28] For a more detailed discussion of Bernard's *Super missus est* and incarnational piety, see Laurel Broughton, 'Ave Maria: The Incarntional Aesthetic and Mary Miracle Collections,' *Studia Mystica* (1999), 1-15.

[29] Gail Gibson, *The Theater of Devotion* (Chicago: Chicago University Press, 1989), pp. 6-7.

[30] Julian makes the connection between Christ and Adam in the parable of the servant, long text, Fourteeenth Revelation, Chapters 51-55. In Chapter 51, she writes: 'By the nerehed of the seruannt is vnderstand the sonne, and by the stondyng of the lyft syde is vnderstond Adam. The lorde is god the father, the servant is the sonne Jesu Cryst, the holy gost is the evyn loue whych is in them both. When Adam felle godes sonne fell; for the ryght onyng

Christ's human nature figures largely in East Anglian marginalia as well. Thus we see the Christ fool riding the goat along the bottom of the Ormesby Psalter (folio 72), a parallel to goat-riding babewins found in the Hours of Mary of Burgundy and the babewin astride a fox in Fitzwilliam MS 242, folio 55v. This sensibility is not confined only to East Anglia. The blackly humorous bickering of the four knights who nail Christ to the cross in the York cycle add to this context.[31] In their attempts to outdo each other in affixing the body to the cross, the hammer-wielding knights, acted by members of the local community, remind the audience that the Crucifixion happens in the here and now, that all people have the potential to drive the nails through the hands and feet.

Not only does Julian emphasize Christ's humanity by equating him with Adam, she recounts the idea of laughing with God in her *Showings* (long text, Revelation 5, chapter 13). She describes the ineffectual nature of the devil:

> God shewed that the feend hath nowe the same malyce that he had before the incarnacion, and also sore he traveyleth, and as contynually he seeth that all sowles of saluacion eskape hym worshyppfully by the vertue of his precious passion. And that is his sorow; and full evyl is he ashamyd, for all that god sufferyth hym to do turnyth vs to joy and hym to shame and payne. [32]

Julian articulates here the cycle of redemption held within the Vaux Beatus B and Fitzwilliam MS 242 Crucifixion. She goes on to say:

> For this syght, I laght myghtely, and that made them to lagh that were abowte me; and ther lawchyng was a lykyng to me. I thought that I wolde that alle my evyn crysten had seen as I saw. Then shoulde all they a lawchyd with me. But I saw not Cryst laghyng; but wele I wott that syght that he shewed me made me to laugh, for I vnderstode that we may laugh in comfortyng of oure selfe and joyeng in god for the feend is overcome.[33]

---

whych was made in hevyn, goddys sonne myght not be seperath from Adam, for by Adam I vnderstond alle man.' *A Book of Showings to the Anchoress Julian of Norwich,* ed. Edmund Colledge and James Walsh, (Toronto: Pontifical Institute of Medieval Studies, 1978), part two, p. 533.

[31] Play xxxv, The Crucifixion, *The York Plays,* ed. Richard Beadle (London: Edward Arnold, 1982), pp. 315-23. Just as they divvy up the parts of the body to nail to the cross, the 'miles' divvy up Christ's belongings at the end of the play.

[32] Julian, *Showings,* Chaper 13, Revelation 5, p. 347.

[33] Julian, *Showings,* Chapter 13, Revelation 5, pp. 348-49.

This understanding Julian articulates enables medieval audiences to laugh at the vaunting but ineffectual devil in the N-Town Passion play, knowing full well that the Harrowing of Hell would show him undone, for all his scheming.[34]

The incarnational aesthetic emphasizes the presence of Christ, the incarnational energy of salvation in the here and now. What we see as anachronism—the Annunciation taking place in a medieval house as in the Merode altarpiece, for example—people in the Middle Ages saw as a spiritual truth. This anachronistic piety that enables the faithful to merge salvation time with personal time prompts Margery Kempe to write herself into the script of the lives of Mary and Christ.[35] And while Margery describes in great detail her uncontrollable outbursts of weeping, an affective result of her incarnational piety, she also delights in holy mirth: 'Alas that euyr I dede synne, it is ful mery in Hevyn'.[36]

Perhaps one of the most incongruous examples of holy laughter is perpetrated by the Virgin Mary. In the N-Town Nativity Play, Joseph scolds her for laughing:

> Why do ye lawghe, wyff? Ye be to blame!
> I pray you, spowse, do no more so!
> In happ the mydwyuys wyl take it to grame,
> And at youre nede helpe wele non do.
> Iff ye haue nede of mydwyuys, lo,
> Perauenture thei wyl gon hens.
> Therefor be sad, and ye may so . . .[37]

---

[34] Play 31, Satan and Pilate's Wife. *The N-Town Play*, pp. 314-17.

[35] Margery Kempe, *The Book of Margery Kempe*, ed. Sanford Brown Meech and Hope Emily Allen, EETS O. S. 212 (Oxford: Oxford University Press, 1940). Margery envisions herself as Mary's handmaid and nursemaid to the infant Jesus in Chapter 6, and at the Crucifixion, Chapters 79-81.

[36] Margery Kempe, Chapter 3, p. 11. Not only does Margery note the mirth in heaven, she uses humour to make her points. Perhaps the best example is found in the story of the bear and the pear tree which she tells to the Archbishop of York (Chapter 52). In this story she tells of a priest who observes a bear overindulge on the blossoms of a pear tree and the distress the animal suffers at his nether end as a result. Margery glosses this story allegorically, providing a link between bodily function and spiritual health. Although no such extreme examples occur in Fitzwilliam 242, Margery's parable relates closely to marginal images of defecation in other manuscripts. Clearly, Margery shows no 'feminine delicacy' in telling this story.

[37] *The N-Town Play*, Play 15, The Nativity, ll. 182-88.

Mary responds:

> Husbond, I pray yow, dysplese yow nowth,
> Thow that I lawghe and gret joye haue,
> Here is the chylde this werde hath wrought,
> Born now of me, that allthynge shall saue.[38]

Mary's laughter and her response to Joseph underscore concepts implicit in Julian's *Showings* and Margery's book: laugher stems from delight in the Lord. It is the natural response to the joy the faithful experience in unity with God, and as Mary demonstrates, it transcends the human propensity to sin which resulted in circumstances normally associated with pain and suffering. Mary's painless childbirth establishes the understanding that human beings triumph over sin and evil, represented by Satan, and in doing so discover their ability to laugh.

That same sense of transcendence may well have informed the reader's perception of marginal images in books of hours, psalters and other manuscripts created for personal devotion. Unlike the cycle plays and other forms of public expression, books of hours present the opportunity for private devotion and contemplation, negotiated between the reader and the book. Joan Clifford would most likely have read her book silently, reciting her prayers in her heart.[39] The book itself, approximately 10 x 6.5 inches, would have been portable and easy to hold. Joan's eyes moving over the page make her an audience of one, a witness to the comic antics on the pages she holds in her hands. The section pages and other traditional illuminations function as windows through which she can enter into the story of salvation. As she moves through her book, as she moves through her day, she traces the progress of salvation from that subtle and sublime moment when Mary says 'yes' to the angelic messenger, through the events to when Mary's son says 'yes' while hanging on the cross and observing the vagaries of human behaviour at play in the bottom margin. Joan is not only audience; she is participant, not just through saying the words, as recommended by Bernard, but by being physically present on the page in various marginal illustrations. The depictions of Joan in the margins and in the capitals bring salvation history into Joan's here and now and conversely, she becomes part of the reality her book of hours celebrates.

Even though they are for private devotion, these books share many traits with their more public counterparts, commingling divine history with everyday life. Scenes

---

[38] *The N-Town Play*, Play 15, The Nativity, ll. 190-93.

[39] Paul Saenger, 'Books of Hours and the Reading Habits of the Later Middle Ages,' *The Culture of Print*, ed. Roger Chartier, trans Lydia G. Cochrane (Princeton: Princeton University Press, 1989), pp. 145-56.

of hunting, farming, fishing sit beside illustrations of bible stories or other religious practices. Thus the decorations encircle the entire realm or realms of spiritual and human physical existence. The frame of the page becomes a metonym for the entire manuscript, which in turn encloses the world. Angels, demons, and buttfaces are all part of the larger totality, and that larger whole is reflected in the range of images and texts contained within these books, coexistence of sacred and profane that constructed medieval reality.

Fitzwilliam MS 242 reflects all these concepts. The manuscript opens with the Annunciation, the sublime incarnational moment and progresses to the Crucifixion, the culmination of the redemption cycle that the reader sees beginning on the first folio. The manuscript captures the cycle, puts the patrons in the middle of it as it is acted out, and allows them and subsequent readers to laugh at the devil and their own human foibles. This all leads to an understanding, difficult for the modern reader to develop, that one can't separate the sacred from the profane in the Middle Ages. They worked together in what medieval people negotiated as the totality of God's creation. They didn't find it odd or irreverent, as we do, to use elements of fabliaux in miracles of the Virgin or the tunes of bawdy songs for hymns. Likewise, the foxes and monkeys, dirty looks and grylli live beneath the dying, redemptive gaze of the body on the cross.

Back to the original question: Did Joan Clifford laugh at the serpentine hybrids and dirty look? Most likely. Just as she probably laughed at the bear and playful puppies. After all, even though serpentine, the hybrids have been domesticated, like the dogs, brought under control through the sacrifice that dominates folio 55v. She can recognize the cosmic power in that voluntary act that renders even Satan powerless and risible, and as a result, she can smile, nay, even laugh outright as she recites the hours.

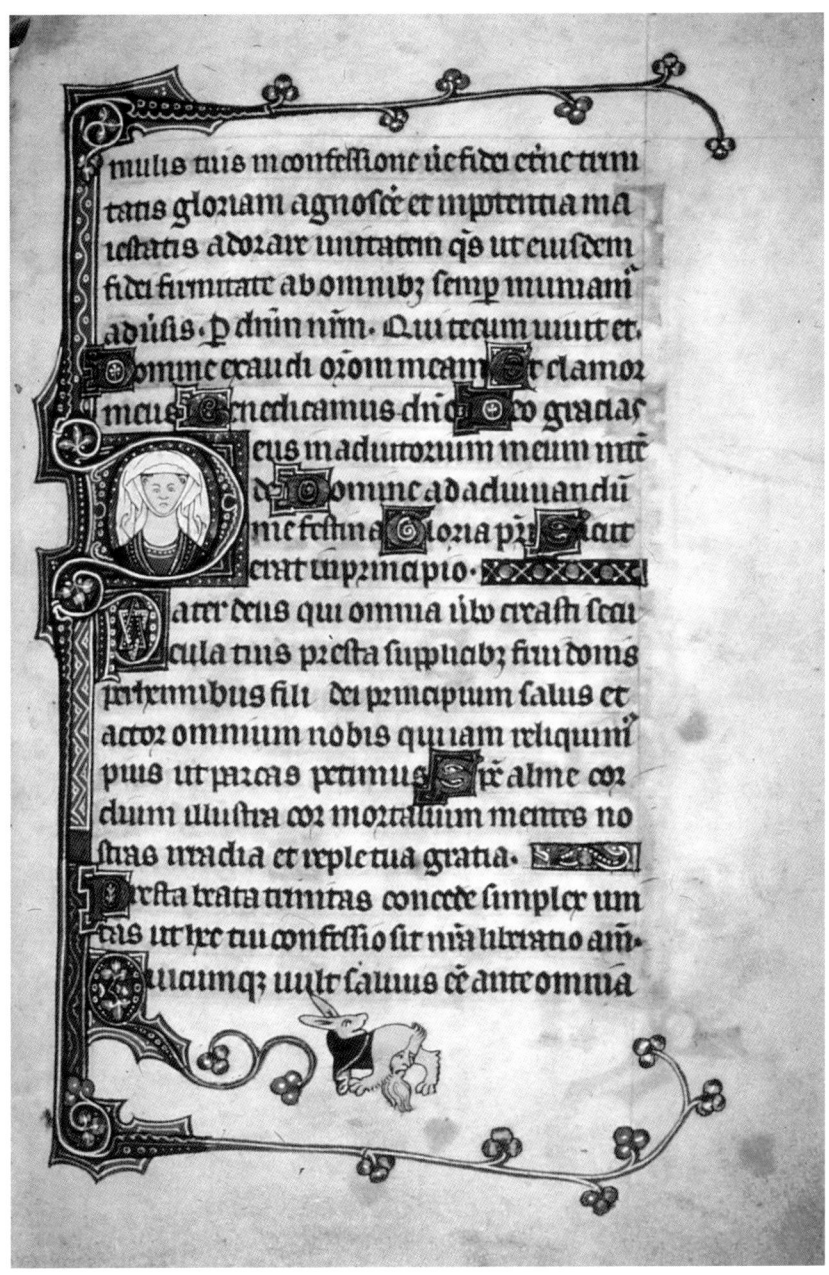

6.01: Hare-gryllus hybrid. Fitzwilliam MS 242, fol. 36r. Reproduced by the kind permission of the Syndics of the Fitzwilliam Museum.

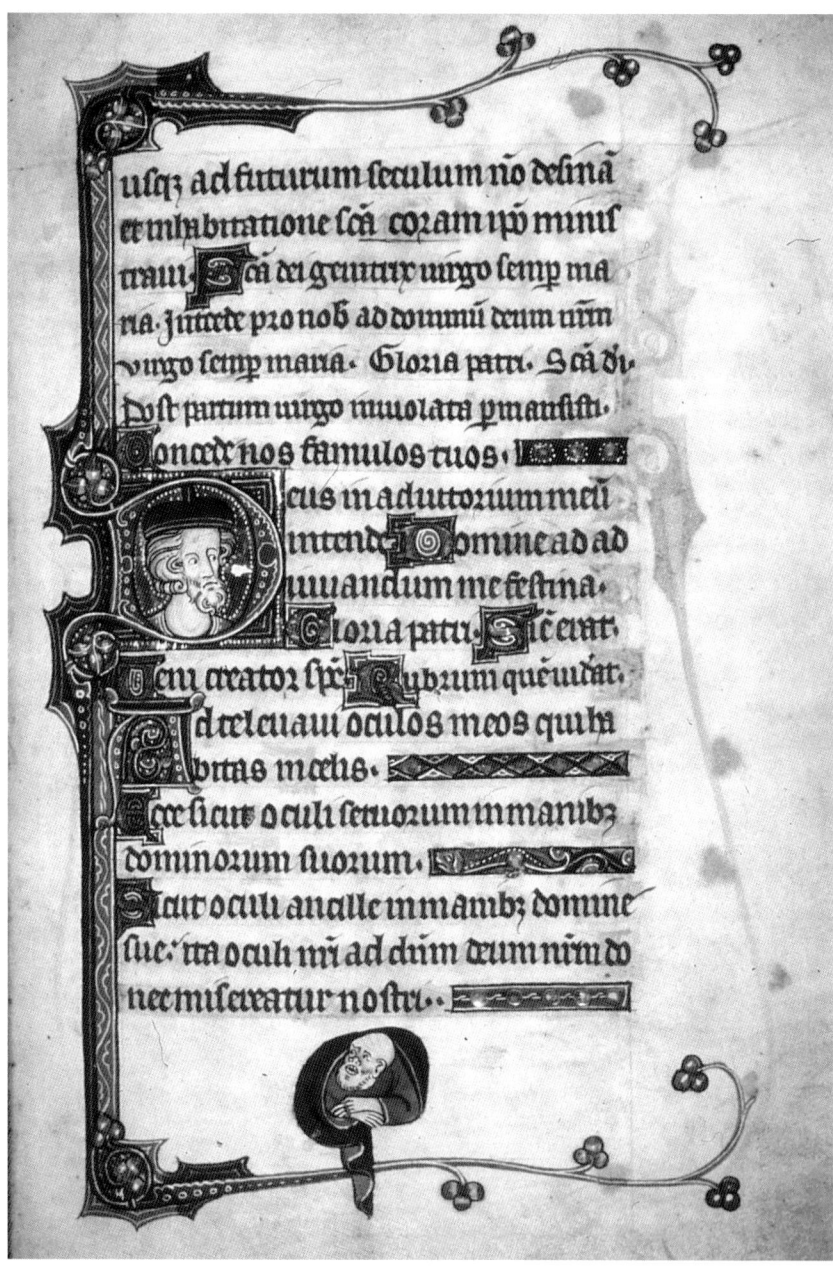

6.02: Marginal grotesque, serpentine block line ending, line 15. Fitzwilliam MS 242, fol. 19r. Reproduced by the kind permission of the Syndics of the Fitzwilliam Museum.

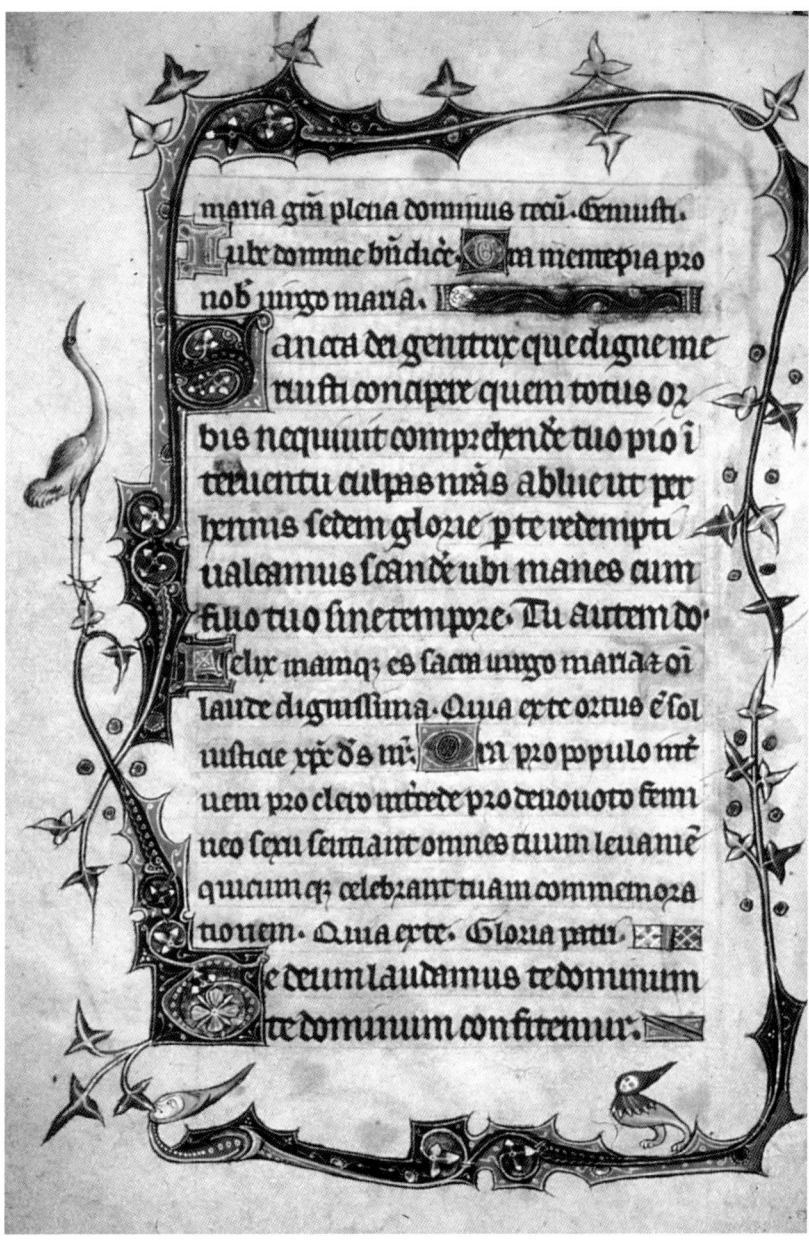

6.03: Marginal hybrids and crane, serpentine block line ending, line three. Fitzwilliam MS 242, fol. 7v. Reproduced by the kind permission of the Syndics of the Fitzwilliam Museum.

6.04: Crucifixion with donors, beasts and gryllus in margins. Fitzwilliam MS 242, fol. 55v. Reproduced by the kind permission of the Syndics of the Fitzwilliam Museum.

6.05: Tree of Jesse with Crucifixion; hybrids, king, beasts and grilli in margins. Lambeth MS 233, fol. 15r. Reproduced by the kind permission of the Trustees of Lambeth Palace Library.

7

Gender Anxiety and Dialogic Laughter in Malory's *Morte Darthur*

SANDRA M. HORDIS

Many of the comic moments in Malory's *Morte Darthur* centre on gender and its ambiguities; indeed, gender roles have been a vital and multifaceted subject of comedy throughout history, from Aristophanes' *Lysistrata*, to Shakespeare's *As You Like It*, to Jack Lemmon and Tony Curtis in *Some Like It Hot*. In all of these examples, cross-dressing, cross-speaking, and alternative gender behaviours problematize the traditionally linked sex and gender categories of 'masculine male' and 'feminine female,' ultimately resulting in a comic troubling of the otherwise strict sex/gender link in interactive social contexts. These cross-gendered moments cause pleasure with their surprising inversions of rigid mores and cultural expectations, recalling Bakhtin's notion of the 'carnival':

> One might say that carnival celebrated temporary liberation from the prevailing truth and from the established order; it marked the suspension of all hierarchical rank, privileges, norms, and prohibitions.[1]

In the carnival, the hierarchical values contained in binaries such as male/female, young/old, and beautiful/ugly become temporarily inverted; attributes which commonly carry a high value, such as youth and beauty, are degraded, and those which

---

[1] Mikhail Bakhtin, *Rabelais and His World*, trans. by Hélène Iswolsky (Bloomington: Indiana UP, 1984), p.10.

are normally constructed as having little or no value, such as age and ugliness, are held in esteem.

In Malory's *Morte Darthur*, the moments of gender comedy also serve the purpose of the carnival. The values contained in the hegemonic sex/gender categories of masculine male and feminine female are disrupted and dialogized when heroic knights dress in women's clothing and damsels valiantly don armour and use swords.[2] The cross-gendered knights and damsels possess value in carnival space and time because they discard the rigid dictates of orthodox chivalric gender roles and revel and laugh in their defiance of those hegemonic discourses. The carnival atmosphere, in effect, rewards them with pleasure (laughter) for their dialogic treatment of chivalric gender, consequently disrupting the coherence of the text and challenging the chivalric ideal.

The difficulty with such reversals, however, arises in their appearance in the heavily codified and rigorous chivalric landscape. During the late Middle Ages when Caxton first printed the *Morte*, chivalry was a cultural institution, permeating much of genteel life and relying on its own literatures to provide a basis of ideas and conduct.[3] Such an idealistic environment, though doomed for its self-referential perspective, seems an odd place for openly defiant comic moments, at first glance seeming to undercut the idiom from which the text claims to come.

But the fifteenth century marked the beginning of great changes in perceptions of the aristocracy and its role in both the culture of England and the country's rule. With the conclusion of the War of the Roses, England was faced with not only replenishing the ranks of the nobility in order to maintain the aristocratic backbone of the English government, but increasingly did so from non-aristocratic families, bestowing titles on landowners, scholars, and wealthy merchants. But this solidifying of England's traditional, chivalric rule had its cost. No longer were aristocratic qualities believed to be inborn, resulting in the loss of confidence of both the peasantry, and the increasingly powerful and influential merchant and middle classes.[4]

---

[2] In using the combined categories of 'masculine male' and 'feminine female,' my motive is to call attention to the hegemonic system which values the connection of sexed individuals with certain behaviours associated with their gender. For example, value is placed on a man who is strong and aggressive (traditionally masculine behaviours), and on a woman who is demure or even a gossip (traditionally feminine behaviours). Thus, traditional categories of biological sex (male, female) become valued when traditional categories of socially constructed gender (masculinity, femininity) are connected.

[3] J. Huizinga. *The Waning of the Middle Ages*. (Anchor Books: NY, 1989), p. 69.

[4] Kate Mertes, 'Aristocracy,' *Fifteenth-Century Attitudes*, ed. by Rosemary Horrox (Cambridge UP: NY, 1996), p. 59.

Caxton addresses this new population of nobles who were wealthy, educated, but lacking the ancestral traditions of inherited titles in his *Preface* by distinguishing 'noble prynces, lordes and ladyes, gentylmen and gentylwymmen' (xv),[5] thereby acknowledging the hierarchical strata which England had generated in itself throughout the Middle Ages. But Caxton also puts the purpose of the text equally to all of these people he later ranks:

> And I [. . .] have doon sette it in enprynte to the entente that noble men may see and lerne the noble actes of chyvalrye [. . .] humbly bysechyng al noble lordes and ladyes wyth al other estates, of what estate or degree they been of [. . .] that they take the good and honest actes in their remembraunce' (xv).

The text, Caxton claims, should serve as a handbook for chivalry for all who read it, whether a prince, lord, or socially-mobile gentleman.

In the absence of comedy, however, such ideals presented in Arthurian tradition might seem bleakly unapproachable or unrealistic.[6] Thomas Malory, I believe, perceived these difficulties and inconsistencies in the practice of ideally based chivalric behaviours, and in the *Morte*, he expanded and developed the comic moments of the sources not to subvert the literary-chivalric ethos which was so important to that late Middle Ages, but to question those inconsistencies in such a way that the more ecumenical values of the chivalric idiom survived the dialogic process.

Malory's Gender

During the feast of the wedding of Arthur and Guinevere at the end of Malory's chapter 'Torre and Pellinore,' the knights of Camelot gather and swear an oath which summarizes and defines the code of chivalry for the text:

> The kynge stablysshed all the knyghtes and gaff them rychesse and londys; and charged them never to do outerage nothir mourthir, and allwayes to fle treson, and to gyff mercy unto hym that askith mercy, uppon payne of forfiture [of their] worship and lordship of kynge Arthure for evirmore; and allwayes to do ladyes, damesels,

---

[5] This and following quotations from Caxton's *Preface* and Malory's text are taken from the one-volume edition of *Malory: Works*, ed. By Eugene Vinaver (Oxford UP: NY, 1971). Only page numbers will be provided.

[6] I have in mind here conflicts of the chivalric ideal such as unrequited love and the generation of heirs, knight errantry and the service due to the king and to the maintenance of one's own lands, and the sometimes hyperbolic descriptions of martial action and the physical abilities of mounted knights.

and jantilwomen and wydowes [succor:] strengthe hem in hir ryghtes, and never to enforce them, uppon payne of dethe. Also, that no man take no batayles in a wronge-full quarell for no love ne for no worldis goodis.(75)

As Thomas L. Wright notes of Malory's oath, it stands quite apart from the oath of spiritual chivalry advocated in the *Suite du Merlin*, which Vinaver identifies as Malory's source for Arthur's wedding.[7] Where the *Suite*'s oath focuses on the spiritual vigour necessary for the upcoming Grail quest, Malory's oath thematically features adventure and earthly chivalry, and makes no mention of piety or reverence. This shift in focus, Wright argues, discards the idea that piety is a specifically knightly trait, and allows the code to encompass not only the knights of the Round Table, but the 'ladyes, damesels, and jantilwomen and wydowes' of society as well.[8]

But beyond their spiritual character, Malory's oath makes clear that men and women have distinctly different roles to play in the chivalric setting. Knights are identified as male ('hym,' 'lordship,' 'men') and are the actors of martial behaviours. Women, on the other hand, fall under a variety of categories, and are positioned as the recipients of knightly deeds ('strengthe hem') and as sexual objects ('never to enforce them'). Malory apparently takes his cues for chivalric gender roles from the standard active/passive gender split delineated in medieval biological and theological tracts; here, men are knights whose masculinity is determined by deeds of prowess and courtesy, while women fall under a variety of noble categories in which femininity is defined by the need for knightly assistance.[9] This apparently fixed construction of chivalric gender identities is reinforced by the absence in chivalric texts of men and women who do not fit these roles, such as peasants, merchants, and all but a small population of clergy; their gender identities are immaterial to the knightly subject of the texts. In assembling a working model of chivalric gender, the question becomes then, how does Malory's construction of chivalric gender compare with other texts on the same subject?

By examining the didactic texts of chivalry from the Middle Ages, we find many constructions of chivalric gender similar to Malory's but which contain much more detail. In Geoffroi de Charny's *Le Livre de Chevalerie*, a text which is made up of

---

[7] Thomas L. Wright, '"The Tale of King Arthur": Beginnings and Foreshadowings,' in *Malory's Originality*, ed. by R.M. Lumiansky (Baltimore: John Hopkins Press, 1964), p. 37.

[8] *Ibid.*, p. 39.

[9] Indeed, Jacques Lacan, in 'The Meaning of the Phallus,' defines femininity in general as having the desire to gain the phallus and the feeling of its lack (*Feminine Sexuality*, ed. by Juliet Mitchell and Jacqueline Rose, NY: Pantheon Books, 1982).

fourteenth-century chivalric commonplaces and therefore can serve as a touchstone for chivalric discourses,[10] the behaviours of men and women contrast in terms of a woman's rich clothing:

> Et a fames d'estat appartient trop bien de estre es meilleurs estaz de riches aornemens sur elles et miex qu'il n'appartient aus hommes. [. . .] [parce que] les hommes vont ou il veulent entre les gens et en pluseurs pays: ce ne font mie les fames. Et si peuent les homes jouster et tournier: ce ne peuent mie les fames. Et si se arment les hommes pour la guerre: ce ne font mie les fames. Et vont et sont en plus de compaignies que les fames ne peuent estre.[11]
>
> [And it is for women of rank to present themselves in rich adornments and it esteems women better than it does men. (. . .) (because) men go where they wish among people and in different lands: women cannot do this. And men can joust and tournament: women also cannot do this. And men can arm themselves for war: women cannot do this. And they can go out more in society than women can.]

De Charny's catalogue of behaviours, like Malory's oath, defines the actions of men in terms of martial pursuits and power, while women's behaviours are described in the negative, suggesting inaction and prohibition. Women, de Charny further argues, have need of fine adornments in order to receive recognition, for they cannot display prowess, honour, and courtesy because they cannot take part in knightly activities. Where knights possess power and physical aggression, women cannot, and therefore must use care for their appearance in order to achieve a properly gendered chivalric status. Such clear behavioural demarcations illustrate traditional conceptions of hegemonic gender by constructing the masculine as active subject and the feminine as passive object, much as Malory does in his oath.

But what is the reader to do, then, with comic scenes where Lancelot is mistaken for a woman, or a damsel dresses in armour and smites the hero of the tale? A number of Malory's scenes problematize the sex/gender categories which are reconstructed in Malory's oath, namely the scenes of Alexander's buffet given to him by a damsel, Lancelot's practical joke of cross-dressing Dynadan at Surluse, and Belleus's mistaking Lancelot for his lady. Such scenes reveal the limits of the chivalric sex/gender categories by showing knights and damsels falling victim to gender mistakes or purposely clouding gender in practical contexts.

---

[10] Geoffroi de Charny, *The Book of Chivalry: Text, Context, and Translation*, ed. by Richard W. Kaeuper and Elspeth Kennedy (Philadelphia: University of Pennsylvania Press, 1996), p. 20. Kaeuper and Kennedy highlight the lack of originality of de Charny's text by examining the commonplaces and valorized self-conception of chivalry presented in the text.

[11] De Charny, *The Book of Chivalry*, p. 192. This and the following translations of the French texts are my own.

The three examples of comic gender-crossing which follow fragment the chivalric ideal by displaying this practical flexibility of gender; however, at the same time, the comedy works to reestablish the limits of chivalric behaviour. Indeed, Malory's moments of gender crossing pull the apparent absolutes of the chivalric gender ideal into an open-ended and flexible dialogic arena, while they also use this flexibility to reinforce chivalric qualities such as honour and knightly authenticity. The laughter in these scenes is therefore ultimately duplicitous: it occurs in the moments when the ideal and the comic join together to dialogize the foundational clarity of chivalry and the carnival absurdity of the gender slips.

Lancelot's Dress

The clearest example of the function of Malory's cross-gendered comic moment occurs in the 'Tournament at Surluse,' on the final day of the event. In the chapters before the event in the 'Book of Tristram,' Dynadan advocates a position contrary to the desires and idealistic attitudes of Arthurian chivalry: he refuses to fight with Trystram against thirty armed knights; exposes King Mark as a coward by tricking him into believing that Dagonet, Arthur's fool, is Lancelot; and he mocks the over-zealous bravery of the knights in the tales. His actions have led scholars to call him 'radically inconsistent' in response to his sporadic courage,[12] a 'misfit' for his criticisms of courtly society,[13] and a rational man in the idealistically irrational world of chivalry.[14] As the varied responses of critics suggest, Dynadan is a skeptic who participates in the structures which he doubts and stands apart from the dogmatism of chivalric discourse while remaining close enough to it to offer insightful criticism and comment through mocking laughter. In effect, the character of Dynadan dialogizes the chivalric world while still remaining active within its structures.

Surluse, however, stands apart from the earlier episodes in which Dynadan plays the skeptic. Lancelot, the accepted representative of the chivalric ideal for which the other knights strive, becomes the mocker. After two days of attempts to mock Dynadan with some success, Lancelot executes the most elaborate practical joke in all of the *Morte*. On the seventh day of the tournament, Dynadan approaches the pavilion where Lancelot, Galehalte the Haute Prynce, and Guinevere sit in judgment

---

[12] D. Thomas Hanks, 'Foil and Forecast: Dinadan in "The Book of Sir Tristram"', *The Arthurian Yearbook* I, ed. by Keith Busby (NY: Garland Publishing, 1991), p. 150.

[13] Keith Busby, 'The Likes of Dinadan: The Role of the Misfit in Arthurian Literature', *Neophilologius* 67 (1983), 166.

[14] Donald L. Hoffman, 'Dinadan: The Excluded Middle', *Tristania* 10 (1984), 3.

over the jousts. He challenges the two knights to meet him on the field, but they both decline, citing their roles as judges for the day:

> 'Perdeus,' seyde the Haute Prynce and sir Launcelot, 'ye may se how we sytte here as jouges with oure shyldis, and allway may ye beholde where we sytte here or nat.' (410)

Twice the two conspirators enthusiastically tell Dynadan that they will remain sitting in the stands, and twice they tell him to watch them there. But couched in their refusal to meet with Dynadan lies their own challenge. They want Dynadan to believe that they sit in the pavilion, and they challenge him to watch them throughout the tournament.

The reader, however, soon discovers their plan. The moment that Dynadan departs from the pavilion and enters the tournament field where he 'mette with many knyghtes and ded passyngly well' (410), Lancelot initiates his joke:

> Sir Launcelot disgysed hymselff and put uppon his armour a maydyns garmente freysshley attyred.(410)

Lancelot chooses to wear a woman's clothes, but the narrative voice makes sure that the textual audience does not forget that he is merely 'disgysed'. Each time Lancelot's feminine garments are mentioned, the narrator focuses on the illusion which Lancelot has created:

> Sir Launcelot, that was *in the damesels aray* [. . .]
> Sir Dynadan sawe *a maner of a damesel* [. . .]
> Hit sholde be sir Launcelot *disgysed* [. . .]
> (410, emphasis mine)

The image Lancelot creates presents an apparent contradiction: Lancelot, who traditionally represents knighthood and masculinity at its finest, wears a dress over his armour, consequently problematizing his gender identity by concealing his armour (the trappings of chivalric masculinity) and accepting a dress for display (the trappings of chivalric femininity). His intent is to gain the attention of Dynadan, and he does so in the manner of the women mentioned in de Charny's *Livre de Chevalerie*: through the intentional display of clothing.

Lancelot's disguise, moreover, is Malory's invention; in the source for the tournament, the *Tristan en Prose*, Lancelot plays no part in the joke on Dinadan. Indeed, Galehalte's plan to embarrass the knight does not begin with a character cross-dressing at all. Instead, Malory embellishes the plan by adding all of the events which Lancelot initiates before the actual encounter with Dynadan on the tournament field.

Malory's version of the practical joke functions in a number of ways which the French version, without Lancelot's involvement and cross-dressing, does not. With Lancelot's scheming, Malory's version points to the flexibility of gender in chivalric culture, despite the categorical gender roles assigned in chivalric discourses. In addition to the visual signs of gender identity in the image of the disguised Lancelot, conflicting behaviours problematize Lancelot's gender, as well. When he is ready, the cross-dressed Lancelot enters the field:

> Than sir Launcelot made Galyhodyn to lede hym thorow the raunge, and all men had wondir what damesell was that. And so as sir Dynadan cam into the raunge, sir Launcelot, that was in the damesels aray, gate sir Galyhodyns speare and ran unto sir Dynadan.(410)

The focus of the narrative rests on Lancelot's control over the image which *he* creates in order to lure Dynadan into a *martial* trap, but the means of his control are the women's garments he chooses to wear. Thus while Lancelot displays his masculinity through his knightly prowess and control, the integrity of his chivalric masculinity is compromised by his choice to dress in drag in order to lure Dynadan into the martial trap.

To those who are not privy to Lancelot's disguise, however, the act is no illusion at all; before Lancelot charges Dynadan, the other knights on the field 'had wondir what damesell was that' (410). They accept that the person being led by Galyhodyn is a woman only by the clothes he is wearing, for they have no knowledge of Lancelot's command to be led on the field, nor do they know of the trap being set. The knights see a person wearing a dress over armour on the tournament field,[15] and as a result of the contradictory signs of masculinity and femininity, Lancelot becomes unintelligible in the chivalric gender system and therefore only vaguely unidentifiable. From the perspective of the unknowing observers, Lancelot's disguise is a successful performance in that it forces the observers to encounter the gender instability of the figure before them.

There is only one knight on the field who comes close to penetrating Lancelot's deception. In a rare shift in the narrative point of view, Malory moves from reporting the development of the scene to a report of Dynadan's perspective:

---

[15] We can assume that the knights can see some of Lancelot's armour beneath the dress because both the knights and later Dynadan 'wondir' at the 'maner' of a damsel which they see. The narrator does not claim that they see a damsel, only a person who, in some ways, appears to be one.

> And allwayes he [Dynadan] loked up theras sir Launcelot was, and than he sawe one
> sytte in the stede of sir Launcelot armed. But whan sir Dynadan sawe a maner of a
> damesell, he dradde perellys lest hit sholde be sir Launcelot disgysed. (410)

Dynadan, unsure if the figure dressed in a maiden's garment is Lancelot, rational-
izes the absence of Lancelot from the judging dais and concludes that the 'maiden'
might be the absent knight. Dynadan's ability to perceive Lancelot's machinations
resides in his position as the chivalric skeptic who continually watches for discordance in chivalric culture: he questions Tristram's honour when his friend charges
against thirty knights, publicly exposes Mark's folly when he writes a damaging
lay for the king, and tells his friends that he would rather not be called a lover than
suffer the agonies and embarrassment of courtly love. When Lancelot disappears
from the dias, Dynadan discovers a discordance in both Lancelot's vehement request to be observed there and the appearance of an unknown woman on the field
of martial play (a site not of feminine participation but of masculine display). These
observations coalesce into Dynadan's fear that the figure in armour and a dress is
Lancelot.

But Dynadan does not have the opportunity to act on his insight:

> But sir Launcelot cam on hym so faste that he smote sir Dynadan over his horse
> croupe. And anon grete coystrons gate sir Dynadan, and into the foreyst there besyde,
> and there they dispoyled hym unto his sherte and put uppon hym a womans garmente
> and so brought hym into fylde.(410)

This shift of cross-dressing from Lancelot to Dynadan under such forced circumstances reveals the purpose of Lancelot's attempt at comedy. Lancelot's drag is
forgotten by the text when Dynadan's appears; we hear nothing more of Lancelot's
disguise or the reactions of the knights when they discover that the maiden is
Lancelot. Such an abrupt shift in the focus of the plot leaves Lancelot's gender
representation in limbo; the text does not resolve his apparently conflicting gender
markers and behaviours.

Dynadan's inability to act, on the other hand, becomes the focus of the text when he
is forced to take on feminine gender markers. It would appear that it is not good
enough simply to defeat Dynadan on the field of battle, thereby diminishing his
honour. To the sensibilities of those characters who attempt to justify chivalric discourses by trying to practice them, Dynadan represents their own failures and fallibil-
ity because of his ability to perceive them. When Lancelot victimizes him in front of
the loyally chivalric court, Dynadan's skepticism is disciplined for all to see and
acknowledge, thus reiterating the knightly norm which Dynadan does not represent:
honour, bravery, and prowess. He must, in effect, be made a visible victim of the
strictures of chivalric discourse if chivalry is to curtail his instability.

The laughter which erupts from the audience at seeing Dynadan dressed as a woman mocks the discordances which he represents. He is put on display as a product of his own unintelligible contradictions; he appears as man and woman, knight and lady, masculine and feminine--many of the binaries which chivalric discourse creates contained in one image. Dynadan's body becomes a sign of the dialogic which his skepticism encourages through the drag, but also through the laughter which it generates. The court turns the tables and is skeptical of Dynadan here, and it reaches this determination by its close proximity to the doubt which Dynadan characterizes. Lancelot embraces the flexibility of gender in his drag, thus calling the dictates of chivalric gender into question and placing himself, and the court which he represents, into a common perspective with Dynadan. In doing so, Lancelot does not reduce the shame of Dynadan's cross-dressing; being a representative of chivalry, he brings the court into a close proximity with Dynadan so that laughter may occur. Considering that Dynadan's skepticism of chivalric behaviour is what the court mocks, and that they themselves participate in that skepticism through gender, the court's laughter at Dynadan lightens a nervous acceptance of their proximity to that which they deem absurd in the otherwise idealistic chivalric setting.

At this moment of comedy, the French text parallels the narrative of the practical joke. The French Dinadan is defeated on the tournament field by a group of knights who, like Malory's knights, drag him into the forest and dress him in a 'guise de dame' (likeness of a woman). The two versions of the crowd's reaction to the sight of the knight in a dress, however, differ drastically, revealing Malory's perceptions concerning Dynadan and the courtly anxiety which he represents.

In the *Tristan en Prose*, Dinadan is unabashed by the joke. Indeed, he bypasses the tent in which the other knights anxiously await his return and goes directly to the tent of Queen Guinevere. Here, he plays the showman and loudly declares his appreciation for the jape:

> Et lors s'escrie Dinadan, et dist: 'Ha! Royne debonnaire, veïstes vous oncques mais chevallier qui s'appareillast en guise de dame et qui en telle guise venist davant les chevaliers et davant les dames et damoiselles? Car j'ay esté jusques a huy Dinadan, or povez vous veoir que je sui une dame.'[16]
> [And then Dinadan cried and said: 'Ha! Beautiful queen, did you never see a knight who dresses himself in the guise of a woman and who in such guise came in front of the knights and in front of the ladies and damsels? For I was Dinadan until today, now you may see that I am a lady.']

---

[16] *Le Roman de Tristan en Prose*, ed. by E. Löseth (NY: Burt Franklin, 1970), II, fol. 397rb.

After a brief and teasing exchange between the queen and Dinadan, he is rewarded for his good humour; Galehaut leads Dinadan to a chamber where he is given rich clothing befitting his sex, thus reinforcing his place in chivalric society through the knights' benevolent acceptance of Dinadan's disposition.[17]

Malory, however, presents a Dynadan who is quite spiteful:

> And than was sir Dynadan brought in amonge them all, and whan quene Gweny-ver sawe sir Dynadan ibrought in so amonge them all, than she lowghe, that she fell downe; and so ded all there was.
> 'Well,' seyde sir Dynadan, 'sir Launcelot, thou arte so false that I can never be-ware of the.'(410)

In Malory's retelling, Lancelot is given the honours for the day 'by all assente.' His mocking joke on Dynadan is the only feat he accomplishes that day, and is appar-ently a popular action--popular enough to outshine the accomplishments of the knights on the field. Indeed, as Donald Hoffman notes, the laughter which the im-age of the cross-dressed Dynadan invokes reinforces the 'communal identity and camaraderie' of the court,[18] but where Hoffman goes on to argue that Dynadan has been constructed and mocked as an outsider to the community, we must remember the skepticism and proximity which the court displays. There can be no doubt that Dynadan is a skeptic of idealistic chivalric practices, but if Dynadan exists in the margins of courtly conduct, so too does the cross-dressed Lancelot and the court which accepts his drag without comment. Thus the fall-to-the-floor laughter of Guinevere and the court does not alienate Dynadan by calling attention to his oth-erness, but instead, it binds the chivalric community together in its skepticism and its contradiction.

Alys's Armour

Where the disciplining of Dynadan's skepticism of chivalric discourses leads to the acknowledgment of the court's own interpretive dialogism at the Tournament at Surluse, the final scene of 'Alysaundir the Orphan' uses gender comedy as a key way to determine knightly authenticity. By the end of this interpolated biography located in the midst of the 'Book of Tristram,' all of the elements of the tale seem to resolve into a denouement typical of Arthurian literature: Alysaundir has escaped his imprisonment by Morgan le Fay in La Beale Regarde with the aid of Alys la

---

[17] Keith Busby argues further on this point, that Dinadan's 'outrageous behaviour has become as much an 'institution'. . . . as Gauvain and Keu' in the French version of the scene ('The Likes of Dinadan', p. 172).

[18] Hoffman, 'Dinadan: The Excluded Middle', p. 12.

Beall Pillaron; he has cleverly upheld his vow of one year of service to Morgan by defending the garden of the recently ruined castle; and he has met and fallen in love with Alys la Beall Pylgryme, who sought him out after hearing of his prowess in defending the garden. But Alysaundir's adventures, though they may seem conclusive to literary-chivalric sensibilities, do not end there. Echoing and manipulating the French source of the tale, Malory writes of another adventure which presents a variety of gender-crossing behaviours and sexually ambiguous innuendoes which culminate in laughter.

In Malory's source, the *Tristan en Prose*, Alixandre vanquishes two knights in joust and takes a respite during which he remembers his beloved:

> Alixandre absorbé par une profonde rêverie où l'a jeté le souvenir d'Aylies, il se pourpensa de le prendre parmi le frain et de le pourmener de ça et de la.[19]
> [Alixandre becomes absorbed in deep thought where the memory of Alyies has thrown him, and decides to take himself by the reign and to lead himself this way and that.]

The French Alixandre displays the characteristic behaviours of a courtly lover; he is, as Andreas Capellanus argues he should be, 'possessed by the thought of his beloved,' and becomes disoriented in his suffering.[20] When Malory rewrites the incident, however, Alysaundir's attentions concentrate not in the memory of Alys, but in the sight of her:

> So whan they were departed sir Alysaundir behylde his lady Alys on horseback as she stood in hir pavylion, and than was he so enamered uppon her that he wyst nat whether he were on horsebacke other on foote.(398)

Alysaundir's male gaze launches the events in the *Morte*, reiterating behaviours which construct Alysaundir as the active male subject and the Lady Alys as the female object, a static statue that is beautiful, silent, and the locus of acute masculine sexual desire. Thus Malory dramatically intensifies the sexual power dynamic of the male gaze in his version of the scene by highlighting the immediacy of sexual desire as distinct from the temporally distanced memory of the beloved in the French version. While both versions of the scene construct chivalric masculinity in relation to a lady, Malory's use of the male gaze makes Alysaundir's masculinity more dynamic through its immediacy.

---

[19] *Le Roman de Tristan,* p. 194.

[20] Andreas Capellanus, *The Art of Courtly Love*, trans. by John Jay Parry (NY: Columbia UP, 1990) p. 186.

With the introduction of the male gaze as the cause for Alysaundir's reaction, Malory highlights the gender and sexuality of the hero as key components to the events which follow in the scene. Alysaundir not only declares his gender and sexuality by establishing himself as the male subject who desires a female sexualized object, but he also reinforces this normalized gender identity through his apparent vulnerability. As Mary Wack argues, the 'mal d'amour' (sickness of love) experienced by lover-knights acts as a buffer between the woman whom his love has ennobled beyond reality and the 'masculine sphere of value' which relegates any sign of weakness to the feminine.[21] The swoons and sighs of lovesick knights become a confirmation of masculine dominance and power through their active distancing of the knightly subject from that which controls him. The 'disease' of love, then, becomes a behaviour which reveals the superior power of the knight in relation to his lady, reiterating the chivalric gender power dynamic of subject-knights and object-ladies. As is the case when Capellanus claims that love ennobles (masculinizes) a lover,[22] or when love inspires the martial feats of Gareth or Trystram, love-longing acts as a masculinizing marker of chivalric gender.

Such an evaluation, however, is not apparent to those characters who are not proponents of chivalric discourse. In Malory's account of the incident, Mordred observes Alysaundir's weakening at the sight of Alys and takes advantage of the lovesick hero's apparent vulnerability:

> Ryght so cam the false knyght sir Mordred and sawe sir Alysaundir was so afonned uppon his lady, and therewithall he toke hys horse by the brydyll and lad hym here and there, and had caste to have lad hym oute of that place to have shamed hym.(398)

Here Mordred acts on Alysaundir's disorientation by leading him 'here and there.' In the episode in the *Tristan en Prose*, Alixandre's random wanderings are the direct consequence of his love-meditation, and the as-yet-unidentified Mordred offers only to joust with Alixandre while the hero is vulnerable.[23]

Mordred's role in Malory's version of the tale affects the audience's perception of Alysaundir's vulnerability in quite a number of ways, not the least of which is to imply dishonour. Mordred does not perceive Alysaundir's disorientation as mascu-

---

[21] Mary Wack, in *Lovesickness in the Middle Ages* (Philadelphia: U Pennsylvania P, 1990), p. 171, asserts that the sighing, swooning illness experienced by lovers in the name of courtly love behaviours is a construct of masculine legitimacy and shows the masculine difficulty with the ascendancy of a woman.

[22] Capellanus, *Art of Courtly Love*, p. 31.

[23] *Le Roman de Tristan*, pp.194-95.

linizing at all; for Mordred, Alysaundir's behaviour is laughable. We are continually reminded here and elsewhere, however, that Mordred, the 'false knyght,' does not represent chivalric integrity. In the community of Camelot, Mordred is a villain, and as such, he cannot perceive the ennobling masculinity of Alysaundir's suffering. He sees only that Alysaundir is not living up to the chivalricly masculine qualities of prowess and power and, in fact, that he participates in the otherwise feminine quality of vulnerability. But because Mordred continually stands as a counter-example, or how *not* to act as a knight, his judgment of Alysaundir's shame for his lovesickness condemns him as one who cannot perceive the subtleties of the chivalric masculine identity. Moreover, because Mordred views Alysaundir's suffering as shameful, the text conversely implies that the hero's behaviours are appropriate to his identity as a chivalric male, in spite of Mordred's mockery and the apparent femininity of Alysaundir's vulnerability.

Mordred's gesture of leading Alysaundir's horse, however, creates a much more ambiguous image of Alysaundir's actions, despite Mordred's falseness. D. W. Robertson has explored the significance of the medieval analogy of the horse-and-bridle to woman-and-marriage.[24] To medieval monastic writers such as St. Gregory and St. Augustine, the horse represents the flesh, with all of its desires and sin; the bridle, therefore, was viewed as an instrument with which to control the animal and the licentiousness it represents. Robertson points out that St. Augustine clarifies the analogy of 'horse' to 'woman' by explaining that those qualities which are represented in the horse might likewise be subjugated in a woman by a similar bridle, namely marriage.[25] Such assumptions concerning the licentiousness of women by medieval religious writers translate easily to chivalric gender orthodoxy; the analogy constructs the male husband as possessing power and control over the female wife, whose sexuality is bridled by marriage.[26] The horse-and-bridle analogy, in effect, reiterates the power structures demarcated in medieval gender discourses.

In the case of Mordred's gesture, the figure of the horse-and-bridle informs the 'false knyght's' actions. Mordred creates the image of the horse-and-bridle by exploiting Alysaundir's lust for Alys and linking it to the shameful licentiousness of the horse. By leading Alysaundir's horse 'here and there,' Mordred exerts the

---

[24] See D. W. Robertson's *Preface to Chaucer* (Princeton: Princeton UP, 1962), p. 254.

[25] Robertson, *Preface,* p. 254. The figure of marriage as a tool of subjugation is likened to the horse-and-bridle image in the criticism of Chaucer's *Troilus and Criseyde* and the play *Mankind*. In Malory, the horse is a prominent image in the marriages of knights, in such cases as the marriage of Gareth and Lyoness and the return of Guinevere to Arthur in the final chapters of the *Morte*.

[26] The trouble with the assumption of church fathers, however, is that in the construction of chivalric gender (masculine display and feminine observation), the female must be sexualized to a high degree in order to generate the conditions for the creation of masculinity.

same control over the licentious male figure in the scene as a marriage-bridle does for the licentious wife in St. Gregory and St. Augustine, Alysaundir's lovesick passivity controlled literally through the horse's bridle. By extension, the horse-and-bridle set-piece figures Mordred as the controlling husband, and Alysaundir as the licentious and controlled wife.

Mordred's position in the horse-and-bridle image and his belief that the image will shame Alysaundir, however, points to Mordred's misinterpretation of chivalric behaviours, and therefore to the fraudulence of his own chivalric identity. Mordred does not perceive the ennobling, masculinizing effects which lovesickness creates in the chivalric setting. To him, Alysaundir's disorientation represents a badge of shame for the weakness and femininity it represents, and it should be made public and mocked. Moreover, Mordred reveals his own disordered sexuality by occupying the role of *husband* while Alysaundir occupies the role of *wife*. In the moment which Mordred constructs Alysaundir as feminized in his role as wife, by choosing to do so with the horse-and-bridle image, Mordred must occupy the position of control, therefore entering a construct of marriage to Alysaundir, whom the text otherwise characterizes as masculine and male. Apparently the unknowing perpetrator of this image of destabilized sexuality, Mordred's interpretation of Alysaundir's lovesick behaviour and his treatment of the swooning knight fails to correspond to the dominant discourses of the chivalric setting, thus reinforcing his position as both sexually and ideologically false according to chivalric discourses.

Despite its knowledge of the masculinizing effects of lovesickness, the narration manipulates the audience to accept Mordred's perception of Alysaundir's vulnerability because it is the only point of view thus far in the text. But when Alys la Beale Pillaron, the damsel who had previously helped Alysaundir escape from Morgan le Fay, sees Mordred leading the hero around the field by the bridle, she perceives the conflicting interpretations of Alysaundir's behaviour:

> So when the damesell that halpe hym oute of that castell sawe how shamefully he was lad, anone she let arme her and sette a shylde upon her shuldir. And therewith she amownted uppon his horse and gate a naked swerde in hir honde.(398)

The perceptions of the damsel confirm Mordred's view of Alysaundir's vulnerability; she can perceive the shame which the horse-and-bridle image holds for the hero. But in her perception of the shame which Mordred intends through his own interpretation of Alysaundir's actions, Alys also sees that the shame is not generated by Alysaundir's love-lorn disorientation. As Malory's phrasing suggests, the shame lies in being led by the bridle, not in the lovesickness. Alys understands that Mordred turns a perfectly normal sexual scene into a disordered one, mistaking his lovesick vulnerability for femininity, and she acts to reconstruct Alysaundir's image.

Malory's dialogic of chivalric gender informs the damsel Alys's preparation to confront Alysaundir and Mordred; while the French source includes a similar gender-crossing by the damsel, the account of her transformation is much more concise:

> Alors la cousine de Morgain se déguise en chevalier.[27]
> [Then Morgan le Fay's cousin (Alyies) disguises herself as a knight.]

Malory's details of the damsel Alys's choice and placement of weaponry emphasize the extent to which she takes on the masculine identity of a knight. She dons the armour with the intent of confrontation and does not 'disguise' herself as a knight as her counterpart does in the French. Malory sidesteps the layering of identities by discarding the idea of disguise and the notions of falsity and play which costumes and masks infer.[28] Malory's Alys hides no identity under the trappings of a knightly identity; Alys herself chooses and places the weaponry, demonstrating a direct participation in the masculine chivalric domain. Even Malory's perception of the damsel Alys's gender slips from feminine to masculine when he writes that she 'amownted upon *his* horse' [emphasis mine]; Alys is the only possible antecedent for the masculine pronoun. Thus Alys's gender becomes not only disrupted for the audience of the scene, but her transformation is so complete that, through the pronoun slip, we hear the narrative voice reconfirming the true ambiguity of gender.

If there is any doubt of the damsel's suitability for her role as knight, she answers us when she confronts Alysaundir:

> She threste unto Alysaundir with all hir myght, and she gaff hym such a buffet that hym thought the fyre flowe oute of his yghen.(398)

In order to rescue Alysaundir from Mordred, Alys becomes not only a masculine figure grammatically through pronoun references, but through her actions, as she demonstrates her martial ability--a distinctly masculine ability in traditional gender constructions. She does not simply 'play' at being a knight by using a disguise; she displays her knightly prowess and succeeds at her martial task.

Alys's blow focuses on Alysaundir's eyes and the way the actions of the scene are linked through sight and seeing. Alysaundir's dilemma results from seeing the Lady Alys and his male gaze constructing her as a sexualized object, one that is at the same time superior and inferior to him. Mordred then sees the lovesickness which

---

[27] *Le Roman de Tristan*, p. 194.

[28] See Louise Fradenburg's *City, Marriage, Tournament: Arts of Rule in Late Medieval Scotland*, especially her chapter entitled 'Soft and Silken War,' for an explanation of the way disguise functions as a tool of display and play in tournament settings.

Alysaundir's gaze creates and interprets it as a sign of weakness to be exploited, but when the damsel Alys sees this exploitation of the hero, she acts to restore Alysaundir by knocking the fire from his eyes. This fire, however, does not result from the shame of Mordred's gesture or the enigmatic 'fire of the soul'; it is the fire of lovesickness, as is apparent from his clear and martial response to the buffet:

> He loked about hym and drew his swerde. And whan she [Alys] sawe that, she fledde, and so ded sir Mordred into the foreyste. And the damesell fled into the pavy-lyon.(398)

Alysaundir regains his control as a result of the trauma to his eyes and responds martially, momentarily forgetting his lady. Such an overt act of chivalric masculinity as drawing his sword reiterates the gender distinctions of the scene, and because Mordred relies on gender's ambiguity to create the horse-and-bridle image, the set-piece fails, Mordred runs away, and Alysaundir's honour is reestablished through the 'false knyght' Mordred's display of cowardice.

Alysaundir quickly realizes the consequences of Mordred's actions after he chases Alys and Mordred off:

> Alysaundir undirstood hymselff how the false knyght wolde have shamed hym had nat the damesell bene, than he was wroth with hymselff that sir Mordred had so ascaped his honds.(398)

In this inversion of the standard chivalric trope of knights saving women, Alysaundir does not direct his anger at the damsel who gave him the buffet; instead, he is 'wroth with hymselff' that he was unable to confront Mordred about the mocking joke. Indeed, Alysaundir's concern does not touch on Alys's cross-gendered state at all, but instead focuses on his own shame and its instigator. The 'false knyght' Mordred was able to take advantage of Alysaundir's lovesick vulnerability, a moment of legitimate masculinity despite its false interpretation as femininity, and victimize the chivalric hero.

But while chasing Mordred reestablishes the control in favour of Alysaundir, one last ambiguity needs to be addressed before the text can neatly conclude. Despite Alysaundir's previous recognition of Alys's role in his rescue ('Alysaundir undirstood . . . how the false knyght wolde have shamed hym had nat the damesell bene'), he and the Lady Alys mock the damsel's actions:

> But than sir Alysaundir and his lady Alys had good game at the damesell, how sadly she smote hym upon the helme. (398)[29]

---

[29] 'Sadly,' according to Skeat's *Etymological Dictionary of the English Language*, may here be defined as 'sorrowfully'.

By belittling Alys's 'sad' action, Alysaundir and the Lady Alys reveal their anxieties concerning the destabilized position which the successfully cross-dressed and cross-gendered Alys occupies; by their reasoning, the damsel Alys fails in her participation in knightly behaviours because she does not possess the physical strength required of the masculine realm. Despite Alysaundir's previous acknowledgment that Mordred would have shamed him 'had nat the damesell bene' and that the damsel's blow made the 'fyre flowe oute of his yghen,' her method of reaching that goal does not accord with the strict gender binary of chivalric discourse. Her success and the disruption of gender definitions which her success causes apparently make Alysaundir and the Lady Alys anxious enough to laugh in reprimand, thereby placing their chivalric sensibilities in a position of control of Alys's dialogized character. We hear nothing more of the damsel Alys following their game, and nothing more of the gender disruption.

Unlike the disciplining laughter of Surluse in the previous example, the mocking 'game' here does not work to build community, nor does it allow the textual audience to encounter the destabilization of chivalric gender at different levels. Alysaundir's reprimand might be a 'game,' but it is a distracting, nervous one; Alysaundir's shame and the perception of his vulnerability as feminine are forgotten in light of the comic teasing of the damsel Alys. Indeed, Alysaundir deflects comment on his own behaviours by presenting a pleasurable re-stabilization of Alys's chivalric femininity, thus limiting the audience's view by using the closeness of comic proximity to distract attention from his own actions.

The fact remains, however, that despite Alysaundir's reprimand with its pleasurable presentation, Alys succeeds in her masculinized role and rescues Alysaundir while he occupies a role which generates clashing gender interpretations. In the end, the only character who occupies a deviant role from chivalric discourse and is censured effectively is Mordred, the 'false knyght,' who troubles the interpretation of masculinizing behaviour, exploits it, and is then shown to be an unchivalric coward.

Belleus's Kiss

The previous two examples present laughter on the one hand as a means to reprimand apparently unchivalric behaviours, and on the other, as a tool for defining a chivalric sphere of inquiry through the determination of community and knightly authenticity. Thus far, despite their tendency to reflect back on the chivalric identity of the mockers in the scenes, the moments of gender-crossing comedy in the *Morte* have been deliberate acts of probing and evaluating the apparently deviant characters' chivalric integrity.

The following example of cross-gendered comedy, however, results from coincidence and mistaken identity. Such accidental gender mistakes shift the purpose of the laughter; instead of revealing the apparent lack of chivalric identity of a character like Dynadan or Alys, comedy and laughter in Belleus's pavilion becomes a tool for healing bruised honours and injured egos. Gender flexibility becomes the dialogic focus of the scene, but it also becomes the means by which characters gain honour and esteem.

As was the case with Alysaundir's victimization following his masculinization through his male gaze and lovesickness, Lancelot's mistaken identity in Belleus's pavilion in the 'Book of Lancelot' occurs directly after the hero is established as a male chivalric model. Taken prisoner by the 'four queens,' among whom Morgan le Fay resides, Lancelot is asked to choose one of the queens for his paramour or else to remain their prisoner. His situation, despite his apparent victimization, places him in a masculinized position: the queens tell him to use his male gaze to sexualize one of them, thereby conversely masculinizing Lancelot by placing him in a position of masculine sexual power.[30] But Lancelot chooses to die instead of picking one of the queens, remaining a 'prisoner' of love for Guinevere, and a bodily prisoner of the vengeful queens.

But once Lancelot, with the help of a damsel, is freed from the castle of the four queens, other events occur which trouble his recently fortified masculinity. The damsel tells him to search out an abbey of white monks, and that she will meet him there in a few days. But Lancelot never finds the abbey. As night falls, he only spots a red pavilion which he decides would be a good place to sleep. Before Lancelot enters the strange pavilion,

> there he alyght downe, and tyed his horse to the pavylyon, and there he unarmed him. And there he founde a bed, and layed hym therein, and felle on slepe sadly.(153)

Lancelot here removes the markers which identify him as a knight, and consequently in the chivalric idiom, his disarming discards the trappings of chivalric masculinity. This is not to suggest, however, that the act of taking off his armour feminizes Lancelot in any way; Lancelot performs no behaviours other than falling asleep, an act which in no way compromises his masculinity, nor is it a distinctly feminine behaviour. What removing his armour and falling asleep does accomplish is that it makes the identity of Lancelot a bit more ambiguous in the strict chivalric environment which, as de Charny suggests of chivalric identity, ultimately is created

---

[30] The sexual power dynamic is extremely convoluted in the scene with the four queens because Lancelot, however masculinized he is by the male gaze, is still a victim of women, just as Alysaundir was a victim of Mordred.

by the actions and clothing of its members. Lancelot is embodied as male, but the naked, sleeping knight's masculinity resists identification.

When the owner of the pavilion, Belleus, arrives not an hour after Lancelot has fallen asleep, he constructs Lancelot's gender according to his own desires and expectations. Unlike the source of the scene in the *Lancelot en Prose* where Lancelot acts by embracing the other knight in bed with him,[31] the action in Malory's version is Belleus's. Belleus sees a figure in the bed in the pavilion and assumes Lancelot to be the lady whom he is to meet there for a tryst:

> [Belleus] wente that his lemman had layne in that bed, and so he layde hym adowne by sir Launcelot and toke hym in his armys and began to kysse hym.(153)

Belleus assumes the femininity of the figure in the bed, a site where he anticipates sexual gratification, and as a consequence acts upon the figure as a sexualized object. What appears to be working here is a male gaze without a specific object; 'The Lady,' as Lacan would argue, literally and figuratively does not exist here because, on the one hand, Lancelot is not a lady, and on the other, because Belleus acts on the fantasmic absolute of 'woman' that cannot exist anywhere except in his own male fantasy.[32] The effects of the perception of his lady, however, still occur as Belleus interacts with the sleeping Lancelot.

One of the troubles with the role that Belleus constructs for the sleeping form is that Lancelot is not aware of it; indeed, Lancelot acts out of his masculine role as knight while he is being acted upon as a feminine sexualized object:

> And whan sir Launcelot felte a rough berde kyssyng hym he sterte oute of the bed lyghtly, and the othir knyght after hym. Ane eythir of hem gate their swerdys in their hondis, and oute at the pavylyon dore wente the knyght of the pavylyon, and sir Launcelot folowed hym.(153)

At the moment when Belleus's beard touches Lancelot's skin and Lancelot recognizes the disruption of traditional categories of chivalric gender and sexuality, he reacts, reclarifying his subjective gender and sexuality by immediately focusing his actions in a martial, and therefore masculine, confrontation. Belleus's reaction of grabbing his sword and exiting the tent to fight also depicts his own martial aggres-

---

[31] *Lancelot en Prose*, ed. by Alexandre Micha, tome IV (Paris: Librairie Droz, 1979), p. 183.

[32] See Jacques Lacan's essay, 'God and the *Jouissance* of The Woman: A Love Letter' (*Feminine Sexuality*, ed. by Juliet Mitchell and Jacqueline Rose, New York: W. W. Norton and Company, 1982) for further exploration of the non-existence of the sexualized feminine object.

sion. But because Belleus's gender is never in question, the motivation for his reaction apparently stems from Lancelot's aggressive response to the mistake which held the potential of threatening Belleus's sexual identity in the site which it exists: the bed on which he was to meet his lady.

But despite the characters' confusion, the textual audience is aware of the conflicting gender constructions from the start; such dramatic irony is driven by the homoerotic potential of the two knights who are identified as heterosexual through Lancelot's love for Guinevere and Belleus's love for 'his lemman.' The homoerotic potential of their encounter, however, is partially realized by Belleus's kisses, but as Carolyn Dinshaw argues of the homoerotic kisses between Gawain and Bercilak in 'Sir Gawain and the Green Knight,' the author 'closes off such a space as quickly as he opens it up.'[33] No sooner does the possibility of a homoerotic tryst appear before Lancelot and Belleus than it is emended by the reactions of the knights who realize the conflicting perceptions of the gender of the figure in the bed.

During the fight of Belleus and Lancelot, Belleus is wounded 'sore nyghe unto deth' (153), but unlike the *Lancelot en Prose* where Lancelot kills the mistaken knight,[34] Belleus yields to Lancelot, who asks for an explanation of his presence. His words are simple and truthful: he planned to meet his lady in the pavilion in order to sleep with her. No other information is given as to why the lovers meet in the pavilion, what status the lady holds, or whether their meeting is a secret. Indeed, no more information is necessary if Malory's purpose is to highlight the dramatic irony which the French source cuts short by the knight's death.

More than highlighting the dramatic irony of the scene, Malory's change also underscores Lancelot's role as 'the floure of knyghtes' (152) by presenting the restraint which Lancelot displays in his fight with Belleus.[35] In the *Lancelot en Prose*, Lancelot fights the unarmed knight of the pavilion, and kills him after chasing him into the forest:

> Et Lanceloz le suit qui atant nel velt mie laissier; si le chace tant sanz robe qu'il l'aconsielt, si le fiert par mi la teste de l'espee si qu'il le fant tout dusqu'es danz et cil chiet morz a terre.[36]

---

[33] Carolyn Dinshaw, 'A Kiss is Just a Kiss: Heterosexuality and Its Consolations in *Sir Gawain and the Green Knight*.' *Diacritics* 24 (Summer 1994), p. 209.

[34] *Lancelot en Prose*, p. 184

[35] Albert Hartung explores Malory's intentions for Lancelot in his changes from the French source in 'Narrative Technique, Characterization, and the Sources in Malory's "Tale of Sir Lancelot"', *Studies in Philology* 70 (1973), 257.

[36] *Lancelot en Prose*, p. 184.

[And Lancelot follows him, for he does not at all want to desist; and he chases him
without clothing until he overtakes him, and strikes him with his sword through the
head so that he splits it right to his teeth and he falls dead on the ground.]

Malory allows Lancelot to proclaim his masculinity in two different ways: instead
of reestablishing his role as a chivalric male solely through martial feats, in Malory's version, Lancelot also clarifies his gender through the mercy which the Round
Table oath also advocates:

> And then he [Belleus] yelded hym to sir Launcelot, and so he graunted hym, so that
> he wolde telle hym why he com into the bed. . . . And so they wente bothe into the
> pavylyon, and anone sir Launcelot staunched his bloode.(153)

By showing such restraint, and giving 'mercy unto hym that askith mercy' (75),
Malory's Lancelot situates himself as a chivalric male by displaying the qualities
of prowess, honour, and control in the space of a few lines. So despite Lancelot's
easy slip from chivalric gender categories, his recovery of a clearly defined masculinity is just as simple, indicating the fluidity of gender even within the highly
structured chivalric iteration.

Belleus and Lancelot seem comfortable enough with the explanation of the mistake
to stay in each other's company, but as Belleus finds, the knights must yet answer
to another audience. When Belleus's lady arrives to meet her lover, she sees the
result of the combat and panics:

> Therewithall com the knyghtes lady that was a passynge fayre lady. And whan she
> aspyed that her lord Belleus was sore wounded she cryed oute on sir Launcelot and
> made grete dole oute of measure.(153)

Her cries of anguish are the result of her realization that Belleus and Lancelot have
engaged in combat, and her anger is so great that she directs her tirade 'on sir
Launcelot,' the knight who wounded her lover. She acts here as a chivalric female,
in effect, as the observer who places meaning on the knightly action by determining
its honour and worthiness, thus masculinizing (or de-masculinizing) the participants. As she perceives the scene, her lover is an innocent victim.

And with the arrival of the lady and her 'grete dole,' Belleus has some explaining
to do. He must not only convince his lady that the wound he received was not given
to him through deceit, but he must also convince her that the homoerotic potential
of the encounter was a misunderstanding. If she is not convinced of these things,
she will carry the knowledge of the homoerotic kisses, questioning Belleus's ideal
chivalric masculinity on account of this act.

Before the lady can formulate the words to question her lover's condition, though, Belleus attempts to circumvent the homoerotic potential of the mistaken identity. His first words to her present an argument regarding the normativity of his own sexuality and Lancelot's gender, the two conditions that constitute the reason for doubt:

> 'Pease, my lady and my love,' seyde sir Belleus, 'for this knyght is a good man and a knyght of adventures.' And there he tolde hir all the case how he was wounded. 'And whan that I yelded me unto hym he laffte me goodly, and hath staunched my bloode.'(154)

Belleus reinforces his own heterosexuality by calling her 'my lady and my love,' in effect pointing out that he is not only heterosexual, but also that his sexual desire is directed at her alone. He then clarifies Lancelot's masculinity twice by reporting that he is a knight and a 'good man.' Then, to buttress his claim of Lancelot's masculinity, Belleus tells his lady that Lancelot takes part in knightly 'adventures,' those honourable and martial exploits which define chivalric masculinity.[37]

Indeed, Belleus's explanation of the kisses is only mentioned in passing by the narrator before Belleus attempts to belittle the seriousness of the moment by pointing out its comic fictionality. Belleus states, 'he laffte me goodly,' without indicating clearly whether Lancelot laughed *at him*, *with him*, or alternately, *made him laugh* at the mistake. Without any preposition to indicate who, exactly, was doing the laughing after Belleus's surrender, we might hesitatingly assume that both knights laughed as an indication of embarrassment, but also of their pleasure, after slipping from the chivalric sex/gender norm.

When laughter emerges from behaviours which resist chivalric categorization, it works to contain those behaviours by rendering them absurd and highlighting their surprising and exciting departure from the chivalric norm. But in the scene in Belleus's pavilion, we cannot be sure that the laughter actually happened at the reported moment; the laughter is mentioned by Belleus only after it supposedly occurred. But Belleus makes this reported laughter work to his advantage. He uses it to control his lady's reaction, claiming the mistaken dialogic of his sexual transgression, thereby reassuring the lady of his own masculinity through his perception of and embarrassment at the mistake, and giving his lady no grounds for punishment on

---

[37] Indeed, Malory never reports whether or not Belleus actually told his lady of the kisses, but his embarrassed laughter following his explanation would indicate that the incident was related accurately. Malory chooses to summarize the incident, perhaps out of a narratorial awareness of his audience's textual experience.

that count.[38] Through Belleus's attempt to manipulate his lady's perception, his own laughter becomes both disciplining of Belleus's own mistake, and liberating for its provision of a means of escape from the lady's censure.

But despite Belleus's attempt to shape his lady's perspective, she feels it necessary to punish their behaviour. She turns to Lancelot and constructs her penance around his role in chivalric discourse:

> 'Sir,' seyde the lady, 'I require the, telle me what knyght thou art, and what is youre name.'
>
> 'Fayre lady,' he seyde, 'my name is sir Launcelot du Lake.'
>
> 'So me thought ever by youre speche,' seyde the lady, 'for I have sene you oftyn or this, and I know you bettir than ye wene. But now wolde ye promyse me of youre curtesye, for the harmys that ye have done to me and my lorde, sir Belleus, that whan ye com unto kyng Arthurs courte for to cause hym to be made knyght of the Rounde Table? For he is a passyng good man of armys and a myghty lorde of londys of many oute iles.'(154)

It would appear that Belleus's lady does not find her lover's mistake as comical as the knights do. She ignores the sexual transgression, just as Belleus hoped she would, by setting a task to requite the 'harmys' done to her lover. Belleus is a worthy knight, she says, and Lancelot has wronged him by giving him a wound; therefore, as a sign of respect to Belleus, Lancelot should sponsor him as a Round Table knight. But when she gives this task to Lancelot, she manipulates the results of the encounter in much the same way as Belleus attempted to manipulate her response through laughter. She recognizes Lancelot, a feat which even his fellow knights have a hard time accomplishing in the *Morte*, and attempts to strategically rehabilitate the masculine relationship of the knights. Her task for Lancelot involves the reestablishing of Belleus's chivalric identity by including him in the Round Table knights, a brotherhood which is at least explicitly heterosexual. By becoming a member of this elite brotherhood, Belleus and Lancelot's relationship is recast in fraternal terms, where two chivalric males are allowed affection for each other without deviant sexual connotations. Thus the knights' kisses are not negated, nor are they forgotten, but instead, the new fraternal relationship of Belleus and Lancelot reinterprets their meaning, pulling them away from the comic and reassigning their significance to the chivalric idiom.

---

[38] Christine Davies similarly argues concerning jokes about intelligence in 'Stupidity and Rationality: Jokes from the Iron Cage', in *Humor in Society: Resistance and Control*, ed. by Chris Powell and George Paton (NY: St. Martin's Press, 1988), p. 5. She asserts that when a person tells a joke about 'stupidity,' the teller reassures him or herself that he/she is not 'stupid.'

Moreover, Belleus's inclusion among the knights of the Round Table also reifies the gender integrity of the relationship of Belleus to his lady. By being included in the knightly goings-on of Camelot, Belleus will be in a position for his lady to watch his exploits. As their relationship exists, the lady has to travel to a pavilion apart from any organized chivalric community where public display defines an individual's gender. The pavilion, isolated from the chivalric community, becomes a place where gender (Lancelot's in this case) can become clouded because of the lady's absence. Belleus's inclusion in Camelot's culture will provide an arena which will codify and recodify his and his lady's gender with every joust and public action.

Unlike the previous two examples of gender comedy in the *Morte*, the scene at Belleus's pavilion allows for a dialogic of gender in the chivalric setting. Lancelot and Belleus are comfortable enough with Belleus's gender mistake to laugh at it for what it is, however anxiously. Their laughter minimizes their deviant behaviour for the sake of Belleus's lady, and liberates their anxieties surrounding the homoerotic potential of the kiss, resulting in a new relationship constructed from Camelot's chivalric brotherhood.

In examining the gender comedy of the *Morte Darthur*, we ultimately discover two apparently contradictory functions of the comic moment: subversion of chivalric gender, and authentication of chivalric culture. The subversion of cross-gendering and the laughter it generates coincide with Christine Davies' arguments concerning ethnic jokes, that social hierarchy is reinforced by humour which creates 'outsiders,' or those who are not a part of the social, ethnic, or political power structure.[39] These outsiders are laughed at not because they are inept or stupid, but because they have been targeted to represent, even for a moment, the anxieties of the dominant culture. Outsiders are laughed at for their 'failures' in order to reiterate the success of the dominant culture and to reassure the mockers of their own subjectivity. In the *Morte*, for example, the damsel Alys is reprimanded through laughter for her attempt to become a knight; Alysaundir and the lady Alys laugh at her 'failure,' and in doing so, discipline the behaviour of the damsel and make legitimate their own subjectivity in chivalric gender.

But this deviance-discipline corollary involves a kind of subversive pleasure, and one that works, in turn, to make legitimate the characters' gender flexibility. The laughter resulting from gender-crossing comedy can build chivalric community, as it does at Surluse, and proclaim knightly authenticity as it does for Alysaundir and the Alyses. Laughter can also act as a tool for social ascension for characters such as Belleus, and as a declaration of knightly honour for Lancelot at the Great Tour-

---

[39] Davies, *Humor in Society,* p. 5.

nament. Despite the dialogizing of the characters' gender roles, the pleasure of the laughter in these scenes has a distinctly constructive purpose: to solidify the role of the knight outside of the gender categories which chivalric discourses advocate.

The audiences' laughter at scenes of cross-dressing and cross-gendering and the apparently contradictory roles such gender confusion serves displays a dialogic between the dictates of dominant culture and the manifestation of pleasure. While dominant thought may determine the definitions of gender in the chivalric idiom, in the scenes of gender comedy in the *Morte*, pleasure resists such categorization by subverting the basis on which chivalric gender is formed and reinforcing other, more distinct truths of knighthood: community, authenticity, and honour.

8

Getting Even:
Social Control and Uneasy Laughter in the Croxton *Play of the Sacrament*[1]

MIRIAMNE ARA KRUMMEL

> Facts never speak for themselves; interpretations create knowledge.[2]
>
> – R. Po-Chia Hsia

The fact is that the Croxton *Play of the Sacrament* presents a willful misinterpretation of Jewishness. Drama, such as the Croxton *Play of the Sacrament*, reveals to us that in medieval, East Anglian culture myths about Host desecration and real presence were interpreted as facts.[3] But facts change, as do

---

[1] A shorter version of this article was presented in the session, Medieval English Comedy, 38th International Congress on Medieval Studies, Kalamazoo, Michigan (11 May 2003). I would like to extend a note of deep thanks to my colleagues Matthew Adkins and Rebecca Potter; their careful attention to my prose has only improved the quality of the text that follows. All mistakes are my own.

[2] R. Po-Chia Hsia, *The Myth of Ritual Murder: Jews and Magic in Reformation Germany* (New Haven: Yale University Press, 1988), p. 13.

[3] For specific details about the Croxton play, see Gail McMurray Gibson, *The Theater of Devotion: East Anglian Drama and Society in the Late Middle Ages* (Chicago: University of Chicago Press, 1989), pp. 19-46. See also Sarah Beckwith, *Signifying God: Social Relation and Symbolic Act in the York Corpus Christi Plays* (Chicago: University of Chicago Press, 2001).

interpretations of those facts. The Croxton play seems committed to repeating antisemitic and Christian anti-Judaic gestures. Simultaneous to the repetition of the anti-Judaic refrain, though, the Croxton play interrogates a philosemitic impulse, which although barely evident, is present and navigates something new, something like philosemitism, in the catalogue of medieval English anti-Jewish gestures.[4] The Jew, a rather multiplex character whose devotionalism is immediately evident, evolves over the course of the play from misled to informed. In the middle of the play, nonetheless, audiences are introduced to the familiar stereotype of the profligate Jew – an integral part of the economy of cultic anti-Judaism – whom we see in all the Jewish merchants' eagerly performed commitments to torturing the body of Christ.[5]

The Croxton play details five Jews, five Host desecrators, acting as community-destroyers by expressing both 'contempt for Christianity and evil intent towards God in His eucharistic manifestation'.[6] By the close of the play, however, these same Jews exhibit signs of kindness and godliness after they receive Christian truth. Through the Jews' transformation – one of the dramas of the play – the audience discovers that, despite its dormancy, a human core can emerge from the Jew.[7] In this way the Croxton play records for us, its twenty first century readers, a fact that by the late-fifteenth century, Jews could be mapped in two sites – the psychic ge-

---

[4] David Katz considers philo-semitism to involve a sympathetic view of Jews: *Philo-Semitism and the Return of the Jews to England, 1603-1655* (Oxford: Clarendon Press, 1982).

[5] The libelous representation of Jew, as features of ritual murder tales, is handled ably by Po-Chia Hsia and Miri Rubin. See Po-Chia Hsia's *The Myth of Ritual Murder*; and Rubin's *Gentile Tales: The Narrative Assault on Late Medieval Jews* (New Haven: Yale University Press, 1999). On cultic anti-Judaism, see Denise L. Despres, 'Cultic Anti-Judaism and Chaucer's Litel Clergeon', *Modern Philology* 91 (1994), 413-27.

[6] Rubin, *Gentile Tales*, p. 28. These Jews exist to destroy the community (of theater and of church). Or rather, as Lisa Lampert-Weissig remarks, the Jew performs as the local East Anglian 'perpetually present enemy ever plotting against Christ and Christendom' (p. 248); see Lisa Lampert, 'The once and future Jew: The Croxton *Play of the Sacrament*, little Robert of Bury and historical memory', *Jewish History* 15 (2001), 235-55.

[7] Importantly for this point, even before Jonathas is converted, his mercantilistic attitude remains respectful of 'Machomet' (l.69); it strikes me that the text is eager to show that Jonathas's conversion is more a result of destiny than force. Forcibly converted identities can stray, of course. All further references to the *Play of the Sacrament*, including citations of the stage directions (cited as s.d.), will be taken from Greg Walker's edition *Medieval Drama* (Malden: Blackwell, 2000), pp. 213-33, and will be cited in the body of the text, according to the line number or, in the case of stage directions, the nearest line number to the cited material.

ography of the imaginary and the physical geography of the territory – two sites that need not be mutually exclusive.[8]

This complex play with its multiple geographies and various semitisms is also negotiating the genres of tragedy and comedy.[9] Tragedy, surfacing in the imaginary pain endured by the Host, is translated into comedy at the expense of the Jewish merchants whose future misery in the imagined geography of Hell is a secret that the Christian audience nourishes. Even more, the tragedy of the Host's torment is rendered comedic through the unspoken but expected anticipation of this future misery. Comedic elements also manifest in the closing marriage celebration of Jewish and Christian bodies as two different identities become one. In this new geography that the Croxton play designs, Jewish bodies can be mapped onto Christian bodies to counteract those Christian bodies, such as Aristorius's, whose abiding belief in the mercantilistic system does not fit into the new Christian economy, where the 'great devocion' (l.928) of five old Jews/new Christians reduces the spiritual flaws of one Christian. Whether comedically or tragically, as Host desecrators or as New Christians, the Jews unite the community and underwrite its need to close ranks and to protect itself from an imagined foreign violence and invasion.

Why continue to rehearse Jewish presence – nearly two hundred years after their expulsion when Jewish pastness was decreed a certainty? Denise L. Despres argues that the rehearsal of Jewish presence signifies a permanent investment in medieval Christian theology.[10] David Lawton theorizes that the Jew and the Host, united in

---

[8] As I have long thought and as David Lawton has recently contemplated, Jews may have reentered the East Anglian landscape by the fifteenth century. See his 'Sacrilege and Theatricality: the Croxton *Play of the Sacrament*', *Journal of Medieval and Early Modern Studies* 33 (2003), p. 293.

[9] John R. Elliott, Jr's. helpful definitions of comedy and tragedy are instructive here: 'Comedy begins in adversity and ends in joy; Tragedy begins in prosperity and ends in misery' (p. 159; capitalizations his). While I may start with these definitions, my work complicates the 'ritual-comic structure' (p. 160) that Elliott explicates. In the piece that follows, I question what precipitates the comedy in and of that ritual comic structure. For Elliott's essay, see 'The Sacrifice of Isaac as Comedy and Tragedy', *Medieval English Drama: Essays Critical and Contextual*, ed. by Jerome Taylor and Alan H. Nelson (Chicago: University of Chicago Press, 1972), pp. 157-76.

[10] See Despres, 'Cultic Anti-Judaism and Chaucer's Litel Clergeon', pp. 413-27; and Despres's 'The Protean Jew in the Vernon Manuscript' *Chaucer and the Jews: Sources, Contexts, Meanings*, ed. by Sheila Delany (New York: Routledge, 2002), pp. 145-64. See also Despres's 'Immaculate Flesh and the Social Body: Mary and the Jews', *Jewish History* 12 (1998), 47-69; in this piece Despres concludes that 'representations of Jewish carnality, physicality, and literalism, which had once served to denigrate corporeality in the here and

their instability, point toward community, theatricality, performance, and illusion.[11] Also thinking of issues of community, Steven Kruger observes that the Jews of the Croxton play are 'chastened Jews [. . .] accepted into the body of the Christian community', for in the end of the play, the Jews convert en masse.[12] In fact, this conversion itself has a performance in the Croxton play, attesting to the needful pastness of Jews: Jews-as-Jews had to be made 'fully *past*' because 'to put Judaism to rest, to kill it off' would 'make way for the new, Christian dispensation'.[13] I see a metonymic link to the construction of the Bible, for just as the Hebrew Bible had to disappear and become a prelude as the Old Testament, the Jews of the Croxton play had to let go of the old order and embrace the new one to fit into the community. No longer needful, the Croxton Jews, like the Old Testament, have become precursors to what is really there and really present. In this piece I speak of slippages that awake a very real anxiety about the internal Otherness that conversion instantiates by exploring the text's negotiations of dark comedy as it anxiously erases the subversion to the sacralized belief in real presence and blurs the racial boundaries between converted Jewish and lapsing Christian bodies.[14]

The Drama of the Croxton Play

The Croxton *Play of the Sacrament* is a fifteenth-century non-cycle text that dramatizes the antisemitic legend of the Jewish desecration of the Christian Host. The main characters in this dramatic effort are five Jews, one Christian merchant, and

---

now, surely evolved to reflect or meet the needs of a dynamic and sometimes conflicting Christian sacramental theology, devotionalism, and ritual culture' (p. 64).

[11] Lawton, 'Sacrilege and Theatricality', pp. 294-97.

[12] Steven F. Kruger, 'The Bodies of Jews in the Late Middle Ages', *The Idea of Medieval Literature: New Essays on Chaucer and Medieval Culture*, ed. by James M. Dean and Christian K. Zacher (Newark: University of Delaware Press, 1992), p. 317.

[13] Kruger, 'The Spectral Jew', *New Medieval Literatures* 2 (1998), p. 11; emphasis his.

[14] A caveat: I understand that categories of race are uninformed claims made at the expense of Black and Jewish bodies (among others). I use this category purposefully. For visual examples of racial differences, see Ruth Mellinkoff who has amassed a fine corpus of such medieval racist gestures in her *Antisemitic Hate Signs in Hebrew Illuminated Manuscripts from Medieval Germany* (Jerusalem: Center for Jewish Art, 1999); and her *Outcasts: Signs of Otherness in Northern European Art of the Late Middle Ages*, 2 vols. (Berkeley: University of California Press, 1993). For a very convincing and lively discussion of the views of medieval racialisms, see Thomas Hahn, 'The Difference the Middle Ages Makes: Color and Race before the Modern World', *The Journal of Medieval and Early Modern Studies* 31 (2001), 1-37; and Robert L. A. Clark and Clare Sponsler, 'Othered Bodies: Racial Crossdressing in the *Mistere de la Sainte Hostie* and the *Croxton Play of the Sacrament*', *Journal of Medieval and Early Modern Studies* 29 (1999), 61-87 (pp. 61-67).

the Host itself. At the hands of each of the five Jews (Jonathas, Jason, Jasdon, Masphat, and Malchus), the sacrament undergoes a series of trials, which include stabbing and burning 'the little biscuit'.[15] The purpose of these trials is to test the doctrine of real presence. Understood another way the five Jews test the Christian story that Christ's body is housed in the sacramental wafer. A test like this invariably unleashes a threat that only the comedy of superiority theory can ably contain.

Although the trials that the sacrament endures establish Jewish villainy, the Jews are not the only villains of this drama. That is, the Jews are not solely responsible for the punishment that the wafer must undergo, for the purchase of what is described as 'Yowr God, that ys full mytheti, in a cake' (1.205) is an arrangement that is made between two merchants, one who is Jewish and one who is Christian. In fact, it is the Christian merchant, Aristorius, who drives the harder bargain by fiercely bartering on the Host: before Aristorius will produce the sacrament, Aristorius demands from Jonathas payment of 'an hundder pownd' (1.208) for the exchange. In return, Jonathas, the Jewish merchant, shows himself to be a worthy foe in arbitration. Jonathas argues that Aristorius's sum is too rich and, thus, resists Aristorius's financial demands by trying to negotiate a much lower sum. Jonathas's resistance is expected because Jonathas cannot know the value of the sacrament as it carries no fetishistic purchase for him as a Jew. Aristorius's act, however, disrupts the social fabric of the Christian economy and that disruption precipitates textual negotiation. Aristorius neither voices concern over his mercantilistic actions nor expresses woe over having sold the host into a situation that will invariably involve bondage and scourging.[16] The eventual outcome is that Jonathas agrees to Aristorius's sum. The Host is produced, sold from a Christian merchant to a Jewish merchant for 'an hundder pownd'.

---

[15] See Sarah Beckwith's 'Ritual, Church and Theatre: Medieval Dramas of the Sacramental Body', in *Culture and History, 1350-1600: Essays on English Communities, Identities and Writing*, ed. by David Aers (Detroit: Wayne State University Press, 1992), pp. 65-89. I use the words of Sarah Beckwith to indicate, as she does, that the 'host, the little biscuit, is a mere stage prop' (p. 68). I mean to underscore that this play, even as it tries to make profound arguments about real presence, cannot completely contain the possibility that the miracle is 'so blatantly theatricalised' that 'the effect is at least potentially parodic' (p. 68).

[16] Gavin I. Langmuir, *Toward a Definition of Antisemitism* (Berkeley: University of California Press, 1990), is very clear on this issue of Jewish and Christian usury: to a public, Langmuir notes, that wants to deny any Christian involvement in the moneylending industry, the Jew was an easy target to 'stereotype' as 'the archetypical usurer' (p. 10). Langmuir explains that Christians were involved in usury and that part of our memory about Jewish involvement in this industry is due to historians who emphasized Jewish involvement and overlooked Christian participation (pp. 26-31).

The tension of this moment between Aristorius and Jonathas is only further com-plicated by later events in the play, for from the reality of bartering for the sacrament emerges the very real issue that personal gain drives both of these merchants. Yet while the Christian and Jewish merchant alike are invested in their worldly efforts, their sense of the payoff widely differs. Aristorius not only wants to maintain his position as 'A merchaunte myghty, of a royall araye' (1.10) but also desires to fos-ter his fame: 'Ful wyde in þis worlde spryngyth my fame' (1.11). Jonathas's desire for goods, alternatively, departs from Aristorius's largely prototypical capitalistic impulse. While Aristorius's interests lie only with himself and what he can attain for himself, Jonathas remains attentive to his God, 'Machomet', whom Jonathas is careful to remember – 'Now, almyghty Machomet, marke yn þi mageste, / Whose lawes tendrely I have to fulfyll' (ll.69-70). Jonathas duly pays homage to his lord, proclaiming 'Machomet' as the author of all his amassed riches:

> For I thanke þee hayly, þat hast me sent
> Gold, sylver, and presyous stonys;
> And abunddaunce of spycys þou hast me lent.
>   (ll.77-79)

Jonathas is clearly more faithful to his (albeit superseded) god than Aristorius is to his. (If there is any possibly present philosemitism, it surfaces in this exchange of the host.)

In writing this moment of exchange into the narrative, the Croxton play points to-ward a deep problem. Jonathas's god, although the superseded and artifactual one, receives more devotion that the spiritual embodiment of the one true God (so the story goes). The crisis of this moment – this shimmer to the fabric of the Christian hegemony – literally sets the stage for what follows. And so the text works urgently to show that God is always present and that once reformed, the evil Others – the Jews with unnatural impulses and misguided beliefs – have the potential to trans-form into community creators.[17]

This moment of the merchants' devotion admits multiple subversions into the text.[18] Both Jonathas's loyalty to Machomet and Aristorius's loyalty to his own personal gain subvert Christian faith. Through both merchants' acquisitiveness another sub-

---

[17] I consciously use the term 'evil Other' rather than Lawton's 'Oriental Other'; see Lawton, 'Sacrilege and Theatricality', p. 284.

[18] My consideration of subversion and containment – and even what later figures as the recorded voices of the Jews – are indebted to the work of Stephen Greenblatt. See, espe-cially Greenblatt's 'Invisible Bullets' in *Shakespearean Negotiations: The Circulation of Social Energy in Renaissance England* (Berkeley: University of California Press, 1988), pp. 21-65; and Jonathan Dollimore, *Radical Tragedy: Religion, Ideology and Power in the*

version, equal in force to the first, filters into the text, and this subversion commands the question: whose faith system and which cultural economy is meant to prevail? Of course, we know what the text wants the audience to answer, but did the audience of the *Play of the Sacrament* know the outcome of these merchants' exchange and acquisitiveness? Probably. Despite this probability, the text remains eager to manage its multiple subversions. Both moments of subversion, for instance, are eventually contained by presenting Machomet as a god that supports any type of fiscal gain for personal ends. Machomet's assistance with Jonathas's financial (and worldly) dreams signifies that Jonathas's god supports acquisition of matters of the flesh and not the spirit.[19] And so the Croxton play illustrates for the audience that both of these merchants need to revise their advocacy of and belief in mercantilism. The other subversion – the one that Aristorius introduces into the text by selling 'the little biscuit' – requires patient textual negotiation to reduce its threat to the fabric of *Christianitas*. Much of this threat to the doctrine of real presence is managed through an epic stage moment when the literal body of Christ emerges from the sacrament: 'Here the ovyn must ryve asunder and blede owt at þe cranys, and an image appere owt with woundys bledyng' (l.632, s.d.). Despite Christ's appearance, some of the aftereffects of this threat to real presence remain.

Importantly, Aristorius does not witness this epic moment seemingly saved for only the Jews to see. In fact, it is here in this moment that the *Play of the Sacrament* forestalls the misapprehension that there could be allosemitic possibilities in the text.[20] While the *Play of the Sacrament* forgives the Jews their transgressions and allows them in the end to fortify the Christian social myth where they had previously worked to destroy it, this complicated impulse – allosemitism (where the Jew who is simultaneously imagined as a community-destroyer and a community-creator) – both underwrites and undermines the Jew.[21] That is, while the Croxton play

---

Drama of Shakespeare and his Contemporaries, 2nd ed (Durham: Duke University Press, 1993).

[19] Lampert's words in *Gender and Jewish Difference from Paul to Shakespeare* (Philadelphia: University of Pennsylvania Press, 2004) encapsulate the matter well: 'Jews were regarded as blinded by the veil of the letter, doomed to carnal understandings of their Scriptures and of the world. [. . .] Christian hermeneutics rely upon a supersessionist understanding of Jewish scripture and of Jews and Judaism that figures Jewish particularity as both origin and stubborn remainder' (p. 10).

[20] I use 'allosemitism' to signify a simultaneous urge to loathe and to love the Jew. For more detailed discussion of allosemitism, see Zygmunt Bauman, 'Allosemitism: Premodern, Modern, Postmodern', *Modernity, Culture, and "the Jew"*, ed. by Bryan Cheyette and Laura Marcus (Stanford: Stanford University Press, 1998), pp. 143-56.

[21] Community-creator and community-destroyer are my own words, but they are informed by Elaine Scarry's work in *The Body in Pain: The Making and Unmaking of the World* (New York: Oxford University Press, 1985).

initially seems to represent the Jews in a positive way, Jonathas is as equally misguided as is Aristorius. The most important difference between Aristorius's and
Jonathas's misjudgment is that Aristorius knows better: Aristorius, presumably
nourished by the Christian economy from cradle to grave, is better informed about
Christian behavior than is Jonathas, who has (only) occupied a space in the Jewish
margins. This point is further emphasized when at the end of the play, the five Jews
are converted, and it is Aristorius who still does not quite fit into the picture and
who must wander the earth as penance for his un-Christian deed. As Aristorius
proclaims, 'Into my contre now wyll I fare / For to amende myn wyckyd lyfe'
(ll.892-93). Aristorius's new peripatetic identity demonstrates for the audience that
it is one thing to be ignorant of Christian revelation, as are the Jews, but to know
and yet have doubt, as does Aristorius, is unacceptable. Aristorius will wander the
world as a nomad, and the Jews (as New Christians) will now be able to settle in
one land. With this lesson about subversive desire disseminated and controlled, the
play ends as it begins by vigilantly reminding its audience that the miracle of real
presence occurred in real time – namely, that the 'myracle was don in the forest of
Aragon, in the famous cite of Eraclea, the yere of owr Lord God Ml CCC. lxi'
(l.927, s.d.).

This play, however it yearns to represent itself, remains deeply mercurial. In many
ways the Croxton play is yet another charge against the Jews who are all too often
fictionalized as Host desecrators. In fact, the Jews' appearance in the role of Host
desecrator is most unfortunate not only for its frequency but also because of the
accompanying Christian anti-Judaic gestures that this role obtains.[22] In such stories
the Jew is permanently fixed as the 'perpetually present enemy'.[23] Always (in)visible
and never really there, the Jew is trotted out to represent important heresies that are
simultaneously present (because heresies are real) and absent (because the national
script disavows the presence of real threats). As such, this play and its Jews have
been understood as part of a device of strategic propaganda, designed to educate
Christians about the doctrine of real presence.[24]

I offer a new possibility. Given that the Jews were expelled in 1290 and that the
power of the Lollard 'heresy' had exhausted itself by 1453, it is probable that both

---

[22] For a more complete sense of the mythology connected to Host desecration, see Rubin,
Gentile Tales; and Lampert, 'The once and future Jew'.

[23] Lampert, 'Once and Future Jew', p. 248.

[24] Of course, the demand to educate and to enlighten was always present in the text, and
many scholars have spoken about this impulse. See Donnalee Dox 'Medieval Drama as
Documentation: "Real Presence" in the Croxton *Conversion of Ser Jonathas the Jewe by the
Myracle of the Blissed Sacrament*', *Theatre Survey* 38 (1997), 97-115 (pp. 107-10); Gibson,
The Theater of Devotion, p. 35; and Clark and Sponsler, 'Othered Bodies', pp. 61-87.

the Jew and the Lollard are more likely to inflame impotent paranoia than to pose a direct threat against Christian hegemony.[25] And so, I read the Croxton text as eager to render the Jew more of an absence than a presence.[26] This is not to say that there is an absence of five very real Jewish characters (with very real Jewish bodies) in the *Play of the Sacrament*. These Jews are very present in the play. But rather than typologically static representations, the Jews serve as a prism. As such, the Jews represent all heresies that pose a threat to the medieval Christian hegemony. Among these heresies, Lollardy is one, and Judaism is another. The Jews, while rendered more overtly than the Lollards, are also more complex than mere presence suggests or even for that matter simple absence indicates. The Jews are absent as Jews – that is, the Jews do not figure as only Jews as much as they signify as Jews, Lollards, and all Other threats. The Jews are at once themselves and also every threat to the national (and national includes religious) unity that their presence lets in. Steven Kruger rightly postulates that questions of 'deep *nervousness* about the body. [. . .] cannot be directly asked by Christians. [. . .] the central ritual of Christianity [. . .] can be projected outward, onto foreign bodies'.[27] To Kruger's point I add that questions about 'the central ritual of Christianity' *must* 'be projected outward, onto foreign bodies'. Like the stock character, Everyman, of the morality play *Everyman*, the Jews of the Croxton *Play of the Sacrament* represent an Everythreat. Even more, the idea of Everythreat explains the narrative strategy of making the Jews responsible for proving the efficacy of the doctrine of real presence. One way of controlling the anxiety about the Jewish threat to Christianity (despite so many efforts to erase Jewishness, Jewishness continues to figure in the medieval world) is deploying dark comedy to ridicule the Jewish Other whose actions threaten the social order of the Latin Church. Here Jewish misprison becomes laughable. Another way of containing the Jewish threat is to diminish that threat by making it appear as if Jewishness is not only completely containable but also controllable like other threats, such as Lollardy.

---

[25] By 1431, it was unlikely, as Dox mentions and as John A. F. Thomson and Margaret Aston particularize, that the Lollards would be able to wage a successful campaign against their religious adversaries. See Dox, 'Medieval Drama as Documentation', p. 108; John A. F. Thomson, *The Later Lollards, 1414-1520* (New York: Oxford University Press, 1965), pp. 1-19; Margaret Aston, *Lollards and Reformers: Images and Literacy in Late Medieval Religion* (London: Hambledon Press, 1984), pp. 1-47. By the time that the Croxton play was performed, the Lollard threat posed itself more as a subversion to the fabric of the national economy than as a visible uprising like that which occurred in 1381.

[26] On the subject of deploying absent and present Jewishness in the cultural and political economy, see Sylvia Tomasch, 'Postcolonial Chaucer and the Virtual Jew', in *The Postcolonial Middle Ages*, ed. by Jeffrey Jerome Cohen (New York: St. Martin's Press, 2000), pp. 243-60; and Steven F. Kruger, 'The Spectral Jew'.

[27] Kruger, 'The Bodies of Jews in the Late Middle Ages', p. 319 (italics his).

Everythreat, as I coin this term, is a character who can usefully disguise the Christian doubt over real presence as a Jewish worry. Everythreat can only be contained through the gestures of comedy – not a glib or light-hearted comedy, but rather a type of comedy that is terrifying in its profundity. The Everythreat, even more, needs to be embodied. I understand the Croxton text to investigate the bodies of Jews and the body of Christ. The *Play of the Sacrament*, that is, specifically queries real presence through a humour that aims to disembody the Jew, the butt of the joke, at the same time that the play embodies Christ, the future of all (Christian) histories. Relying upon a grotesque humour and the grotesquerie of the Jews whose Jewish bodies become a postcolonial palimpsest that drives the forward movement of the *Play of the Sacrament*, the grandeur of Christ's body appears in all its awesome presence at the conclusion of the Croxton play. In this way visual embodiment resolves the crisis: Everythreat is contained through Christ's visible, speaking body.[28]

Comedic Anxiety and the Tragic Self

Both the Wakefield *Noah* and the Towneley *Second Shepherds' Play* provide examples of medieval comedy.[29] *Noah* borrows from medieval fabliau and fashions a 'comic war of the sexes' when Noah's wife stubbornly refuses to enter into the ark because, as she explains disdainfully, 'I was never bard ere, as ever might I the, / In sich an oostré as this!' (328-29).[30] The *Second Shepherds' Play* similarly dramatizes lack of insight through both the display of general confusion about the faux baby and the interactions among the characters who play the shepherds and the

---

[28] I have in mind Bakhtin's closing thoughts to 'The Grotesque Image of the Body and Its Sources': 'in the grotesque concept of the body a new, concrete, and realistic historic awareness was born and took form: not abstract thought about the future but the living sense that each man belongs to the immortal people who create history' (p. 367). See Mikhail Bakhtin, *Rabelais and His World*, trans. by Hélène Iswolsky (Bloomington: Indiana University Press, 1984).

[29] For a non-allegorical, secular view of the comedic moments in these plays, see Charles Mills Gayley, *Plays of our Forefathers and Some of the Traditions Upon Which They Were Founded* (New York: Duffield, 1907), pp. 166-68, who discusses the comedy in *Noah*. Jeffrey Helterman, *Symbolic Action in the Plays of the Wakefield Master* (Athens: University of Georgia Press, 1981), explores the comedic elements in *Noah*, pp. 59-69; and in the *Second Shepherds' Play*, pp. 95-103.

[30] See *Medieval Drama*, ed. by David Bevington (Boston: Houghton Mifflin, 1975), p. 290. All further references to the Wakefield *Noah* are taken from *Medieval Drama*, pp. 290-307, and will be cited in the body of the text.

country folk, Mak and Gyll.[31] The play is nearly over (586 of the 754 lines have been spoken) before the epiphany occurs. Until that moment shepherds one and three remain duped:

> Gyf me lefe hym to kys, and lyft up the clowtt   [cloth]
> What the Dewill is this? He has a long snowte.

To which shepherd one responds:

> He is merkyd amys. We wate ill abowte.   [We do wrong to pry]
> (584-86)

So eager to believe that the sheep is a baby, the shepherds prefer illusion over reality. The second shepherd, however, recognizes the depth of their delusion: 'Ill-spon weft, iwys, ay commys foull owte/ [. . .] / It was hee frawde (the foulness of ill spun material, indeed, will always be apparent [. . .] It was high fraud) (ll.587, 594). Yet more shenanigans unfold before heavenly intervention (in the form of an angel, l.637 s.d.) interrupts the comedy.

The Croxton *Play of the Sacrament* also engages with comedic design as do *Noah* and the *Second Shepherds' Play*, yet the comedy of superiority theory – so comfortably deployed when a woman and when poor country folk are the butts of the joke – is, perhaps, less easily recognizable when five Jews compel the sacramental wafer to undergo a series of painful trials. As with *Noah* and the *Second Shepherds' Play*, the serious nature of the *Play of the Sacrament* does not foreclose comedic possibilities. The comedy of the Croxton play, like that of *Noah* and the *Second Shepherds' Play*, is at once comedic and not comedic (if we reflect on what generates humour). The Croxton play invites a response fraught with stupefaction at the absurd behavior of the Jews just as the inappropriate fastidiousness of Noah's wife and the inane naivete of the shepherds obtains a sense of superiority: Noah's wife does not know that the ark will save her; the shepherds cannot distinguish between a sheep and a baby; the Jews do not know that Christ's body rests inside the sacramental wafer. (How stupid they all are!)

The Jews of the Croxton *Play of the Sacrament* are agents of absurdity in their darkly comedic and farcical attempt to disprove Christ's presence in the sacramental wafer. It is not enough that five strokes make the Host bleed or that 'the Host sticks to [Jonathas's] hand' (l.418, s.d.) to avoid being thrown into a cauldron of boiling oil. The Jews then 'fasten the Sacrament' – and presumably Jonathas's hand – to a 'post' (l.431, s.d.). Still, not finished with their tests, Jonathas's four fellow

---

[31] See the Towneley *Second Shepherds' Play* in *Medieval Drama*, ed. by Walker, pp. 42-57. All further references to this play are taken from this edition.

Jews rip off his arm ('pluke þe arme') while the hand – with the Host nailed to it – remains on the post: 'þe hand shall hang styll with þe Sacrament' (1.435, s.d.). Now the Jews have a problem. And having forgotten why they started this trial, they march off to a doctor, and there discover that the doctor's servant is smarter than the doctor. In an episode that reminds us of the narrator's slow-witted incredulousness in Geoffrey Chaucer's *The Book of the Duchess*, Master Brandyche arranges to have his servant approach Jonathas, who is missing a hand, and ask Jonathas 'In a pott yf yt please yow to pysse' because only then 'he can tell yf yow be curable' (ll.568, 567). Very Three Stooges. But there is more: Jason pulls the nails out of Jonathas's dismembered hand, drops the hand into a cauldron, and out pops Jesus who addresses (and here the text negotiates a moment of doctrinal seriousness) the Jews' questions and their doubt.

The Croxton play remains always aware of its theatricality and of its play-fullness. The three scaffolds, a presumably large table, and the various other items necessary for performance, including a cauldron large enough to admit a man, instantiate the presence of theatrical self-awareness.[32] Croxton, thus, represents a religious moment through a text that has the potential to figure as a 'jeu', a game, and part of that game involves playing with Jewish perspicacity in the interlude with Master Brandyche and his servant Colle.[33] This moment of certain slapstick reminds the audience that servants know more than masters, that insight resides in the unlikeliest of places. Indeed, sometimes, as Jody Enders reveals, these medieval scripts proximated the gestures unique to contemporary snuff film.[34] This link that Enders pursues might also apply to the Croxton play. Profoundly aware of deploying medieval production technology, the Croxton play overtly directs the Jewish merchants to 'pluke þe arme' so that Jonathas's 'hand shall hang styll with the Sacrament'. This is the same hand that with 'an hamer and nayles iii [. . .] They fasten the Sacrament [and Jonathas's hand] to the post' (ll.428, 430 s.d.). Perhaps, 'the "playing" of violence' is enacted 'just for laughs'?[35] Even more, the doctrinal message – carefully negotiated only after Jonathas has suffered a bit – is disseminated through two bodies in pain: one, Christ, whose absent present body in pain morphs

---

[32] Darryll Grantley, 'Saints' Plays', in *The Cambridge Companion to Medieval English Theatre*, ed. by Richard Beadle (New York: Cambridge University Press, 1994), pp. 265-89, discusses the technology necessary to perform the Croxton play.

[33] See Lawrence M. Clopper, *Drama, Play, and Game: English Festive Culture in the Medieval and Early Modern Period* (Chicago: University of Chicago Press, 2001), pp. 1-24 (pp. 19-20).

[34] Jody Enders, *The Medieval Theater of Cruelty: Rhetoric, Memory, Violence* (Ithaca: Cornell University Press, 1999), pp. 202-22. Enders remarks that both the medieval stage and the contemporary snuff films literally 'promise dramas of life and death' (p. 24).

[35] Enders, *The Medieval Theater of Cruelty*, p. 199.

from disembodied to embodied and the other, Jonathas the Jew, whose presently doubting Jewish body in pain slowly transforms into a presenting believing Christian body in peace.[36] The play tells us that Jonathas cannot be reborn as Christian until he has suffered like Christ, for 'torture is a process which not only converts but announces conversion of every conceivable aspect of the event and the environment into an agent of pain. [. . .] the production of a fantastic illusion of power, torture is a grotesque piece of compensatory drama'.[37] The closing celebration of five converted Jews, in this way, necessitates pain as does Jesus's seemingly endless array of thrusts, jabs, and nailing, a succession of violent acts that mimics the crucifixion scene and details the deliberate, sanctioned, pleasurable cruelty that underwrites the spectacle of violence that both Jesus and Jonathas endure. In fact, the one Jew who expressed himself as god-fearing suffers the most.

In all, the fifteenth-century Croxton *Play of the Sacrament* is at once certain and uncertain about its dramatic identity and its interventions into the manifold conversations of late-medieval society. Among the many possible subjects that become important to this late-medieval culture, the *Play of the Sacrament* interrogates the validity of Christ's presence in the sacrament; underscores the wrongful nature of mercantilism; argues for the false belief system of the Jewish religion; and specifies the violent nature of the Jewish people.[38] The Croxton drama presents these four issues, what Seth Lerer considers to be signs of the 'narrative and performative transformations of the legal and social practices of bodily torture and corporeal mutilation', because these issues have immediate relevance to the doubting Christian.[39] In fact, the *Play of the Sacrament*, as its title foretells, imagines itself as focusing on one key motif that runs throughout the play: real presence, the doctrine that Christ's body is present in the sacramental Host.

---

[36] On this subject, see Scarry's *The Body in Pain*.

[37] Scarry, *The Body in Pain*, pp. 27-28.

[38] These subjects are addressed, respectively, by Norman F. Cantor, *The Civilization of the Middle Ages* (New York: HarperCollins, 1993), pp. 480-505; Jeremy Cohen, *Living Letters of the Law: Ideas of the Jew in Medieval Christianity* (Berkeley: University of California Press, 1999), pp. 317-63; and Langmuir, *Toward a Definition of Antisemitism*, pp. 197-262.

[39] Seth Lerer, '"Representyd now in yower syght": The Culture of Spectatorship in Late-Fifteenth-Century England', in *Bodies and Disciplines: Intersections of Literature and History in Fifteenth-Century England*, ed. by Barbara Hanawalt and David Wallace, Medieval Cultures, Vol. 9 (Minneapolis: University of Minnesota Press, 1996), pp. 29-62 (p. 31).

Overriding sacramental doubt is enacted through a narrative that relies on the ethics of history.[40] Organized around the need to present the irrefutable evidence of a
miracle, the Croxton play works hard to face down any uncertainties and deploys
the furniture of real time and real histories – what has been rightly characterized
as 'historical specificity' – to do so.[41] As the opening Banns insist, the miracles and
marvels 'off þe Holi and Blyssed Sacrament' (l.8) occurred in specific, historical
sites – namely, 'Aragon' (l.11), 'Eraclea' (l.12), and 'þe cyte of Surrey' (l.19). The
Croxton drama, thus, geographically maneuvers itself into mapped locations, in
this way fixing the authority of the miraculous events that follow. 'Aragon', 'Eraclea', and 'þe cyte of Surrey' affirm the miracle's truth even as the text proclaims
that the story is 'þe sothe to saye' (l.11); that 'þis full trewe!' (l.19). Another aspect
of this truth, in addition to its appearance in real time and at real places, is acquiring institutional instantiation. The Banns carefully affirm the play's events by re-
marking that 'thys marycle at Rome was presented, forsothe' (l.57). With so many
avowals of truth – 'sothe to saye'; 'full trewe'; 'forsothe' – it hardly seems necessary for the play to worry over doubt. Still, the play is very careful about conveying
its didactic message as evidenced in the doctrinal and geographical repetitions of
the play's close through the recitation of Episcopus's certain doctrinal imperatives
in the text's (final) mapping of place and time – 'in the forest of Aragon, in the
famous cite of Eraclea, the yere of owr Lord God Ml CCCC. lxi' (l.927, s.d.). The
Croxton play's anxieties about its genre – whether that genre is historical truth or
dramatic representation or something in between the two – speak to a certain urgent
desire to obviate doubt.

The Croxton play deploys humour to cleanse the English nation of all heresies.
Through the comedically absurd behaviour of an already Othered group emerges
a carnival of fools and clowns that erases sentiments of marginality in the audience

---

[40] There has been a fair amount of discussion about the genre of the Croxton play. My
claim, based on the presence of a (constructed) history, argues that the play forges a relationship between itself and a historical document. Martin Stevens finds that the Croxton play
exemplifies the qualities of a 'saint play' in addition to being a 'type of popular play' (p.
41); see his 'Medieval Drama: Genres, Misconceptions, and Approaches' in *Approaches to
Teaching Medieval Drama*, ed. by Richard K. Emmerson (New York: Modern Language
Association of America, 1990), pp. 36-49. In *Non-Cycle Plays and Fragments*, Norman
Davis understands the play to be 'the only thing of its kind in medieval English. [. . .]
concerned neither with Biblical narrative nor with the lives of the saints, but with an extraor-
dinary legend of the desecration of the Host by Jews and their ultimate conversion by the
miracles that follow'(p. lxxiii). Walker, however, considers the *Play of the Sacrament* to be
both a Miracle Play and a Conversion drama; see his *Medieval Drama*, p. 213-14. For the
mixture of features common to comedic mimes and tragic texts, see Miriamne Ara Krummel,
'The *Tale of Ceyx and Alceone*: Alceone's Agency and Gower's Audible Mime', *Exemplaria* 13 (2001), 497-528.

[41] Clark and Sponsler, 'Othered Bodies', p. 71.

and promotes feelings of both moral superiority and social homogeneity. In fact, in its humorous impulses, the Croxton play is very Bakhtinian, for in taking Christ's body down to size, the Jews unmake a disabling 'cosmic terror'.[42] In their ultimately grotesque actions, the Jews, importantly led by Jonathas – a character who also believes in a mystical and invisible Other – is the one whom all believers can certainly connect to, for Jonathas leads the Jews (and the audience) to obtain God's physical form. Even more, pushed off onto the Jews, the Jewish grotesquerie is a reasonable assumption because the Jews are imagined as believing in the flesh over the spirit (anyway). The laughter, then, in the *Play of the Sacrament* is humour derived at the expense of cultural Others (the Everythreat) who occupy the margins of society. Given this reading, whenever the Jew (the Everythreat) appears on the stage, a moment of (dark) comedy enters into the performance of the play as this figure, this Jew, this Everythreat, this stock character that represents 'the fool', always already poised to behave in some absurd and anti-social manner, walks onto the stage. The moral of the comedy is that Everythreat must be ridiculed to be contained.

Comedy That is Not (So) Funny

The space created by time fashions a site where what was once funny ceases to be funny: jokes, Guy Halsall explains, change 'through our interactions with other cultures'; if humour were to remain 'static' we would still be laughing 'at fifth-century western-European ethnic stereotypes and at hunchbacks wearing armour'.[43] We might also still be laughing at five Jews who are testing the efficacy of transubstantiation.

The hegemonic gestures within the *Play of the Sacrament* and the hegemon's transformation of fearsome things into laughable nonsense leads us to a theory of comedy first outlined by Thomas Hobbes in his *Leviathan*. Setting out to consider human nature, Hobbes discusses a sort of laughter that he terms 'sudden glory'.[44] Hobbes, identifying one of man's passions as 'sudden glory', theorizes that it

---

[42] 'Cosmic terror' are Bakhtin's words: see his *Rabelais and His World*, pp. 335-37.

[43] Guy Halsall, 'Introduction: "Don't worry, I've got the key"', *Humour, History and Politics in Late Antiquity and the Early Middle Ages*, pp. 1-21 (p. 11).

[44] See Thomas Hobbes, *Leviathan*, ed. by Michael Oakeshott (Oxford: Basil Blackwell, 1960), p. 36. Hobbes's 'sudden glory' is now known as 'superiority theory' by contemporary critics who study humour. A recent article in *The New Yorker* by Tad Friend, entitled 'What's So Funny? A Scientific Attempt to Discover Why We Laugh' (11 Nov. 2002), pp. 78-96, attributes the 'first full explanation' of 'superiority theory' to Hobbes (p. 80). See also Leonard Feinberg, *Introduction to Satire* (Ames: Iowa State University Press, 1967), concurs and identities Hobbes as 'the authority most often quoted' (p. 206). Ross, *The Language of*

is the passion which maketh those *grimaces* called LAUGHTER; and is caused either by some sudden act of their own, that pleaseth them; or by the apprehension of some deformed thing in another, by comparison whereof they suddenly applaud themselves. And it is incident most to them, that are conscious of the fewest abilities in themselves; who are forced to keep themselves in their own favor, by observing the imperfections of other men.[45]

Through the theory of 'sudden glory', Hobbes specifies in what ways comedy can reflect the more iniquitous impulses of human nature, such as the xenophobic gestures that pervade the *Play of the Sacrament*. This Croxton play, then, depicts the actions of the Jews (as Hobbes writes, 'some deformed thing') as equal parts of absurd and sinister humour. The Jews are, that is, inane enough to doubt the validity and realness of Christ's presence in the host. The play is also eager to illustrate the Jews' idiocy and 'applaud' Christian truth ('by the apprehension of some deformed thing [. . .] they suddenly applaud themselves'). The Croxton play, in portraying Jewish doubt, actually celebrates (in Hobbes's word, 'applaud[s]') what is Same about the Christian majority culture, a culture that is wiser than the Jewish one that believes in a superseded belief system (a 'deformed thing').

In the Croxton play, the Christian anti-Judaic trope of the Jews as continually engaging in 'the ritual murder of a Christian child or stealing, profaning and mutilating the Host', has fused with the comedic impulse of 'sudden glory' to fashion the joke of the-Jew-as-blind-to-truth.[46] In this fusion the *Play of the Sacrament* is most likely attempting to utilize the technique of 'sudden glory' in order 'to keep themselves in their own favor'. As a device of propaganda, the play would have been deployed as a weapon both against Lollardy and against Judaism in order to maintain social stability and deflect the anti-Catholic sentiments and desires of two groups that openly wonder over the medieval Latin Church's mission. Such denial, according to Hobbes's theory, results when an institution, such as the medieval church, is 'forced to keep themselves in their own favor, by observing the imperfec-

---

Humor, p. 53, also cites Hobbes as the source of our contemporary notions about 'superiority theory'. See also John Morreal, ed. *The Philosophy of Laughter and Humor* (Albany: State University of New York Press, 1987), pp. 19-20. Henri Bergson, *Laughter: An Essay on the Meaning of the Comic*, trans. by Cloudesley Brereton (New York: Macmillan, 1912), while historical, offers compelling theories about laughter that derive from crowd psychology wherein the majority culture finds humour in the actions of the outsider (pp. 1-66).

[45] Hobbes, *Leviathan*, p. 36.

[46] Christie Davies, *Jokes and Their Relation to Society* (New York: Mouton de Gruyer, 1988), p. 141.

tions of other men'. For these reasons it is likely that the play aims to speak against – to undermine the position of – Everythreat.[47]

Hobbes is not alone in recognizing that the least socially integrated member of the culture – whether that Other be sexually, socially, or religiously inferior – is selected out as the one most suitable to figure as the butt of the jokes.[48] Because whether we find humour in Noah's wife's rejection of the filth of the ark or the shepherds' inability to distinguish a sheep from a baby or the Jews' stubborn refusal to accept the apparent embodiment of Christ in the sacrament, these comedic Others are also framed by the furniture of violence common to what Christie Davies describes as 'nasty urban legends'.[49] These Others, by and large rendered humorous through the absurdity of their actions, behave in 'inflammatory rather than amusing' ways.[50] Performing within the frame of 'the nasty urban legend', we recognize that Noah's wife – the sexually Othered – nearly disrupts the integrity of her family by threatening their lives through her obstinate and even passive aggressive refusal to enter the ark; we see that the shepherds – the economically marginalized – are prepared to harm Mak until an angel interrupts their abuse; and we witness the Jews – the religiously different – as they repeatedly force the host to endure socially destructive acts of violence.[51] As the furniture of violence in 'nasty urban legends', moreover, these characters occupy space in the geography of the 'periphery of the

---

[47] Walker, ed., *Medieval Drama*, believes that 'such plays were designed to explore and proclaim the universal truth of Christian doctrine in the face of criticism or disbelief. [. . .] the unbelievers against whom it was directed may well have been the Lollards and other influenced by the opinions of the fourteenth-century heretic John Wycliff, who denied the real presence' (p. 213). Dox, 'Medieval Drama as Documentation', ably proves that the 'language' of Croxton *Play of the Sacrament* 'with its references to current doctrinal controversies, clearly links the script to Lollardy' even though the link is not a 'one-to-one correspondence' (p. 109). See also Gibson, *The Theater of Devotion*, p. 35.

[48] See Shanzer, 'Laughter and humour in the early medieval Latin west', pp. 25-47 and Halsall, 'Funny foreigners: laughing with the barbarians in late antiquity', pp. 89-113, both in *Humor, History and Politics*.

[49] On the subject of nasty urban legends, see Davies's work in *Jokes and Their Relation to Society*.

[50] Davies, *Jokes and Their Relation to Society*, p. 141. Davies importantly notes that 'urban legends have often been treated as a completely separate genre from jokes but in fact there is often a considerable similarity between the two, both in content and in structure' (p. 8). See also Jos Enders' fine discussion of the role of the Jew in legends that involve violence to the host: 'Burnt Theatrical Offerings', pp. 118-30, in her *Death by Drama and Other Urban Legends* (Chicago: University of Chicago Press, 2002).

[51] Rubin fully details this unjust story of alleged Jewish abuse to the Host in her *Gentile Tales*.

joke-teller's country or culture'.[52] Provocatively in the case of the *Play of the Sac-rament*, the periphery is simultaneously distant and proximate, at once absent and present, seemingly detailing the story of misled neighbours (the Jews) whose ex-otica (Jewishness) culturally situates them as Other. Transported back and forth between a physically distant land (Aragon) and a physically proximate site (the stage in East Anglia), the entire play wittingly negotiates the audiences' imaginary so that the Jews, an expelled community since 1290, are psychically returned to English territory in the fifteenth century.

Sacramental Jews and A Miraculous 'Little Biscuit'

In importing Hobbes's political theories about crowd psychology into a discussion of a medieval text, I mean to interrogate the more invidious urges that surface in the miraculousness of the equally sudden (only 23 lines spoken by Jesus compel conversion) and prolonged (nearly 70% of the play transpires before this act) con-version of five Jews in the Croxton play. Certainly, the entire play rides on this eventual conversion because without the conversion of the Jews, there is no miracle and no evidence of real presence. Or so it would seem.

Freud's analysis of the intersection between humour and psychology provides re-vealing answers to the delayed conversion of the Jews.[53] Jokes, like dreams, Freud finds, express the content of the unconscious's surfacing in the conscious state – a way of managing fear of the unknown and a fear management akin to the Bakhtin-ian 'cosmic terror'. That fear, that 'terror', manifests as a joke in our conscious states, the place where we reconcile our unconscious fears with our conscious knowledge. The result of this joke-work is pleasure. Through joke-work what is feared can be made 'allowable' (it is more 'allowable', that is, that the Jews test the Host than a Christian) and 'sensible' (it is more 'sensible' for this Jewish Everyth-reat to have doubt about the fabric of *Christianitas* than a Christian).[54]

The *Play of the Sacrament* begins by carefully negotiating its joke-work:

---

[52] Davies, *Jokes and Their Relation to Society*, p. 1, p. 138.

[53] Sigmund Freud, 'The Relation of Jokes to Dreams and to the Unconscious', in *Jokes and Their Relation to the Unconscious*, trans. by and ed. by James Strachey (New York: W. W. Norton, 1960), pp. 159-160; Freud, *On Dreams*, trans. by and ed. by James Strachey (New York: W. W. Norton, 1952). On the difference between dreams and jokes, Freud writes, 'dreams serve predominantly for the avoidance of unpleasure, jokes for the attainment of pleasure; but all our mental activities converge in these two aims' ('Relation of Jokes', p. 160).

[54] Freud, 'Relation of Jokes', p. 172.

> We be ful purposed, wyth hart and wyth thowght,
> Off our mater to tel þe entent,
> Off þe marvellys þat wer wondursely wrowght
>   Off þe Holi and Blyssed Sacrament.   (ll.5-8)

This miracle – 'marvellys þat wer wondursely wrowght' – would seem to be the eventual appearance of Christ 'with woundys blody' (l.47). By all accounts Christ's appearance in an oven rent 'asondre and all to-brast' (l.48) is most assuredly part of the miracle. But there are other critical moments that are equally miraculous and that could not have occurred without the laughable and comically absurd Jewish doubt. One of those miraculous moments is the Jews' conversion – 'Thus in our lawe they were made stedfast' (l.49) and 'In contrycyon thyr hertys wer cast' (l.51). Another miraculous moment is the forgiveness of the Sacrament – 'The Holy Sacrament sheuyd them grette favour' (l.50). All the same this marvel is rather prolonged by a dismaying kaleidoscope of the comedy of superiority theory and the drama of torture, given that the Sacrament's forgiveness follows upon a fair amount of torment that Jasdon particularizes: 'surely wyth owr daggars we shall ses on thys bredde, / And so wyth clowtys we shall know yf he have eny blood' (ll.371-72). Jasdon is not alone, for each of the five Jews strike the 'bredde' with their 'daggars' that are both 'sharpe and kene' (l.382), incisive and critical.

This Jewish persistence in querying the authenticity of real presence only heightens the comedy of superiority theory in that the Jews' ability to read right is clearly flawed. That the bleeding Host does not obtain enough proof for the Jews to believe in real presence is evident because more tests follow (the joke-work continues). The directions following line 400 are explicit in this – 'that ylke cake' (l.415) is dropped into a fiery 'cawdron full of oyle' (l.406). In the midst of all this proof that there is real presence, the sacrament 'sticks to [Jonathas's] hand' (l.418, s.d.). Still, the Jews remain 'thus blynd' (l.308). In fact, the Jews need to hear Jesus, and it is only after Jesus speaks – 'Here shall þe image speke to the Juys' (l.636, s.d.) – that the Jews' response allows the text to close most of the textual subversions as the Jews 'knele down all on ther kneys' (l.665, s.d.). Reduced to complete humility for their stupidity and in total abnegation for their sins, the comedy of the Jews' misprison ends.

I wonder over this prolonged torment that figures as an almost tantalizing delay of the actual marvelous miracle itself – a miracle that was already occurring even as the play began:

> Thus in our lawe they were made stedfast;
> The Holy Sacrament sheuyd them grette favour.
> In contrycyon thyr hertys wer cast.
> And went and shewyd ther lyves to a confesour. (ll.49-52)

So it would seem that if the opening Banns are correct – and they prove themselves to be – the text permits the eucharist to be subjected to torture. It is into that prolonged history, moreover, that the Croxton play eagerly explores pain, endurance, and the final outcome of the marvelous miracle. What we fear most, Freud finds, manifests as a joke.

The representation of the miracle (of the body of Christ responding to the Jews' testing) certainly suggests elements of laughter at the Jews' absurd stubbornness and grotesque behaviour. Enders cites a document that remembers the representation of Christ's blood as having 'shot upward from the aforementioned Host, *as if it were a child pissing*'.[55] It is hard to imagine the moment of mock crucifixion (that is, the five wounds exacted by each of the five Jews) being taken seriously when the image of 'a child pissing' is evoked (by a medieval audience member) as the verbal / written representation of what the visual image reproduces. This superabundance of blood, this pissing child, positions the Jews as the fools in a drama that approaches the carnivalesque.

There are other places where the Croxton play touches the genre of comedy. The *Play of the Sacrament*, while always remembering its objective to detail the 'purchase' of and the desecration to the Host, includes a comic subplot – the story of the servant Colle and his master, the physician Brandyche. This interlude is itself problematic, for even the comic subplot scripts the Jews as humorous in their ineptness. Through this interlude the idiocy of the Jews' behaviour in the main action of the play is mocked again. In this way – through a mimicry of mockery – the comic subplot serves to clarify the comedy of the main plot through a moment that involves the 'ontawght' (l.558) or blindly ignorant physician Brandyche whose servant Colle has the capacity to see more clearly and to read better than he. On the one hand, the interlude cautiously reminds the audience that those who claim to have more knowledge often do not know very much. These Jews who worship the Old Testament and the doctor of medicine Brandyche, for instance, are unnecessary, lacking useful – if any – knowledge. On the other hand, the proximateness of the subversive interlude to the main plot (servants are smarter than masters; Jewish merchants are more god-fearing than Christian ones) blends with – and in blending with challenges – the near tragedy of the purchase of and desecration to the Host. In the end the comedy of superiority theory contains the subversion of Artistorius's mercantile urges. Similarly, the actions of the Jews are rendered just as comedic as the subplot interlude of Colle and Brandyche. The interlude, then, reveals that servants can read situations better than masters; the main plot illustrates that the Host

---

[55] Qtd. in Enders, 'Burnt Theatrical Offerings', p. 124; italics hers. Enders is not alone in documenting a vast amount of blood: Darryll Grantley attempts to reimagine the medieval stage effects of the Croxton play; see Grantley's "Producing Miracles," in *Aspects of Early English Drama*, ed. by Paula Neuss (Totowa: D. S. Brewer, 1983), pp. 78-91 (pp. 84-87).

can (and will) survive – and thus defy – the interrogation of Everythreat. And so, the play closes in comedy: the Jews are converted, or rather wedded, to Christianity.

All the same, the *Play of the Sacrament* rides on acts of subversion. Just at the moment when the drama nearly questions the doctrine of real presence – at the moment when the audience wonders whether the Host will respond to the injustices of the Jewish testing of real presence – Jonathas responds: 'It bledyth as yt were woode, iwys!' (l.403). Through this bleeding Host, subversion is contained. In fact, through mimicry of the Crucifixion scene and through 'sudden glory', the *Play of the Sacrament* simultaneously manages two dramatic events.[56] One of those managed moments is organizing Christian anxiety and feelings of inferiority in the portrayal of the five Jews-as-clowns who exist only to be converted and to run misguided tests, such as desecrating the Host. It is here that the Jews' blindness (Jonathas does not know how right he is in realizing that the Host will prove him blind when he comments, 'thys bred that make us thus blynd' [l.308]) speaks of the issue of supersessionism (representing Judaism as a superseded and, therefore, an outmoded religion). A second dramatic event that the Croxton play controls is the deployment of a comedic interlude. That is, although the comedic economy never unsettles the doctrine of real presence, it does come dangerously close to total subversion. Comedy, at least in the case of the *Play of the Sacrament*, underwrites the hegemony, the centralized majority. The marginalized majority (Christians who wonder over the doctrine of real presence) are made a bit more central when the story of those whose expulsion from the land – namely, the Jews – are rendered even more absurd than their own.

In a sense the legal absence of real Jews in England makes their reality in the play more present. Everythreat is real, and heresies are real even though their presence is denied. At the same time, the disturbance that subversion causes to the hegemony is also very real: in fact, that disturbance is just as real as is the denial of the presence of that disturbance. And while the *Play of the Sacrament* is eager to erase Jewish presence – to render that presence Christian – the play is just as eager to make the entire text a comedy. For even in that marriage of five New Christians to

---

[56] This moment involves a dangerous interrogation made possible through the gestures of sudden glory and of joke-work. Subversion still enters into the text, for in having five Jews (who are really Christian actors) perform a mock Crucifixion, the play admits multiple subversions; one of those possible subversions is sanctioning five Jews' testing the doctrine of real presence. The act of mimicry, as articulated by Homi Bhabha, reveals the farce of mimicry in that mimicry does not build up; mimicry tears down. The effect causes a loss of 'representational authority' (p. 92). See Bhabha's 'Of Mimicry and Man: The Ambivalence of Colonial Discourse', in *The Location of Culture* (New York: Routledge, 1994), pp. 85-92.

Christianity, there is uneasiness because the Jewish conversion to Christianity only suggests that our neighbours are subversives.

When Resistance is Futile

Up to this section, I have explored the manifold gestures of this play that render the text comedic. The Croxton *Play of the Sacrament* is far more than a simple comedy, of course. This medieval play also survives on an array of levels and speaks as a mercurial text. In fact, the *Play of the Sacrament* figures as a document that under-writes the medieval Catholic hegemony – as a complicated story that wonders over allosemitism and as a comedy that celebrates 'sudden glory'. In this way the Crox-ton play educates its audience about the doctrine of real presence; stipulates that failure to acknowledge the efficacy of the sacrament can effectively make one an outcast, in a word be typed as Jewish; argues that some Christians, typified through the character Aristorius, behave in even worse and more antisocial ways than Jews; and enables the marginalized members of the audience to achieve some agency and access an, albeit false, sense of centrality. All of these impulses speak of serious issues of hegemonic control. One of these gestures of the hegemony involves con-taining any spectators who most likely would have flirted with heretical notions and whose economic marginalization would have created feelings of inferiority.[57]

In closing, I would like to return to Davies's notions about the comedic impulse to inflame anti-Other sentiments despite – and perhaps because of – the possible gestures toward allosemitism and philosemitism. In the Croxton play, these senti-ments surface as anti-Jewish gestures and are not completely transfigured even though as Everythreat, the Jewish subversion to the social fabric is eventually con-tained through conversion. Hyam Maccoby finds that medieval culture imagined the Jew as maintaining a rather key position in affirming the medieval social econ-omy. It was necessary, Maccoby explains, 'to build up [the] image of the Jew as well as to break it down. [. . .] As long as Christians feared the Jews, regarding them as figures of established power, they resorted to the weapons of ridicule and

---

[57] John C. Coldewey understands the audience of the *Play of the Sacrament* to be mem-bers of the economic underclass whose spectatorship at outdoor plays may have demanded a more carnivalesque atmosphere. See his 'Some Economic Aspects of the Late Medieval Drama', in *Contexts for Early English Drama*, ed. by Marianne G. Briscoe and John C. Coldewey (Bloomington: Indiana University Press, 1989), pp. 79-80. In *Christ's Body: Identity, Culture, and Society in Late Medieval Writings* (New York: Routledge, 1993), Beckwith reasons that the late medieval audience – after much committed fetishizing (the selling, the touching, the pricking, the puncturing) – may have come to 'dismiss' or to have 'lost sight of' (p. 79) the miracle of transubstantiation.

vilification'.[58] Alternatively, only 'when it became clear that the Jews were defeated and had become harmless objects of contempt', is the Jewish threat contained.[59]

While the Croxton play is overt in representing the absurdity of the Jews' eucharistic tests as expressions of ignorance and as subversions that are (easily) managed through conversion, these Jews will destroy neither society nor community because the Jewish threat is contained. Even more, this shift from evil Other to the misguided Other returns us to the gestures of comedy. Comedy affirms the social fabric by ending with various marriages (unions); with real presence affirmed. The 'cosmic terror', in this way, is contained.

In all, the darkly humorous comedy of the *Play of the Sacrament* utilizes uneasy laughter to navigate Jewish caricatures of Christian anxiety. By the fifteenth century, the dominant ideology of the medieval Church was less able to manage its hold over the Christian imaginary. Medieval Christians had come to wonder over the efficacy of the practice of administering the eucharist.[60] I believe that there was great worry over this doubt, and this terror surfaces in the (vile) representations of the Jews, who labour to disprove the efficacy of real presence only to prove its validity. Jewish inanity signifies Christian doubt, and laughter reduces the fear about what is unknown. The subsequent failure of the five Jews to disprove satisfactorily the doctrine of real presence acts as a sort of wish fulfillment for the medieval Christian who wants to discover that there is a Body in the wafer – and to become a better Christian in that discovery – by vicariously testing the validity of real presence. In the end the act of transubstantiation is at once safely mocked and rigorously defended by the Christian (through the Jew). All the same the failure to negate the efficacy of the eucharist does not leave us without the memory of the uneasy laughter even in reminding us that resistance is futile.

---

[58]   Hyam Maccoby, 'The Wandering Jew as Sacred Executioner', in *The Wandering Jew: Essays in the Interpretation of a Christian Legend*, ed. by Galit Hasan-Rokem and Alan Dundes (Bloomington: Indiana University Press, 1986), pp. 236-60 (p. 238).

[59]   Maccoby, 'The Wandering Jew', p. 239.

[60]   See Beckwith, *Christ's Body*, p. 37.

9

From Snickers to Laughter: Believable Comedy in Chaucer's *Miller's Tale*

T he closest we will probably ever have to Chaucer's source for the *Miller's Tale* is the Middle Dutch tale *Heile van Beersele*. Of the various analogues, it is the only one old enough that Chaucer could have been familiar with it. Also, it is in a language that Chaucer probably knew and is from a region that Chaucer had visited and with which he had family, business, and other ties. There are, furthermore, many parallels in plot and phrasing that make a connection almost inevitable.[1]

A comparison of *Heile van Beersele* with the *Miller's Tale* shows that while both tales are funny, Chaucer's tale is far more believably funny than the Middle Dutch tale. Time after time, Chaucer shows that he wanted to make his story more realistic than his source was. In this essay, however, I will generally use the term 'believable' rather than the term 'realistic' because the term 'Chaucerian realism' is so

---

[1] I present the full argument for the connection between the two tales the chapter on the *Miller's Tale* in *Sources and Analogues of the Canterbury Tales*, ed. Robert M. Correale and Mary Hamel (Woodbridge, Suffolk: D. S. Brewer, 2005), volume 2 (forthcoming). All of my quotations are taken from the edition of *Heile van Beersele* in that volume. The translations, though based on the version given there, reflect at times an alternative phrasing. My quotations from the *Miller's Tale* are taken from the first fragment of the *Canterbury Tales* in the *Riverside Chaucer*, 3rd edn., ed. by Larry D. Benson (Boston: Houghton Mifflin, 1987).

fraught with multiple meanings that to use it is to invite confusion.[2] There may have been a number of reasons for that greater believability, but I propose that one of them was that Chaucer wanted his audience to feel that the characters were not just made-up people in an unlikely anecdote, or cartoon characters in a frame, but more like folks who act within the realm of imaginable human action. Indeed, it is almost as if Chaucer wanted his audience to be able to imagine the actions of the story as taking place on a stage with live actors performing the actions before our eyes. The plot is, of course, still pretty outlandish, but at least the people in Chaucer's little comedy act within the realm of human possibility.

The increased believability of Chaucer's version of the tale alters the nature of the comedy. It is one thing to laugh at the words and actions of characters whom we cannot quite believe in. It is something different to laugh at – and sometimes with – people who seem to be more like ones we know, people who are more nearly like ourselves. I do understand, of course, that we can know little about the responses of audiences to tales told or read six centuries ago, and I shall not attempt to speculate in any detail about the quality of the laughter that Middle Dutch audiences would have given to the story of Heile and her customers, or about the different quality of the laughter English audiences would have given to the story of Alison and her suitors. I do, however, invite readers of my comparisons below to assess the nature of their own responses to scenes that seem to be made-up or cartoon-like, as opposed to their responses to scenes that seem far more likely actually to have happened to actual in-the-flesh people.

Dating from the second half of the fourteenth century, the Middle Dutch *Heile van Beersele* is a short fabliau-like tale of ninety-five octosyllabic couplets. It is about an Antwerp prostitute who makes appointments on the same evening with three customers, a miller named Willem, an unnamed priest, and a blacksmith named Hughe. The humour of the piece lies mostly in the fact that the three appointments

---

[2] In his *Chaucerian Realism* (Cambridge: D. S. Brewer, 1994), Robert Myles identifies some of the kinds of realism that philosophical and semiological semanticists talk about: foundational realism, epistemological realism, ethical realism, semiotic and linguistic realism, intentional realism, psychological realism, Cratylic realism, scholastic realism, and so on (see pp. 1-2 of his book for some preliminary definitions). In this chapter by 'realism' I mean something much simpler: that the actions of the characters would have been recognized as plausible by readers, who would be more likely to say, 'yeah, that is sort of outlandish, but I can almost believe it,' rather than, 'hey, no way would people I know do that.' My thinking here is in line with that of Dieter Mehl, who speaks in *Geoffrey Chaucer: An Introduction to His Narrative Poetry* (Cambridge: Cambridge University Press, 1986) of 'the precise details of observed every day life' in the *Miller's Tale*. We get, Mehl says, 'a sense of watching a more familiar world, a world that does not demand abstract reflection but only an immediate human fellow-feeling' (p. 175).

that are intended to follow each other begin to bump into each other. While the miller is still with Heile, the priest comes a-knocking. Heile hides the miller in a hanging trough, then lets the priest in. After the priest has satisfied himself sexually, he preaches a little sermon about a coming flood, a sermon that the miller up in the trough hears. When the third visitor, the blacksmith, knocks for his turn with Heile, the busy lady tries to send him away, but he begs for at least a kiss. Heile persuades the priest to let the smith kiss his buttocks. Afterwards the angry smith rushes home to his forge and returns with a hot poker that he then uses to scorch the butt of the priest. The priest's cry for 'Water, water' signals to the miller that the predicted flood has come. He cuts the rope holding up his trough and comes crashing down, breaking an arm and a leg.

The nine examples I give below show Chaucer transforming the unlikely fictional materials of *Heile van Beersele* into more likely fictional materials. I do not pause after each one to say, 'Gee, isn't that funny?' I do, however, invite readers to consider whether in his making his own tale more believable, Chaucer transformed an audience's snickering at the outlandish plots and characters in the Middle Dutch tale into something more like genuine amusement.

Tale of a Tub

Heile happens to have hanging from the beams in her house a large trough. We do not learn ahead of time that it is there, and the only explanation we get of why it is there is Heile's to her first customer, Willem, on the arrival of her second customer, the priest. The explanation that it sometimes comes in handy:

> Heile seide, 'daer boven hangt .i. bac,
> Dies ic hier voermaels ghemac
> Hadde te menegen stonden'. (67-69)

> [Heile said, 'up there hangs a trough that I have found convenient here on many previous occasions'.]

We are left to imagine in what ways it may have been 'convenient' to her in the past – presumably to hide other clients who did not want to be discovered in the arms of a prostitute. And because the Middle Dutch author does not say, we are left to imagine how Willem manages to climb into the tub. We are not told how high the tub hangs, though we are presumably to imagine that it is pretty high off the floor, because Willem later breaks his arm and leg when he falls from it. Are we to imagine him initially climbing into the tub by standing on a high table, or shinnying up a rope, or climbing a ladder? In fact, we do not know because the author does not tell us.

Chaucer leaves far less for us to be puzzled at. We know why the three tubs are hanging from the beams – because at Nicholas's direction, foolish old John collects them, provisions them, and suspends them from the beams. And we know how the three characters get into the tubs – by means of ladders that, following Nicholas's instructions, John has built. We 'see' the old carpenter hanging the tubs and provisioning them, see him using the ladder he has built to climb into it. Is it funny? Well, yes. I find no humour in the fact that a tub hangs in Heile's bedroom and that a man somehow gets into it. I find great humour in old John's feverishly acquiring the tubs, hanging them, provisioning them, building ladders for them, and finally, exhausted, climbing a ladder into his private little Noah's ark.

Counting the Times

The Middle Dutch author tells us that the priest makes love with Heile three times before the third lover, Hughe the smith, arrives:

> Heile dede den pape te ghemake
> Ende alsi die wiekewake
> Driewerf . . . . (75-77)

[Heile made the priest happy, and they made love three times . . . .]

Some readers or hearers may find the priest's stamina impressive, but I find it just puzzling. We are not told that priest is a randy teenager in the prime of his youth. Whatever his sexual recovery time, it would eat up a lot of the evening for him to perform three times, even with the skilled professional that we imagine Heile to be. More puzzling is why Heile, who knows that she has one client hanging in the trough above and another hanging around outside waiting his turn, would let the priest proceed at such a leisurely pace. We can perhaps imagine an explanation – that she is afraid of him, for example, or that she needs his priestly blessing, or that she does not want him to summon her to the ecclesiastical courts, or that he offers her more money – but in fact the text offers no such explanation. Three times is not impossible, but little is gained, except perhaps a snicker, by giving him an exaggerated number of 'wiekewakes' with so unprofessional a prostitute.

By being less specific Chaucer makes the sexual activity of Alison and Nicholas more credible:

> And thus lith Alison and Nicholas,
> In bisynesse of myrthe and of solas,
> Til that the belle of laudes gan to rynge,
> And freres in the chauncel gonne synge. (3653-56)

We presume that the two young lovers, finally united in bed, are an active pair, but Chaucer does not strain our credulity by specifying precisely how often they make love.[3] The humour comes not in the number of times the randy-handy Nicholas makes love with Alison, but in the success of his clever plan to fool old John and bed his wife. Of course, there is more humour coming, as we come to see that the too-too-solid flesh of young Nicholas is soon to pay the price for his cleverness.

Preaching a Sermon

After he makes love three times with Heile, the priest preaches her a little mini-sermon:

> Ghinc die pape liggen ghewaghen
> Uter ewangelien menech woert.
> Oec soe seidi dit bat voert,
> Dat die tijt noch soude comen
> Dat God die werelt soude doemen,
> Beide met watre ende met viere;
> Ende dat soude wesen sciere
> Dat al die werelt verdrinken soude,
> Grote ende clene, jonge ende oude. (78-86)

> [Then the priest quoted many words from the scriptures. He also said that the time would soon come when God would destroy the world with water and fire, drowning everyone in the world, great and small, young and old.]

The priest's motivation here is not clear. Why, after making love with a prostitute, would the priest preach such a sermon? Perhaps we can imagine a plausible reason – for example, that he feels guilty about his sinful lust and so warns both himself and Heile that they should get right with God before death takes them – but in fact the Middle Dutch author gives no such explanation, and the priest's sermon remains a puzzling anomaly.

---

[3] By not mentioning the number here, Chaucer is consistent with his technique elsewhere. In three of the four most likely sources for the *Reeve's Tale* (conveniently gathered together and translated in volume 1 of *Sources and Analogues of the Canterbury Tales*), the first lover brags that he has made love to the young woman six or seven times. Chaucer tells us only that Aleyn and Malyne 'were aton' (4197). To be sure, Aleyn later brags that he has 'swyved' Malyne 'thries' (see lines 4265-66), but the context suggests that the number is probably the result of a bragging college-boy exaggerating his prowess to a chum. There is no bragging in *Heile van Beersele*, where the number is stated by the narrator as a simple fact.

Chaucer's Nicholas makes a somewhat similar prediction about a coming flood that will drown all the world, but he does so not after he has sex with Alison, but before. Indeed, his goal is to make it possible for him to have sex with Alison, not somehow to atone for his having had it already. Nicholas's prediction to the foolish John that a second Noah's flood is coming is part of an elaborate plan to convince Alison that he is cleverer than John and to get rid of John so that he can spend a joyous night in bed with Alison: 'For this was his desir and hire also' (3407). Nicholas's plan, of course, is outlandish and, on the face of it, so improbable that it can never work. It does work, however, because Chaucer has worked hard to make John precisely the sort of funny old fool who would believe the prediction. He is foolish enough to imagine that he can cage his wife, even as he allows into the cage a randy young college boy. He is foolish enough not to imagine that his wife could be attracted to Nicholas or indeed to Absolon, who one night serenades his wife outside their bedroom window. He is foolish enough to imagine that God could select him to be a second Noah, even though God had made a covenant with Noah never to send another such flood. We believe the forecast flood in neither tale. In Chaucer's tale, however, we accept it as a funny ruse that works precisely because its intended fictional audience, old John, is foolish enough to swallow it, hook, line, and trickster.

Rejecting a Suitor

Heile is a prostitute in need of money who does what prostitutes in need of money sometimes have to do: makes appointments with three different men spaced far enough apart that she can make a good night's wage by pleasuring them all. That part seems logical enough. What is strange, however, is that an experienced professional would not have spaced the appointments farther apart so that the men's visits would not overlap, or that she would not have kept better track of the time so that she could have sent one on his satisfied way before the next came knocking. A reader's puzzlement at the Middle Dutch story is even more pronounced when Heile rejects Hughe the smith, her third appointment. Hughe is, after all, both a neighbour and a customer who would have been good for additional business in the coming weeks and months. Instead of apologizing to him or whispering that she is busy and asking him to return later that night or another time, Heile cruelly spurns him. When he asks for at least a kiss, she tells the priest to humiliate him:

> 'Ay, here, laet cussen desen knape
> U achterste inde, hi sal wanen wel
> Dat ict ben ende niemen el;
> Sone saeghdi boerde nie so goet'. (110-13)

> [Ah, sir, let this fellow kiss your behind, and he will surely think that it is I and no one else. You've never seen such a good jest.]

We might imagine, if we want to, that Heile is exhausted after her four sexual encounters (one with the miller and three with the priest) and is therefore motivated to spurn a fifth, but in fact the text offers no justification for such an imagining. Besides, surely we have reason to doubt that a prostitute-for-hire, even if she were weary, would insult a paying customer. No, the plot requires the buttocks-kissing so that the smith will be angry enough to go fetch the hot iron, but no actual prostitute could afford to treat her appointed clients so outrageously. It is just bad business.

Chaucer makes the whole scene more believable by making Alison a wife rather than a prostitute. Frustrated by a marriage to a man perhaps thrice her age, she arranges to take one lover, not three. The overlapping of the lovers in the *Miller's Tale* happens only because the uninvited Absolon insists on coming by. The first 'suitor', her husband John, belongs there, since it is his home, and he is properly aloft snoring away. Alison rebuffs and insults her third suitor, Absolon with a cruel jest because she does not like him and because she has a lover she likes better. Absolon has no appointment with her and is not welcome. When he will not take no as her answer but begs instead for a kiss, she is for that reason motivated to play her nasty trick on him. She behaves just as a frisky young wife, in bed with her lover, would react to the foolish other suitor who begs for a kiss. Rather than being puzzled about why Heile insults a paying customer she had invited to visit her, we are free to be amused at the obscenely clever way Alison quite justifiably punishes a suitor she quite rightly spurns. Puzzling, no. Funny, yes.

Listening in a Tub

The Antwerp priest in the Middle Dutch tale does not know that he has an auditor other than Heile when he preaches his illogical little sermon, but Willem, sitting in the trough above, overhears the priest's sermon:

> Dit hoerde Willem daer hi sat
> Boven hoge in ghenen bac,
> Ende peinsde het mochte wel waer wesen
> Sidermeer dat papen lesen,
> Ende dewangelie gheeft getughe. (87-91)

> [Willem heard this from where he sat high above in the trough and thought it might well be true, since priests read the gospels, and the gospels bore witness to it.]

Immediately, however, there is a problem: if Willem is close enough to the bedroom that he can hear the priest's sermon, how is it that he has apparently not also heard the sounds, however muffled, of the priest's triple-encounter with Heile, and how is it that, immediately after he hears the sermon that is not intended for his ears, he apparently does not also hear the conversation between Heile and Hughe? If he had heard it, and had heard Heile telling the priest to let the smith kiss his buttocks, why does Willem know so little about what goes on down there that he does not realize, a few minutes later, that there really is no flood? He has, after all, been awake the whole time, has heard no thunder, seen no lightning, observed no patter of rain on the roof over his head. His assumption that the predicted flood has come makes no sense whatever.

Chaucer's tub-scene is more believable. After his hard day's work of acquiring, provisioning, hanging, and laddering the three tubs, poor old John is exhausted. Almost immediately he falls asleep:

> The dede sleep, for wery bisynesse,
> Fil on this carpenter right, as I gesse,
> Aboute corfew-tyme, or litel moore. (3643-45)

Old John does not hear Absolon's or Nicholas's conversations with Alison because he is dead asleep the whole time. He sleeps nervously 'Awaitynge on the reyn, if he it heere' (3642). The next thing he hears in his slumber is the 'thonder-dent' (3807) of a fart and then Nicholas's cry, 'Water! Water!' (3815). He groggily assumes from the thunderclap and from the cry for water that the flood has come. It turns out to be a wrong assumption, but Chaucer, unlike the Middle Dutch author, has set things up in such a way that we accept that assumption as believable. Rather than be puzzled at or merely snicker at Willem's strange actions, we laugh at the foolish John's absurd and well-deserved fall.

Penetrating I

When Hughe kisses the priest's bottom, he does so with such zeal and force that his nose penetrates the priest's anus:

> Ende Huge waende that Heile ware
> End custe spapen ers al dare
> Met soe heten sinne,
> Dat sine nese vloech daer inne,
> Soe dat die smet sonder waen
> Harde well waende sijn gevaen
> Gelijc der mese inder cloven. (117-23)

> [And Hughe thought it was Heile and kissed the priest's arse right there with such hot desire that his nose shot inside, so that the smith undoubtedly thought that he was caught like a titmouse in a trap.]

That may be good slapstick comedy, but it is not believable. We all know that the human sphincter would not permit the penetration of even the most Pinocchio-like human nose. And as for the bird with his beak in a trap, can we really, except in a cartoon sequence, imagine such a thing as the result of a human kiss?

Chaucer eliminated the impossible nose-penetration:

> And Absolon, hym fil no bet ne wers,
> But with his mouth he kiste hir naked ers
> Ful savourly, er he were war of this. (3733-35)

The penetration in the Middle Dutch story we cannot believe; 'savourly' in the English story we can. The 'savourly' is, for Absolon, a believable detail. His mouth has 'icched al this longe day' (3682) and at night he has dreamed that 'I was at a feeste' (3684). At the window he tells Alison that he yearns for her 'as dooth a lamb after the tete' (3704). It is not strange at all that a young man who so consistently associates love with eating should kiss his beloved 'ful savourly'.

Getting the Hot Iron

Deeply insulted by his misdirected kiss, Hughe angrily rushes home to his smithy and heats up a hot iron:

> Hi liep thuus alse die was erre;
> Hine woende van daer niet verre.
> Een groet yser nam hi gereet
> Ende staect int vier ende maket heet
> Soe dat gloyde wel ter cure. (131-35)

> [He ran home as if he were mad. He lived not far from there. He immediately took a big iron, stuck it into the fire and made it so hot that it glowed, just the way he wanted it to.]

On the one hand it seems both logical and economical for a blacksmith in need of a hot iron to run home and fetch one. On the other, we might perhaps assume, though we are not told, that he had let his hearth go cold at the end of the day in anticipation of his visit to Heile, so his returning home to heat up the hearth again would have taken some time – perhaps enough time for his rage to cool enough that he would approach the fateful window the second time more cautiously.

Chaucer changed that by having Absolon visit a friend, Gerveys, who already has his smithy up and running, with a hot coulter already there in the forge – 'that hoote

kultour in the chymenee heere' (3776). He can then, after a very brief conversation
with Gerveys, grab the coulter 'by the colde stele' of the handle (3786) and rush
back with it. In the heat of his anger he knocks again at the window, never thinking
that the woman he intends to punish may be cleverer than he, never anticipating
that the buttock he scorches may be that of a man rather than of the woman he has
come to loathe. Rushing back he applies his instrument of revenge effectively
enough, but does so in such a way that he is punished again, this time with a blind-
ing fart in the face. Hughe the smith is not punished a second time. There is no need
for him to be punished even the first time because he has done no wrong. Absolon,
however, deserves not only the first punishment but the second as well, since he is
a vow-breaking fraud of a parish clerk who presses his suit on a clever woman who
has twice rejected him. Chaucer carefully sets the smithy-scene up so that Gerveys
has the hot coulter ready, thus permitting Absolon to act quickly and without considering the possible consequences, thereby hilariously bringing on his own second
and much-deserved punishment.

Penetrating II

When the priest puts his buttocks out the window to receive a second kiss, Hughe
strikes while his iron is hot:

> End die smet stac ongelet
> Tgheloyende yser in den ers. (146-47)

> [And the smith immediately stuck the red-hot iron into his arse.]

While it may be funny to have the priest sodomized twice, once by Hughe's nose
and once by Hughe's hot iron, the second sodomizing is as contrived as the first. It
is, after all, pitch dark, the human anus is a narrow target, and Hughe has no hint
about where to aim his hot iron, unless we are to assume that he is aided by its own
red glow.

Chaucer treats the second window scene more believably. For one thing, the weapon
is a coulter, the broad plow-knife designed to cut the earth vertically before the
plowshare cuts it horizontally and turns it over. It is just the sort of implement that
a blacksmith would be likely to have heating up in his hearth in the very early dawn
of a spring morning, prior to sharpening it for the Oxford farmer who would use it
that day.[4] For another thing, since it is not yet dawn, Absolon's aim cannot be so

---

[4] J. A. W. Bennett tells us in *Chaucer at Oxford and at Cambridge* (Oxford: Clarendon
Press, 1974) that 'blacksmiths customarily worked at night to early morning – the best time
to repair gear or "tip" ploughshares that were needed on the morrow' (p. 41).

precise. He has, after all, only the sound of the fart to guide him – the fart itself being a believable human response to a man like Absolon. Hughe, we recall, had no clue about where to aim. Even if the early dawn light were beginning to bring the outlined forms out of the darkness, Chaucer tells us that Absolon has been blinded by the fart:

> This Nicholas anon leet fle a fart
> As greet as it had been a thonder-dent,
> That with the strook he was almoost yblent. (3806-08)

Striking blindly, the angry Absolon hits Nicholas not in the anus, even if he had been aiming for that specific part of the anatomy, but 'amydde the ers' (3810). And, given the flattened breadth of the plow coulter, it seems appropriate that 'hende' Nicholas receives not a puncture wound but, rather, a hilariously funny and appropriate buttocks-burn 'an hande-brede aboute' (3811).[5]

Falling into a Cesspit

The priest in *Heile van Beersele* is double-punished. First, he has his anus scorched by a cauterizing hot iron wielded by Hughe the blacksmith. His shout 'Water, water' leads Willem to cut the rope[6] suspending his tub, and Willem's crashing down so surprises the priest that he thinks the devil has come. The fearful priest rushes into the corner, where he receives his second punishment by falling into a cesspit:

> Die pape scoet in een winkel
> Ende waende dat die duvel ware;
> In enen vulen putte viel hi dare,
> Alsoe alsmen mi doet weten
> Quam hi thuus all besceten
> Ende sinen ers al verbrant. (172-77)

---

[5] I cannot agree with the strain of criticism that sees Absolon's act as sodomitic. See, for example, Edmund Reiss, 'Daun Gerveys in the *Miller's Tale*', *Papers on Language and Literature* 6 (1970), 123, and Roy Peter Clark, 'Christmas Games in the *Miller's Tale*', *Studies in Short Fiction* 13 (1976): 'The "kultour" is a phallus-shaped weapon. . . . Absolon's thrusting of the hot iron up Nicholas's rear is an act of symbolic buggery' (p. 283). There is no penetration in the *Miller's Tale*.

[6] A minor change in the direction of believability in the *Miller's Tale* is that Nicholas has John provide the tubs with 'an ax to smyte the corde atwo' (3569), and that John at the appropriate time uses it: 'And with his ax he smoot the corde atwo' (3820). Willem is not said to have any cutting instrument in the trough with him, but manages in his panic to produce a knife from somewhere: 'Sijn mes hi gegrepe / Ende sneet ontwee den repe' (161-62) [He gripped his knife and cut the rope].

[The priest ran into a corner, thinking [Willem] was the devil, and fell into a foul pit, as I have been told, and then went home all beshitten and with his arse branded.]

Chaucer makes a significant change in moving the cleric from the inside of the house, where he is in the Middle Dutch tale, to the outside. Absolon is not yet a full-fledged priest, of course, but this sensor-swinging parish clerk apparently aspires to be one. In any event, he is the referent of the anticlerical theme so characteristic of the fabliaux. By moving the clerical figure outside and putting Nicholas inside, Chaucer switched the scheme of punishment. Still wanting the priest to receive a double-punishment, Chaucer replaces one scatological element for another – and more logical – one. How logical is it, after all, to find a 'vulen putte' (174) inside the house? Certainly we are not told in advance that one is there, and there is no mention of the reek or vermin that must have been associated with such a foul pit. Perhaps we are to assume, rather, that the pit is outside in a corner of the garden, but in fact the Middle Dutch poet says no such thing. The plot needs a cesspit, so the author provides it. We snicker when we see the priest tumble into it, but we have no reason to believe such a tumble because the author has not explained it. It seems to be a puzzling afterthought to a puzzling tale.

Chaucer makes no mention of the sanitary facilities associated with John's house in the *Miller's Tale*.[7] His plot, of course, requires no such site, so there is no reason for him to have mentioned it. Chaucer does, however, provide a double-punishment for the cleric Absolon. The first is the foul arse-kiss, the second is the foul fart. Both of these are logical enough given the details of characterization that Chaucer gives to the fair Alison who presents her buttocks for Absolon to kiss, and to the raunchy Nicholas, who produces the fart. Both of these punishments, given the preparation Chaucer has given them, are entirely logical and entirely funny in the context of the story Chaucer has so elaborately set up.

Chaucer's *Miller's Tale*, then, is far more believable than *Heile van Beersele*. It is so believable that some readers have even assumed that the story is based somehow on 'real life'.[8] My purpose here is not to prove that Chaucer's version of the story

---

[7] Little is known about the typical location of latrines in or around medieval houses. For a hint about what is known, see Georges Duby (ed.), *A History of Private Life*, volume II, *Revelations of the Medieval World* (Cambridge: Harvard U P, 1988), especially pp. 460, 463-64.

[8] For example, see Robert A. Pratt, in 'Was Robyn the Miller's Youth Misspent?' *Modern Language Notes* 59 (1944): 47-49, and Charles Long, 'The Miller's True Story', *Interpretations* 6 (1974), 7-16. Long thinks that the events of the *Miller's Tale* actually took place 'on a dark night, some twenty years ago in the home of John from Osenay, that is of Osewold'

of the multiple lovers is superior to the Middle Dutch one. Most modern readers will of course prefer the *Miller's Tale* to *Heile van Beersele*. It has a more fully developed plot and more fleshed-out characters. And it supports a more consistently developed set of themes by punishing the self-deceiving foolishness of old John, the prideful randiness of young Nicholas, and, especially, the self-serving religious pretensions of clerkly Absolon. *Heile van Beersele* is quite different from the *Miller's Tale*. It is much shorter – only a fifth the length of Chaucer's – and is by genre an anecdote that does not pretend to believable development of anything. It is a smirk-inspiring story about the troubles that three men make for themselves when they associate with a prostitute who has a bad sense of timing. We cannot help but be amused when three sexual encounters meant to be sequential turn out to be simultaneous. The Middle Dutch tale does what it sets out to do, and does it all with admirable economy. That economy, however, comes at the expense of verisimilitude. The characters are not believable, nor are they meant to be. Their actions could not really have happened, and we are not meant to think that they could really have happened.

In Chaucer's *Miller's Tale*, as in *Heile van Beersele*, we readers are aware always that we are dealing with fiction, not actual life. In reading the *Miller's Tale*, however, far more than in reading *Heile van Beersele*, we imagine the events as happening to human beings. Unlike the Middle Dutch author, clever though he was in telling a funny anecdote, Chaucer made a series of narrative moves that help us to believe that the events of the story might actually have happened to people whose behaviour is in basic accord with human nature. Instead of scratching our heads in puzzlement at the strange actions of the strange people in *Heile van Beersele*, we readers of the much more believable *Miller's Tale* can react with amusement at the human comedy that unfolds before us.

(pp. 8-9). Long discusses some of the changes that I discuss here, but reaches quite a different set of conclusions: 'Chaucer intends for the story to be biographical or even autobiographical. . . . The Miller . . . had observed the events in his youth' (p. 9). According to Long, although Robyn was himself off in London with Gille on the fateful Monday night in question, he 'could easily have satisfied his curiosity by gleaning the varying tidbits of information from the stories of neighbors or from Nicholas and Alison as well. The Miller's story, then, is almost certainly based on an episode in his life, and Robyn the Miller is Old John's young apprentice, also named Robyn, who would have been a near "eye witness" of the Nicholas-Alison-John triangle' (p. 10). Long's argument is variously flawed. He never explains why a future miller would have apprenticed himself to a carpenter, for example, and the name and age of Osewald the Reeve do not sort well with those of old John or with the twenty-years-past events of the tale. Long's argument is even more tenuous when he surmises that John has long since separated from Alison and married 'a new young wife', while Alison is currently the Wife of Bath on the pilgrimage to Canterbury. My own reasoning requires no such house of cards. A useful counter-reading to the Pratt-Long kind of 'realism' is that of Charles A. Owen, Jr., 'One Robyn or Two', *Modern Language Notes* 67 (1952), 336-38.

Perhaps in dwelling so long on the differences between the Middle Dutch tale and the Middle English one that Chaucer derived from it, I shall be thought to be doing just what Chaucer asked us to NOT to do, that is to making 'ernest of game' (3186). On the contrary, I want to emphasize far more the 'game' of the tale than its earnestness. In Middle English, the word 'game' meant not only 'playfulness', but also 'play' in the sense of a piece of drama. One of the key differences between the *Miller's Tale* and what came before it is that Chaucer was, by means of dialogue and setting and imaginable human action, moving British fiction in the direction of drama. If I may return for a moment to the cartoon analogy, *Heile van Beersele* is like a comic strip. It is a series of static frames that, together, tell a story. The people have short speeches in the bubbles above their heads, but they are essentially frozen in place, immobile, in each rigid frame. We do not expect verisimilitude when we read a cartoon strip or comic book. Cartoons are, by definition, funny, but their humour derives more from situation than from logical action or psychologically complex motivation or truth to life. The *Miller's Tale*, on the other hand, is like a stage play with real actors. They move around in fluid frames. They speak more. They are played by human actors who are doing, for the most part, the kinds of things that people do. Because the actors are alive, their actions seem more believable and more motivated. We find out how and why the props got there and we come closer to understanding the human motivation of the actors. I cannot, of course, press these analogies too far, but if I am right, then one of the central changes Chaucer made was to transform the cartoon-anecdote that lets us respond by saying, 'My, those characters sure did funny things', into the kind of dramatic action that lets us respond, rather, 'My, those funny characters are a lot like you and me'.

10
Musical Comedy in the
Medieval Choir: England

Elaine C. Block
With the participation of Frédéric Billiet[1]

It is crucial to remember that choir stalls in cathedrals, abbeys, chapels and other churches were built for music and the liturgy offices linked to chanting the psalms. The seating by the main altar was the most sacred part of the church although prayers could be recited not only in the choir, but in chapels dedicated to particular saints, before painting of holy events, or even in an ordinary seat that fostered meditation and the recitation of the rosary. The choir was designed for sacred singing and prayer; and its construction took account of that.

Near the close of the twelfth century the popular Benedictine order of monks programmed eight hours daily to sing the Psalms of David. The choral singing involved antiphony so the singers needed to face each other to keep in time. The stalls therefore were required to have at least two rows of facing seats. The dorsal panels and canopies, in addition to keeping out the winter cold and violent winds, acted as resonance boards to make the sound worthy of its subject – sacred music. The carvings which glorified the stalls sometimes mimic silently the music that was heard in the choir and at other times explains why it was there. Documentation on these subjects is scarce but it does pay to go directly to the source – the choir stall carv-

---

[1] Frédéric Billiet, as one of the authors of this chapter, is covered by international copyright laws. No part of this article nor its illustrations may be reproduced without the written permission of the authors.

ings on arm-rests, dorsal panels, jouees and misericords, the focus of study for Misericordia International and the heart of the *Lexicon for Medieval Choir Stalls*.[2] Many of these images show the performance techniques and liturgical furnishings used at the time, the lectern and candelabras, the song books and the *tactus*. Churches which could afford the expense created their own Albert Hall or Carnegie Hall for the glory of God.

Music in the Medieval Choir Stalls

I have found in my studies of ten thousand misericords in thirteen countries that music is not treated the same way in each region. In France, for example, on one misericord we see – and imagine – a concert performed by a group of seven musicians in courtly dress: a singer, an organist, a lutist, a piper and a fiddler, with two others too mutilated to describe (10.01). At the extreme right of this group stands a robed man who is obviously not a musician. He holds an object which is difficult to identify since it is broken, but a close look reveals it to be a set of scales. The figure is visibly similar to a seventeenth century emblem by Alciato which presents a monk holding scales, defined as a symbol of harmony. I have not found such a harmonious concert in any other country. Outside of France each musician operates alone or at most as part of a pair. It is not obvious if the musicians are performing in a town or for a special observance, since the allotted space under the alternative seating provided by the ledge of the misericord carving is too small to show an entire scene.[3] Additional misericord carvings in France reinforce the importance of the harmonious concert by showing a number of musicians cleaning and tuning their instruments (10.02). The instruments seem to take care of themselves in other regions.

Theatre and Music in the English Choir

In England the theatre and comedy overtake the concertizing. Some choir stall carvings in England are derived from theatrical performances. The brewster to whom we will refer below is mentioned in one of the mystery plays performed at Chester and also adorns a misericord at Ludlow in Shropshire. At Chester one

---

[2] Elaine C. Block and Frédéric Billiet (ed.), *Lexique pour les stalles médiévales* (Turnhout: Brepols, 2005).

[3] In our work we consider the misericord to consist of three parts: the ledge on which the religious singers can perch when they are supposed to be standing, the console or block of wood which supports this ledge, and the carving which may or may not cover the console. Misericord derives from the Latin *misericordia* or mercy and these mercy seats were originally intended for use by aged and handicapped monks, canons and nuns.

10.01: The Harmonious Concert, *from the chapel of Gaillon (Eure) now at Basilique Saint-Denis. Courtesy of Elaine C. Block / Misericordia International.*

10.02: Tuning the Lute, *Saint-Chamant (Cantal). Courtesy of Elaine C. Block / Misericordia International.*

misericord illustrates a tale told by the Wise Men of Gotham, in which geese are enclosed in a pen but they fly away anyway no matter how high the pen is built (10.03). There are scenes analogous to Chaucer's *Canterbury Tales* and from the epic *Renard the Fox* (10.04). At Bristol Cathedral we see Bruin the bear with his snout caught in a wedge of a tree, and Tybert the cat trapped in the barn and later biting the testicles of the nude priest. Finally, Renard is judged by Noble the lion. One of the supporters shows an ape piper, certainly providing the musical background for these stories. While some of these motifs exist in choir stalls of other countries, they are presented there as isolated images rather than as comical accompaniments to a story.

Very little attention, however, has been paid to the role of music while telling these stories. I propose that in English choir stalls we have the beginnings of the musical comedy. The actions of musicians may be distorted and the instruments they play may be unusual. We will consider in the English choir the roles of angels, humans and animals as musicians and compare them to their analogues in other regions.

Angels and Sacred Music in the Choir

Most of the angels who play musical instruments on misericords strum lutes or skim a bow over a fiddle. A few play the hurdy-gurdy (10.05), blow horns or manipulate the keyboard of a portative organ. The imagined music could represent the heavenly sphere.[4] While some angels ocupy the entire misericord others, especially in England, generally occupy the sidelines and provide music for the central scene. For example, a visit by the Magi on Twelfth Night at Lincoln Cathedral is accompanied by two angels sitting on the supporters and strumming instruments (10.06).[5] We know from the Bible that the angels did not travel with the Magi but we may assume that they awaited the visitors and struck their strings when they heard the first steps – as in the overture to a current musical. Also at Lincoln Cathedral, the Coronation of Mary is accompanied by two seated angels each strumming a lute and singing (10.07). The monks undoubtedly knew what they were singing as today we would know *Silent Night*. Everyone could join the singing angels. The presentation is theatrical; the scenes, in heaven and on earth, are directed at an audience; and they are so arranged – like a Broadway or a West End musical – with the music from the supporting angels focusing on the central scene with its holy characters.

---

[4] See Frédéric Billiet, 'Concert imaginaire', *The Profane Arts of the Midlle Ages* 6:1 (Spring 1997), 68-78.

[5] Supporter is a heraldic term which refers to the animals or objects supporting a coat of arms and the extended meaning includes the side scenes which exist on a number of misericords, mainly in Great Britain.

10.03: Wise Men of Gotham and the Geese, *Chester (Cheshire) Cathedral. Courtesy of Elaine C. Block / Misericordia International.*

10.04: Renard and Tybert, *Bristol Cathedral. Courtesy of Elaine C. Block / Misericordia International.*

10.05: Angel with Hurdy Gurdy, *Ricey-Bas (Aube) Saint-Pierre-les-Liens. Courtesy of Elaine C. Block / Misericordia International.*

10.06: Angels and the Magi, *Lincoln (Lincs.) Cathedral. Courtesy of Elaine C. Block / Misericordia International.*

10.07: Angels and the Coronation of Mary, *Lincoln (Lincs.) Cathedral. Courtesy of Christa Grössinger.*

As an encore to the angelic accompaniment of the holy story, three angels at Enville (Staffs.) occupy the entire stage (10.08). Each is seated in his own space and may, for all we know, be actors in disguise. The angel at left plays a harp, the one in the middle plucks a large lute and the angel at right plucks what appears to be a small lute.[6] The middle lutist, certainly the star of the show, is sitting under a type of elaborate arch usually reserved for a holy scene. However, careful scrutiny reveals a pair of devil masks as pendants on the central arch. Is this supposed to be funny? Is it just a comment on the angelic voices – that is, bold laughter – or is it the real essence of the scene? The angels are taking over for the devils but the devils keep an eye on them.

I imagine that the reader is asking how these angelic scenes are related to comic presentations in England. Are not misericords the same all over Europe? All angels play lutes and harps and they are certainly present at the holy scenes such as the Nativity and the Annunciation to the Shepherds. While I cannot claim to have seen all medieval choir stalls I have not missed many, and I have found these dramatic angels only on misericords in England. Perhaps the English found them humorous while others did not. Or perhaps the tradition of story telling was so strong in England that it invaded the field of music. In any case, I trace these musical accompaniments directly to the structure of the English choir stall. Basically, with the central carving and the pair of supporters each misericord may present three scenes, whereas the stalls in other countries are generally limited to a single central carving.[7] The side scenes, or supporters, may have several functions. They may, first of all, continue the story. Yet the examples given above do not continue the Visit of the Wise Men or the Coronation of the Virgin. Rather, they are concerned with music and provide an atmosphere in which the central story can be told. The supporters, in addition, can contrast with the main scene or criticize it. Therefore the fact that the English stalls have three scenes makes it possible for musical angels to be accessories rather than the main focus of the misericord. Consequently, they can illustrate the musical context of the main scene whereas this is rarely possible on continental stalls.

---

[6] The condition of these carvings sometimes makes their identification problematic.

[7] There are some exceptions. The choir stalls at Barcelona Cathedral each have three scenes but here the side scenes are larger and generally more important than the central scene. At Celanova Monastery (Orense) several of the seats have side scenes but they are mainly decorative. The cathedral at Albi (Gironde) has small side scenes on a number of seats but no central carving.

10.08: Three Angel Musicians, *Enville (Staffs.) St Mary. Courtesy of Elaine C. Block / Misericordia International.*

10.09: Annunciation, *Gresford (Wales) All Saints. Courtesy of Elaine C. Block / Misericordia International.*

Musical Comedy and the Bible

Another reason why the musical angel is basically a dramatic phenomenon in England is that scenes from the New Testament and the Apocryphal tales associated with the Bible are carved mainly for English churches. There is no set of English choir stalls devoted solely to a Christological or Marian cycle but there are isolated New Testament scenes among others at the cathedrals of Lincoln (Nativity, Visit of the Magi, the Ascension and the Coronation of the Virgin), Leintwardine (Annunciation and Resurrection), the Abbey of Sherborne (Last Judgment) and even at the small church at Gresford in Wales (Annunciation) (10.09).

This is not to say there are no angels or, specifically, musical angels in other countries but there are significantly fewer and their functions are vague. At Erfurt Cathedral (Thuringen), for example, four angels occupy a jouee,[8] each playing a different stringed instrument. At Ricey-bas (Saint-Pierre-les-Liens) in the departement of the Aube, a number of misericords show angels playing a variety of instruments, including a hurdy-gurdy (10.05). These angels act alone and are not visibly connected with any overall iconographic programme. At Amiens Cathedral angels concertize at the Coronation of the Virgin and other biblical scenes. However, these images are carved on the expansive panels of the jouees rather than on the limited space of misericords.

One angel in England, however – and I have found only one such example on a misericord – does not play a stringed instrument but bagpipes (10.10). While angels allegedly have no gender, this one is distinctly feminine. It has wavy hair and the clouds from which it issues are arranged as a ruffled skirt. It holds the instrument as intended, with the drone over the shoulder, and its fingers operate the pipe professionally. The angel, in fact, appears to be a trained musician. Bagpipes are commonly assumed to be the instrument of the devil, so what are they doing here in the hands of an angel? Or is this really an angel? All those who lived in the celestial kingdom were winged, even those contaminated by the sin of Pride. It is possible that the carvers distinguished the proud angels, the rebel angels, by the instruments they played. The raucous bagpipes certainly shut out the heavenly music and the monks would have had to sing better and better to counteract the sounds of the devil's own instrument. I can even imagine a test for the sounds of glory by having someone play bagpipes during rehearsals in an effort to drown out the sacred psalms.

Act I of the musical comedy in the choir: the angels are telling a story.

---

[8] There is no English word for this part of the choir stall, the end panels that bind the seats together. The term 'bench end' is sometimes used but there are no benches. The French word, *jouee*, has therefore been adopted for the end panels of the choir stalls. See Elaine C. Block and Frédéric Billiet, *Lexicon for Medieval Choir Stalls*.

10.10: Angel Bagpiper, *London Royal Foundation of St Katharine. Courtesy of Elaine C. Block / Misericordia International.*

10.11: Harpist, *Chichester (Sussex) Cathedral. Courtesy of Elaine C. Block / Misericordia International.*

Act II: Human and Hybrid Musicians and how they Play

The closest image to a traditional concert in England is at Chichester Cathedral where a harpist and probably a piper (now mutilated) are seated side by side (10.11). The supporters show the heads of a man and a woman, presumably representing the audience. While there are only two performers they seem serious about their work, possibly entertaining a small group at a castle. A dance scene at Chichester might earn a laugh, for the dancer, as she floats by the fiddler, turns up her head for a kiss (10.12). This may connect Lust to the dance or just be a comic addition to the concert. Elsewhere, music is linked to Lust as a pair of nude musicians accompany a concupiscent pair of lovers in, of all places, Westminster Abbey.

Most of the human musicians in English choir stalls are not doing what we expect them to do; that is, to play musical instruments as they should be played. A couple at Lavenham (Suffolk), gaily strumming away, have turned into hybrids, creatures with baser instincts then humans (10.13). They wear funny hats, while their hind quarters are bare. The woman strums a fiddle while a second head at the end of her tail turns to her, mouth open, probably singing or, rather, making noises. The female head, wearing a hat with flaps to drown out sounds to her ears, looks intently at her fiddle. Her partner on two clawed legs has what looks like a fox's tail at the end of his body. His hat looks like the woman's except that it has a scarf blowing in a high wind, his ears free instead of covered by flaps. He holds a set of bellows in one hand; his bow is a pair of fire tongs![9] Perhaps this shows his position in the household. His instrument is more likely to produce squeaks than heavenly sounds. Neither the bellows nor the tongs have strings. Their surfaces are metallic and animal skin; they could probably drown out the fiddle. We might be seeing here an image of marital conflict. Is the husband about to beat the wife with his tongs? Is the wife trying to bring the sacred back into their union? Or is the man showing us what the woman's fiddling really sounds like? Another hybrid playing the fiddle is in Walsham (Norfolk). This may be a monk in disguise, celebrating one of the world turned upside-down days when children or even animals take over the church rituals.

When the humans are not disguised as hybrids, they may be jesters in scalloped jackets and eared hats with bells on various parts of their costumes. They can be cruel to animals. At Lavenham, not far from the bellowing hybrids,[10] one jester sits

---

[9] A word of thanks to Malcolm Jones, who turned a crutch into a pair of fire tongs. Remnant describes this scene as the male hybrid 'mimicking (the female) by playing a pair of bellows with a crutch.' G. L. Remnant, *A Catalogue of Misericords in Great Britain* (Oxford: Oxford University Press, 1969), p. 146.

[10] Since puns were regular tricks of the carver's trade we might consider this pun intentional.

10.12: Fiddler Kisses Dancer, *Chichester (Sussex) Cathedral. Courtesy of Elaine C. Block / Misericordia International.*

10.13: Hybrid Musicians, *Lavenham (Suffolk) St Peter and St Paul. Courtesy of Elaine C. Block / Misericordia International.*

with a pig on his lap. He is biting its tail and pressing some of the pig's most sensitive organs to make it squeal and thus amuse the crowd for whom he is obviously playing. At St Botolph in Boston, two jesters sit side by side, each with a cat on his lap (10.14). Their hoods have large ass-ears, their jackets are scalloped and bells cover the tips of their shoes – costumes for entertainers. Each jester is biting the tail of his cat while squeezing those animals as bagpipes. The resulting pain makes them squeal to delight the audience. Both jesters, cat tails in mouths, glance at the audience as they manipulate their cats.

Act III: Animals in the Upside–Down World of Music

Animal musicians are on misericords in most countries, probably to critique the human musicians. The scenes described above at Lavenham and Boston are repeated at Beverley Minster. Here, however, an ape replaces the human. As part of the world upside-down, the ape, biting the tail and squeezing the rump of his dog, replaces the human jester. The situation of this scene on a supporter may indicate that it was not the main event of the show. The central carving shows bear baiting with dogs turned loose on a trapped bear. The ape musician probably entertained the crowd between the main acts and very possibly scampered through the audience making his dog squeal at will.

Several distinctive scenes of animal musicians appear only in Great Britain. For example, at Winchester a pig plays the viol (10.15), and while bagpiping pigs are found on misericords in Spain, they appear in a different context in Great Britain (10.16). In five or six English choir stalls the sow plays bagpipes for her little ones, usually three in number, to dance (10.17). Other items set the scene; the trough in the centre creates a barnyard and a house in the back shelters a woman and child. A fox has just stolen a chicken and carries it off in his mouth as the woman runs after the fox wielding her distaff. If successful, she will down the fox and return the chicken to the barnyard. The animal musician has thus become part of a literary tradition and is inserted into the story of Chanticleer found in Chaucer's *Canterbury Tales*. The pigs are irrelevant to the story, but the pig's ineptitude in trying to get the piglets to dance may be contrasted with the success of the fox running off with the chicken as the widow contends with this crisis. In other countries, and sometimes in England as well, the fox runs off with the goose. But there is no barnyard, no widow and no sow piping for her piglets. We are left just with the fox and goose.

On the continent, the pig is the major musician and his instrument is usually bagpipes, but sometimes a harp. This may illustrate a proverb – originally about an ass – 'you can teach a sow to read music but she can only squeal'. In Great Britain the fox and the bear get a chance to be musical. At Castle Hedingham, in the world

10.14: Jesters with Cats, *Boston (Lincs.) St Botolph. Courtesy of Elaine C. Block / Misericordia International.*

10.15: Pig Playing Viol, *Winchester Cathedral. Courtesy of Elaine C. Block / Misericordia International.*

10.16: Pig Bagpiper and Piglets, *Winchester Cathedral. Courtesy of Elaine C. Block / Misericordia International.*

10.17: Chaucerian Pig, *Manchester Cathedral. Courtesy of Elaine C. Block / Misericordia International.*

turned upside-down, a fox marches home carrying over his shoulder – slung from a pole – a priest with his head on the ground and his feet attached to the pole. The supporter before this upside-down couple shows a cowled fox blowing a trumpet (10.18). He is probably announcing his victory in capturing the priest, forming a little story that might be Renardien. On a misericord at Chichester, a seated fox plays a harp for an ape, now mutilated but originally a flute player or dancer. We know the fox is not a serious musician since he has trapped a goose under one foot (10.19). We can only imagine the sounds of his harp as the fox sets his mind on his forthcoming dinner.

Another musical scene is at Beverley St Mary (Yorkshire), where two cowled foxes each hold down a page on their side of an open book (10.20).[11] Both foxes have open mouths so they must be singing, or at least reading chorally. Behind the open book stands what appears to be an eagle but is actually the carving on a lectern, which often is crowned with an eagle, the attribute of St John the Evangelist. Each fox has a cowl around its neck, and these cowls are flat so we know that no stolen goods are hidden. The function of these foxes is much more spiritual; they are singing from this book. We are just able to see the staff and to read the notes, so we know that the foxes are singing the *Magnificat*! What is the response of the audience to this song of the sly fox? What will happen next? At Hereford Cathedral we see the same necessity of holding the book open so the singers can read the music. Here, however, the book is sedately held by a pair of angels, one of whom is evidently singing very loudly. There is no music notation in this book; perhaps, unlike the foxes, angels do not need musical notation. The divine, angelic music is as far as it is possible to be from the raucous music we have heard from the beasts (10.21).

Epilogue: Bedevilling the Music

The devil has important work to do and we cannot expect him to play a large role in the musical comedy beneath the seats in the choir stalls. Yet we do see him occasionally with his bagpipes and realize that he too is a musician. His skills are apparent on a misericord at Ludlow (Salop.) (10.22). We have here an illustration of a story, commonly seen on church frescoes, of the devil pushing a brewster, ac-

---

[11] I wish to acknowledge the perspicacity of Professor Billiet who first recognized these foxes as singers. In Remnant, *Op. Cit.*, the scene at Beverley St Mary (Yorkshire) is described as 'eagle holding an open book from which two foxes are reading' (p. 178). See also the chapter on these foxes by Billiet in *Grant risee. The Medieval Comic Presence / La Présence comique médiévale. Essays in Honour of Brian J. Levy*, edited by A. Hindley and A.Tudor and dedicated to the memory of Brian J.Levy (Turnhout: Brepols, 2005).

10.18: Fox Trumpeter, *Castle Hedingham (Essex) St Nicholas. Courtesy of Elaine C. Block / Misericordia International.*

10.19: Fox Harpist with Goose, *Hereford Cathedral. Courtesy of Elaine C. Block / Misericordia International.*

10.20: Foxes Sing the Magnificat Beverley *(Yorkshire) St Mary. Courtesy of Elaine C. Block / Misericordia International.*

10.21: Animal Bagpiper, *Norwich (Norfolk) Cathedral. Courtesy of Elaine C. Block / Misericordia International.*

10.22: Devil Sends Brewster to Hell, *Ludlow (Salop.) St Lawrence. Courtesy of Elaine C. Block / Misericordia International.*

10.23: Currying Fauvel, *Ely (Cambs.) Cathedral. Courtesy of Elaine C. Block / Misericordia International.*

cused of serving watered beer in her tavern, feet first into the mouth of Hell.[12] Nude, except for a horned head-dress which was known as a place for the devil to nest, she still holds – right side up – a stein of beer. The chief devil, clutching his bag-pipes, announces her imminent arrival in Hell. On one supporter the devil Tutivil-lus writes down her name, thus reserving her an infernal space. On the other supporter, as a continuation to the story, a woman is tossed into the Hell mouth as another emerges. The brewster's sin was considered so devastating that Christ left her in Hell when he rescued all the other sinners.

The Musical Comedy

At least one medieval musical comedy has survived: the *Romance of Fauvel*. Here a horse becomes the most corrupt mayor the town has ever known. He is not a musician, but musicians accompany him on his missions. A manuscript illumination shows the audience watching from box theatre seats. However, the two related misericords in England – and originally there were probably more – show no music or musicians. Instead they show three ordinary people currying a horse (10.23). What does this scene have to do with Fauvel? Simply, it is a pun; one of the carver's comic elements which remains while the music is off stage. We see farmers curry-ing a horse – Fauvel – while we are currying Favour (Fauvel). We must remember that our theatre is beneath the seats in the choir rather than in an auditorium with a stage. Our performers are a mixture of the angelic and the grotesque. And our audi-ence consists of demons trying to dislodge our holy men and women from their path to glory.

A New Audience

Music in the choir stalls differs by region and it is especially prominent in England. The context for this music varies as it brings biblical scenes, folk tales, jokes and different types of comedy into the programme of the English misericords. Here the angels have stories to tell and a stage set worthy of their presentation, while the animals convey the impossibility of a harmonious earthly concert. The musical comedy in England is tied to its story-telling tradition combined with the value of comic effects. The jesters play animal bagpipes, the dancer kisses the fiddler, the sow teaches her young to dance while the widow in the background handles a crisis. An actual musical comedy, the *Romance of Fauvel*, depicted on two miseri-

---

[12] We use the word *brewster*, instead of the more common *aylewife*, to show that the lady in question was a spinster. Allegedly, she later married one of the devils in Hell.

cords in England,[13] seems to be without music as only the comic elements remain. These elements are major parts of the musical stories as they are in other aspects of English literature: Chaucer, Shakespeare, Goldsmith. Today, we have lost most of the angels and most of the animals. And, as the musical has evolved to its twenty-first century audience and we listen to Sondheim or Bernstein, our seats are more comfortable.

The curtain comes down.

---

[13] The currying scenes are at Ely Cathedral (Cambs.) and at Greystoke (Cumbria).